THAT'S RIGHT!

An Introduction to Ethical Theory

Michael S. Russo

SophiaOmni

ISBN: 978-1490-381435

SophiaOmni

Visit our website at:
www.sophiaomni.org

CONTENTS

II. Utilitarianism

III. Deontology

IV. Moral Rights Theory

V. Virtue Ethics

preface

I know exactly what you're thinking: does the world really need yet another college textbook on ethics? I mean, after all, if you do a book search on Amazon.com and put in the word "ethics" you are likely to find more books on the subject than you can read in a lifetime. And the list of these books would include works like Aristotle's *Nicomachean Ethics* that were written centuries ago (and which are still relevant today) as well as more than a few works by some fairly impressive moral theorists that were published only within the past few years.

So why, then, is this short study of ethical theory necessary at the present time?

I'll pass over the fact that, given the persistent moral ambiguity that seems to reign supreme today, we probably can never have too many books published that help individuals clarify their own moral thinking. If anything, there is probably too little ethics being read and discussed in our own society rather than too much.

The real reason why I wrote this book is much more practical than that. You see, I've been teaching ethics for over twenty-five years now, and I've done so in a variety of settings. I've taught ethics in one form or another to junior high school students in the South Bronx, to prep school students at a prestigious Academy, and at several colleges and universities in both graduate and undergraduate programs. What I discovered over these twenty-five years is that most texts in ethics are written in a way that often fails to serve the most basic needs of the average eighteen-year-old, who may be sincerely looking for some degree of moral clarity in his or her own life.

These students come into ethics classes, often during their freshman or sophomore years of college, and encounter books which are chock full of complex theories, obscure language, obtuse case studies, and issues which often seem somewhat esoteric, to say the least.

Nor do many of these texts provide simple, straightforward guidance that can help typical college students with the complex issues that they have to face every day of their lives. The first years of college can often seem like a moral mine field in which young men and women are free for the first time to make decisions on their own, and have to live with the consequences of these decisions. I believe a text in ethics should serve as a resource tool that actually aids in the moral decision-making process.

That's the reason why I developed *That's Right: An Introduction to Ethical Theory*. Among the features that I believe make this text different from others currently used in college ethics classes are the following:

It is short and easy to read. Most texts in ethics tend to be a bit long-winded because the authors of these texts and their publishers need to justify the high costs they charge to readers by adding more words. These texts also tend to be filled with complex jargon that can throw off the average reader. In an attempt to make the study of ethics as accessible as possible to the widest audience possible, I have intentionally made each chapter of this text as brief as possible while still allowing for a comprehensive discussion of the theories presented. I have also attempted to keep the technical philosophical verbiage that one often finds in typical ethics texts to a minimum. Where it has been necessary to use discipline-specific terms, I have attempted to explain these terms as clearly as possible so that they don't become stumbling blocks as you work your way through the text.

It focuses on down-to-earth issues. While many courses on ethics focus on the most dramatic and controversial issues—abortion, infanticide, war, etc.—I believe that the vast majority of moral dilemmas that individuals face occur in our ordinary everyday dealings with other human beings. It is for this reason that many of the examples and case studies in this text focus on everyday moral issues, particularly those likely to affect the average college student such as yourself.

It has a very specific goal in mind. The aim of this text, as I have already pointed out, is to assist you in developing your own framework for moral decision-making. I have focused most of this text on explaining five of the most influential moral theories in the history of Ethics—ethical egoism, utilitarianism, deontology, rights theory, and virtue ethics. By the end of the text you should be in a position to determine which of these theories—if any—makes the most sense to you and why. After that, it will be up to you to attempt to apply this theory as consistently as possible to your everyday moral decision-making.

This text would not have been possible without the contributions of several wonderful individuals who took time to proofread the completed work and offer many helpful suggestions. Allow me, therefore, to express my sincerest thanks to Marie Dollard, Laura Hefele, Una Milella, Elisa Rapaport, and Ashley Lantz for their assistance in producing this text.

WHY WE NEED ETHICS

Case Study: A Day in the Life

It is Tuesday morning around 7am. You got to bed late last night after an evening of partying with friends, and now you are having trouble getting up for your morning classes. Your alarm keeps blaring its warning to you that you are running late, but you keep hitting the snooze button for just a few more minutes of sleep.

You hear some pounding on the door and your mother's grating voice telling you that if you don't get up right now you will be late for your 8:15 accounting class. You manage to pull yourself up from bed, covering your ears to block out your mother's voice and in frustration scream out to her, "Shut the hell up and leave me alone for two minutes, will you!" She leaves in a huff, offended as usual by your abrupt morning behavior.

It is now 7:40 and you know you will have to rush if you are to make it to class on time. You quickly brush your teeth, shower, and get dressed. Before you leave the house, you stop into your older sister's bedroom on an important errand. Seeing that she has left already, you "borrow" $25 from the funds that she keeps in her dresser drawer, promising yourself that you will return this money after you get paid from work this evening.

Since you don't have time for a real breakfast, you stop off at 7-11 on the way to school and get some cigarettes and a large coffee, which lately has become your typical morning fare. Determined to get to class on time, you gulp your coffee, knock off a couple of cigarettes, search for the books you will need for class in the wasteland that is your car, all the while driving well above the speed-limit on the local expressway. No harm done though: there were no cops around today, so you made it through without getting a ticket, arriving on campus at exactly 8:15am.

Unfortunately, you didn't account for how long it would take you to find a parking space on campus and you arrive to class ten minutes late. As you enter the classroom, you can tell that the professor is annoyed that you are once again late for his class, but you pretend not to notice and slump into an available seat. You know that you should be paying attention to what he is saying—especially since the midterm is coming up soon—but you are so tired that your mind wanders aimlessly.

During a break in the class, you go into an empty stairwell with a classmate to smoke a cigarette. You bump into a friend named Karen, who is in your Philosophy of Existence class and ask her how she is doing on the paper for that class which is due on Thursday. Karen confesses that she simply bought a paper from an on-line academic paper site and that she is very happy with the results. Since you know that you will not have time to write a decent paper by Thursday, you get the web address of the site from Karen, determined to follow her example.

After class you bump into some of your friends hanging out in the cafeteria. They are talking about a mutual friend, who, it turns out, is pregnant and is considering having an abortion so she won't have to drop out of school. Although some of the people in the group clearly are concerned about their friend's welfare, most simply enjoy gossiping about her situation, speculating about the specific circumstances of her pregnancy. Delighting in the misfortunes of other people—they make your own life seem a little brighter in comparison—you offer up some particularly graphic information about this girl's sexual history that you heard about from one of her former boyfriends. Although this has nothing to do with her current predicament, your friends enjoy hearing all the sordid details you have to offer.

At 4:20pm you finish your classes for the day and head off for your job in the children's department of Macy's. Because you spent so much time gossiping, you are late once again, and, since the store manager already dislikes you intensely, you fear that you could very well lose your job. Fortunately, the assistant manager of the children's department is "really into you." Flirting outrageously with this lonely and pathetic individual, you con the assistant manager into covering for you with the hint of going out together at some point in the future. Of course you have no intention ever to do so. You spend the rest of the night trying to do as little work as possible, goofing off with your co-workers, and avoiding the store manager at all costs.

You end your day as you always do. Hanging out with your friends at one of their homes, drinking assorted alcoholic beverages, smoking some pot when it is available, and occasionally "hooking up" if the right person happens to come along.

FOR DISCUSSION

Read through the above "typical day" in the life of a college student like yourself. Do any of the events or reactions described in this case study seem implausible to you (i.e., unlikely to happen to any real college student)? Which of the actions of the typical college student described would you characterize as morally problematic or wrong? What do you think it is that makes these acts wrong?

In the first case study in this text, you were offered a "typical day" of a fictitious college student. Of course the events described are compressed into a day to make the scenario a bit more interesting for you. I personally think that it would be rather unlikely that the average college student—even one as ethically challenged as the one portrayed in the case study—would make quite so many bad choices in such a short amount of time.

And yet, I also have no doubts that the kind of moral situations that our imaginary student faces are not at all unlike those which confront most college students at one point or another during the course of their everyday lives. I would go even further than this arguing that the moral choices that this student makes in the case study would probably be not unlike those that many college students would make in similar circumstances.

Our Moral Crisis

Perhaps you think that I am exaggerating the extent of moral confusion rampant in our colleges. In fact, college students are probably no more confused about the right way to live their lives than Americans in general. In study after study of ethical attitudes and beliefs, however, social scientists have detected an alarming decline of moral standards among average Americans. In one such study, James Patterson and Peter Kim surveyed 2000 people chosen at random about their moral attitudes. In their work, *The Day America Told The Truth* the authors shared the following statistics:

- Only 13% of Americans believe in all the Ten Commandments.
- 91 % of Americans lie regularly, at work and at home.

- 20% of women say they were raped by their dates.
- 33% of AIDS carriers have not told their spouses or lovers.
- 31 % of married people are having or have had an affair.
- 7% of participants say that for $2 million they would commit murder (Liszka 2).

One could argue that statistics like these are symptomatic of a deep moral crisis affecting Americans. Indeed, for many of us living at the beginning of the 21st century, it often appears as though the state of the world that we inhabit is about as morally bankrupt as it has ever been. Every time we open the newspaper or turn on the news, we are confronted with reports of corporate malfeasance, government corruption, sexual scandals, and assorted acts of cruelty and violence that boggle the mind.

Objectively, we have more than enough moral guidance in our daily lives to help us make the right moral choices. There are countless individuals around us—family, friends, co-workers—who are more than willing to tell us exactly how to live our lives, often bombarding us with their unique ideas about right and wrong, good and evil. If you go to any decent library or bookstore, you will find scores of books that have been written over the centuries by some pretty smart people in the field of ethics, trying to help us clarify our moral thinking. We are also constantly reminded of how we should behave by pulpit preachers, radio talk show hosts, and an eclectic collection of gurus and sages.

With all this help one would think that it would be relatively easy to figure out the right way to live our lives. And yet the sad fact is that more individuals than ever in our society are completely befuddled when it comes to making moral choices. The problem is not that we are making the wrong moral choices; the problem actually is that we don't have a framework in place for understanding what makes an act right or wrong in the first place. The average college student today probably believes that there is no objective basis for moral decisions and that the best one can do when confronted with a moral dilemma is to muddle one's way through it as best one can.

I do not wish to suggest that people weren't confused about moral matters in the past—of course they were—or that previous generations were more scrupulous in their moral practices than we are—of course they weren't. The difference is that although our grandparents might have had some questions about the right way to live their lives, they probably didn't doubt that there was a right way to live. And while they probably engaged in the same kinds of bad moral behavior that we do, at least they knew that they were behaving badly.

It appears that the unshakable certainties of previous generations have instead given way to disconcerting feelings of ambiguity. We no longer know what the right answers are to our moral dilemmas. We may even have a sense that we are living in a world where there are no longer any clear norms for moral behavior, a world in which each individual must look to him or herself to find the answers.

The Purpose of Ethics

Every day of our lives we are confronted with moral questions that demand answers. Some of these questions are fairly innocuous (whether, for example, to tell the truth or not to the telemarketer who calls during dinner and asks if you are home); other are significantly more complex (for instance, whether to cheat on your income taxes, have an abortion, or support government policies that may be unjust). The point here is that you just can't bury your head in the sand and pretend that these dilemmas don't exist or that they can just be imagined away.

It is precisely because each of us is confronted with so many difficult moral choices in our every day lives that the field of ethics becomes so very important. Ethics differs from most other fields of human inquiry in that the goal of studying about ethics is not simply to attain some sort of theoretical knowledge, but to acquire the kind of practical wisdom necessary to live a better life. Ethics may begin with theories, but always ends with how these theories can help clarify your moral decision-making process and ultimately help make you a more moral human being. As the philosopher Aristotle put it several centuries ago, "The purpose of [studying ethics] is not, as it is in other inquiries, the attainment of theoretical knowledge: we are not conducting this inquiry in order to know what virtue is, but in order to become good, else there would be no advantage in studying it." (*Nicomachean Ethics* II.2).

Fortunately, we don't have to solve all of our moral dilemmas completely on our own. Like any other complex field of human endeavor, ethics has its own set of "experts" who have struggled to find clear, consistent, and rational principles to guide human activity. When confronted with our own moral dilemmas, it is not always necessary to refer to what the great ethicist of the past and present have to say on these matters, but it may be comforting for you to know that there are thoughtful men and women who have reflected upon the same sorts of issues that you are facing, and may have some meaningful guidance to offer you as you attempt to sort through the moral issues that will undoubtedly arise throughout your life.

Finally, some individuals mistakenly presume that the purpose of ethics is to brainwash people into believing certain ideas about right and wrong. Nothing could be further from the truth. The purpose of ethics is to provide the broad theoretical framework to help you make intelligent moral decisions that fully reflect your own unique values and ideals. In the end what you choose to think or how you choose to act is entirely your own business.

Arguing Ethics...Civilly

There's one final thing you have to be prepared for now that you have chosen to undertake the study of ethics. Some students who enter ethics classes are put off by the argumentative nature of these classes. They might be coming from subjects like chemistry, math, or accounting, where there is very little debate at all over the topics being discussed. Then, when they enter their ethics classes, the kind of conversations that typically go on can often seem like a free-for-all.

Believe it or not, the fact that discussion, debate, and even vehement arguments are occurring in your ethics class is a good sign. It means that there is an honest, open exchange of ideas and that students feel comfortable enough to express their views candidly. Although this sort of dynamic exchange doesn't occur in every ethics class, it usually does in the best sorts of ethics classes—those in which faculty members are open to hearing students' ideas and the students themselves are intellectually invested in the subject matter.

Although debate is a natural feature of ethics classes, this debate should always be civil. As you read this text and discuss the topics found within it, there will undoubtedly be ideas presented by your classmates that you find silly, stupid, or even morally repugnant. Although it's perfectly fine to disagree with the moral positions of others, you should strive to do so in a way that is never demeaning or degrading.

Too often in our society the discussion of important ideas devolves into personal attacks that end in acrimony and discord. All this does is entrench individuals in their own partisan and dogmatic views, and nobody is enlightened as a result. While you can and should disagree with positions you find false—and disagree forcefully at that—ethics is also about being open to the possibility that you can learn something from those with whom you disagree. This doesn't mean that by giving the positions of opponents an honest hearing your own positions will change dramatically, or even at all. But your own moral perspective might very well be enhanced by exposure to ideas that you may not have considered before.

How to Use This Book

As I have previously mentioned, the aim of this work is not to turn you into some kind of preeminent scholar in the field of ethics (although that wouldn't be so bad); nor is it to provide you with esoteric ideas that you can use to dazzle your friends at the next party you attend (although that might actually make the party much more interesting). The aim of this work, quite simply and pragmatically, is to provide you with the tools you need to begin to live an ethical life.

You're probably thinking right now: "But I already am living a perfectly moral life. So what on earth do I need to read a book like this for, anyway." In fact, you may be a terrific, kind-hearted, generous, and responsible person...But this doesn't necessarily mean that you are an ethical person. As you'll see throughout this book, living an ethical life presupposes that you understand the reasons why you behave the way you do, and, even more importantly, that you have certain clear, consistent, and rational principles that you follow when deciding how you are going to act in a particular situation. These are precisely the tools with which you will be provided as you work your way through the ideas being presented.

To get the most out of this work, I would ask you to observe a few simple recommendations:

1. Each chapter of this text begins with a case study that typically involves an ordinary person just like yourself confronted with a moral situation that demands resolution. These case studies are intended to introduce the main ideas in each chapter and to illuminate your own attitudes and beliefs about these issues being discussed. Make sure to read through these case studies and carefully reflect on the questions being posed by them *before* reading the rest of the chapter.

2. As you read through the ideas and theories presented in each

chapter, do so with a critical mind. No particular theory in the field of ethics is sacrosanct, and there is no theory without its own limitations. It is your job as a reader to assess the merits of each theory and then to consider how useful each of these theories may be if applied to your own life situation. It's my hope that, by the end of this text, you'll find at least one theory that resonates with you, and that you can begin to use to guide you when confronted with your own personal moral dilemmas.

3.   Each chapter ends with exercises that help reinforce the theories that you have just read. Take the time to do these exercises and make sure you understand how each theory can be applied before moving on to the next theory. Remember, if you can't apply moral theories to concrete situations, these theories won't serve you very well in life.

4.   For those who wish to delve more deeply into the ethical theories presented in this work, I've included a selection of primary sources at the end of the text that presents the ideas of some of the greatest thinkers in the field of ethics. You might find some of these selections a bit challenging, so you are advised to read them only after going through my basic overview of each moral theory in Part 2 of this text.

And above all else, try to have a good time!

For Further Discussion

1. Rank the following moral issues in terms of how important they are to you and using the following scale...

   VI = very important
   SI = somewhat important
   SU = somewhat unimportant
   VU = very unimportant

   _____ global poverty/hunger
   _____ overpopulation
   _____ war
   _____ global warming
   _____ premarital sex
   _____ racial discrimination
   _____ sexual discrimination
   _____ the death penalty
   _____ abortion
   _____ environmental pollution
   _____ teen pregnancy
   _____ criminal violence
   _____ genetic engineering
   _____ illegal drug use (including marijuana)
   _____ same sex marriage
   _____ destruction of wilderness areas/deforestation
   _____ religious fanaticism
   _____ illegal immigration
   _____ poverty/economic inequality
   _____ animal cruelty

2. Which of these moral issues do you consider to be the most serious one confronting human beings today?

3. What is it that makes this issue so morally significant for you?

4. Is there any other moral issue that is extremely important to you that isn't on this list? What is it about this issue that makes it so important to you?

Sources and Further Reading

Aristotle. *Nicomachean Ethics*. Trans. Martin Ostwald. Englewood Cliffs, NJ: Prentice Hall, 1962.

Eberly, Don E. *The Content of America's Character*. Lanham, MD: Madison Books, 1995.

Liszka, James Jakob. *Moral Competence: An Integrated Approach to the Study of Ethics*. Upper Saddle River, NJ: Prentice-Hall, 1999.

PART ONE

WHAT IS ETHICS ANYWAY?

FIRST THINGS FIRST

Case Study: A Case of Revenge

On a Saturday afternoon in April, Billy Slotnik, an eighteen-year-old college freshman, goes with his friend Arnie to the mall to pick up some new Ipod speakers. On this particular Saturday, the mall is very crowded and Billy has been forced to drive around in his 2004 green Honda Civic for some time in order to find a parking space. Eventually he gets lucky and spies an elderly woman leaving a space very close to the entrance of the mall. After waiting patiently several more minutes until this woman leaves her spot, Billy gets ready to park there only to discover that a guy in an expensive, large, black SUV has cut him off and has pulled into the spot that Billy was waiting to occupy.

When Billy confronts this man about his behavior, he dismisses Billy with some disparaging comments and tells him to go $%&# off. He then walks into the mall, leaving Billy seething with rage. Wanting to teach this guy a lesson, Billy tells his friend Arnie that he is going to deface the man's car. Arnie has serious reservations about what Billy is planning to do, but decides that he doesn't want to get involved and says nothing. Billy then takes out his house key, makes a long, deep scratch along the entire left side of the SUV, and takes off feeling vindicated.

Unfortunately for Billy, someone had witnessed the entire incident and was able to provide the police with the color and model of Billy's car as well as the first three digits of his license plate number.

A few days later the police show up at Billy's house, having tracked him down through the partial license plate number that was provided to them. Not wanting to pay to repair the damage he caused or get a police record, Billy lies and says that he was home the whole day on Saturday and had nothing to do with the damaged car. Although Billy's parents know that he was at the mall that day, they decide to back their son up and support his story, since they don't want him to get in any trouble with the police.

Without any hard evidence and with Billy's parents supporting his alibi, the police have no option but to drop the case. As they walk out of the house, one of the policemen, Officer Murphy, confides to his colleague that he is sorry that they didn't have enough evidence to nail Billy, since he really dislikes Eastern Europeans. He goes on to make some ethnic jokes about Eastern Europeans, which his partner laughs at, even though he is a bit uncomfortable with Murphy's overt bigotry.

FOR DISCUSSION

How would you characterize the behavior of the SUV owner, Billy, Arnie, Billy's parents, Officer Murphy and Murphy's partner? If you were present during any of the incidents in question, what would your advice be to these individuals?

Do the actions of the individuals in question seem to fit into the scope of ethics as you understand it (are these really moral or ethical issues)? Why or why not?

In academic circles ethics is considered to be a major subdivision of the field of philosophy. The term philosophy, derived from the Greek words *philia* (love) and *sophia* (wisdom), literally means the love of wisdom. Philosophy is that field of study that explores the meaning of human existence. Philosophy begins in wonder and asks questions about our place in the cosmos, questions like, "What is the purpose of life?" "Why are we here?" "Where are we ultimately going?" Sometimes these questions can lead to answers that help to make our lives more meaningful; at other times, it is enough simply to raise important philosophical questions, even if the answers to these questions remain somewhat obscure or contentious.

As a discipline, philosophy is usually divided into four main areas: metaphysics (the study of the nature of reality), epistemology (the study of human knowledge), aesthetics (the study of beauty), and, finally, ethics.

The word ethics itself comes from the Greek word *ethos*, meaning custom. The Latin equivalent of this term is *mores* (customs), from which we derive our words moral and morality. Although for our purposes we can use the terms ethics and morality interchangeably, there are those philosophers who argue that the two terms have slightly different meanings. In general, morality usually refers to specific moral codes that different communities or societies impose upon their members to prevent harm to others or to promote group cohesion. The Amish, for example, have their own very unique moral code and this code would be dramatically different from that of, let's say, conservative Jews or Western European liberals. The moral codes of different groups or cultures typically develop over long periods of time, and rarely are subject to intellectual scrutiny or critical examination.

Ethics, on the other hand, begins with an attitude of skepticism. It examines all moral views, including those that are perceived as sacrosanct, with a critical eye. This critical reflection on the truth or validity of moral positions is the hallmark of all legitimate ethical inquiry.

The scope of ethics is vast, indeed. As it is commonly understood, ethics addresses questions about how we ought to live our lives, what the nature of the good life is, and what is the proper way to interact with our fellow human beings (and perhaps with non-humans as well). Needless to say, there is very little in the realm of human activity that is not included somehow in the scope of ethics.

Since it is important to define fields of study as precisely as possible at the onset of any intellectual journal, our definition of will have to be broad enough to encompass the vast scope of ethical inquiry, while at the same time maintaining the focus on skepticism as the hallmark of this endeavor. For our purposes, then, we can define ethics simply as *the critical and rational examination of questions of right and wrong in human action.*

The Origin of Ethics

Although human beings have probably engaged in some form of moral reflection since the beginning of time, the formal study of ethics probably began with the ancient Greeks, who made a conscious effort to apply logic and reason to the study of moral questions. One of the first people to systematically begin to inquire about the right way to live was a fellow named Socrates, who lived in the fifth century before Christ in Athens. Socrates was the son of Sophronicus, a sculptor, and Phaenarete, a midwife. During the early part of his life, he seems to have followed in his father's footsteps, working as a sculptor. When he was a young man, however, Socrates turned his attention to Philosophy, and soon devoted himself almost exclusively to studying questions of ethics. He came to believe that it was his mission to act as a kind of "gadfly" to the Athenian people, provoking them into recognizing their moral ignorance. Socrates' goal in interrogating his fellow citizens was not simply to drive them crazy (although he probably unintentionally succeeded in doing this as well). Through the act of moral questioning, he hoped to find some objective standard right and wrong that would aid human beings in determining the right way to live their lives.

Needless to say, his constant interrogation did not endear him to all the citizens of Athens. While Socrates developed a following among many of the more idealistic young men of Athens, he soon incurred the wrath of some of the most powerful men in the city. In 399 B.C. Socrates was put on trial for atheism (not believing in the gods of Athens) and corrupting the youth of the city (by teaching them to question everything). In the end, the jury found Socrates guilty as charged and condemned him to death by the drinking of hemlock.

Socrates' goal of trying to discover some objective criteria for determining right and wrong was taken up by his equally famous disciple, Plato. In his dialogues, in which the character of Socrates plays a central role, and in his great work, The Republic, Plato attempted to ground moral behavior in some transcendent Good that is absolute, eternal and unchanging. Plato's own student, Aristotle, took a decidedly different turn from his master, rejecting Plato's otherworldly approach to ethics. Instead, his approach focused on goods—or virtues—that are extremely practical and down-to-earth. The differences between these two giants of ancient philosophy can be noted in Raphael's famous painting, "The School of Athens." Plato, on the left, is portrayed as pointing upward towards the transcendent realm; Aristotle, on the right, is stretching out his hand horizontally, clearly indicating his comfort with this world of change and impermanence.

Since ancient times, scores of philosophers in various countries have struggled to find the basic principles of moral living. Like Plato and Aristotle, many of these philosophers came up with radically different, and sometimes even opposing, moral principles. Throughout this text, we will examine the ideas of many of these great philosophers and attempt to assess how successful they were in finding an objective basis for moral action.

Divisions of Ethics

There are two traditional subdivisions in ethics:

Non-Normative Ethics is descriptive or empirical. This form of ethics does not attempt to tell us how we ought to behave, but rather simply describes how people typically behave. Anthropologists , psychologists, and sociologists, for example, also study human behavior. The anthropologist might examine certain customs among members of an East African tribe; a sociologist, the group dynamics of certain inner city gang members, the psychologist, the behavior of individuals diagnosed with a specific psychological disorder. They would study all of these forms of behavior, however, without any reference to the rightness or wrongness of the actions in question.

Let's take a rather extreme example: Certain tribes in East Africa engage in what is known as female circumcision (also known as genital mutilation). Using a blade or some kind of sharp device—occasionally even shards of glass have been known to be used—the genitalia of unmarried girls are mutilated with the result that sexual intercourse is extremely painful for these young women after they are married. This serves a dual purpose: first, because the vaginal opening is now smaller, husbands derive greater pleasure from the sexual act, and, second, the girls are less likely to engage in adultery, because the sex act is so unpleasant for them.

Now an anthropologist would certainly study this practice, attempting to understand the origins of the custom and the rationale behind it. What an anthropologist would not do, however, is pass a value judgment upon the actions being performed. His job is simply to describe the behavior and attempt to explain it. That's why non-normative is described as descriptive in nature.

Normative Ethics, on the other hand, is prescriptive rather than descriptive. Take the example of female circumcision once again. The ethicist studying this action might very well start from the same place as the anthropologist. She would want to understand the action completely—its origins, history, rationale, etc.—but the ethicist would go one step further than the anthropologist by evaluating the moral status of the act in question and attempting to justify the rightness or wrongness of the act by referring to clear, consistent, rational principles. In this specific case, almost all ethicists would argue that female circumcision is morally wrong, although they might base their judgment on widely divergent principles (respect for the individual, human rights, the effects that this tradition has on the common good of the societies in which it is performed, etc.).

As you can see from this example, normative ethics attempts to tell us how human beings ought to behave. Normative ethics also provides guidelines and norms that can be used in real life situations when one is confronted with moral dilemmas. This is the form of ethics that we will focus on in this text.

Normative Ethics in turn can be broken down again into two major divisions.

General Normative Ethics is the study of the general principles that determine rightness or wrongness in human conduct. This area of ethics answers the question of how one ought to behave in all circumstances.

Although there are numerous principles that can be studied in the field of normative ethics, most ethicists focus on a few main ones that have stood the test of time: ethical egoism, utilitarianism, deontology, rights theory, and virtue ethics. In principle, almost any moral question can be resolved by referring to one or more of these theories. Furthermore, after studying these main theories for some time, most people find that their own moral position fits quite nicely into one or more of these great ethical traditions. Since this text focuses mainly on general normative ethics, these are the theories that we will eventually be examining in the second part of this book.

Applied Normative Ethics takes general principles of rightness and wrongness in human conduct and applies them to specific areas or realms of reality. Areas of applied ethics include business ethics, environmental ethics, medical ethics, communication ethics, and sexual ethics. Basically just about any domain of human activity could be examined through the lens of applied ethics. A course in environmental ethics, for example, might examine moral issues related to animals—factory farming, animal experimentation, hunting, etc.—by applying theories like those we will be studying in this text to these sorts of specific issues.

Although this text focuses on general normative ethics, we will certainly be using examples from several different areas of applied normative ethics to help elucidate the theories we are discussing. For the most part, however, the cases studies and exercises that are included in this text come from an area of applied ethics that is sometimes referred to as "everyday ethics." In everyday ethics, we apply the great moral theories to the kinds of moral questions you will inevitably struggle with throughout your life—for example, whether to lie to a sick family member, have sexual relations on a first date, or betray the trust of a friend.

Now that we know how ethics fits into the general scheme of philosophy, there are just a few more terms we need to deal with before we can begin to explore the field of ethics in greater depth.

Getting Our Terms Straight

When the average person makes moral statements or judgments, they usually use certain terms interchangeably. For most people the terms *moral, right,* and *good* all refer to behavior that is judged to be acceptable or correct from their perspective, while *immoral, wrong* or *bad* refers to behavior that is judged to be unacceptable or incorrect. Although these terms carry more nuances than the person on the street may be aware of, for our purposes we can also use them interchangeably.

Quite often moral terms are used not only to describe behavior or action, but also to describe a person's character. Thus when we refer to someone as being a *moral person* we are making a judgment that his character is good or virtuous; conversely, when we refer to someone as being an *immoral person* we are claiming that his character is bad, wicked or evil. We should be very careful, however, when we label individuals, rather than their actions, as moral or immoral, good or bad, since we often lack enough information about an individual's character or motivations to make these judgments properly. It might be easy enough to make a moral judgment about Hitler's character, but it is a bit more difficult to do so in the case of, let's say, Richard Nixon.

There are two other terms that are often used in ethical discourse that should be kept in mind.

The term *amoral* means having no sense of right or wrong. Babies, small children, severely mentally handicapped individuals and sociopaths can be said to be amoral and, as such, are usually not deemed to be morally responsible for their actions. The word *non-moral* means outside the realm of morality. Fields of study, such as genetics and physics, or inanimate objects, such as guns or nuclear weapons are essentially non-moral. The old cliché, "Guns don't kill people, people do," therefore, is correct because guns themselves are neither moral nor immoral.

For Further Discussion

Which of the following individuals would you describe as behaving immorally? Be prepared to explain what it is about these acts that you believe to be immoral:

1.   A 27-year-old man who has no ambition in life, who still lives in his parent's house, and who is content to hang out and smoke pot every day rather than trying to be a "productive" member of the community.

2.   A 17-year-old high school junior who frequently gossips and reveals information told to her in confidence.

3.   A 20-year-old college junior who thinks that women are simply

objects to be used for his pleasure.

4. A 25-year-old woman who accidentally gets pregnant after casual sex and opts to have an abortion because she feels that having a baby will prevent her from advancing in her career as a corporate lawyer.

5. A 30-year-old man who believes that all minorities are inferior but who doesn't act upon his racist tendencies.

6. A wealthy, attractive, and stylish 35-year-old woman who never says "thank you" or "please."

7. A middle-class mother of four who believes that her only moral obligation is to her family and does nothing to help those in need in the larger community.

8. A 40-year-old man who regularly eats chicken and hamburgers.

9. An affluent 60-year-old woman who owns several expensive fur coats and wears them regularly during the winter.

10. A teenager who carves the name of his girlfriend in the trunk of a tree so deep in a forest that no one will ever notice it.

Further Reading

At one point or another, as you read this text, you may become interested in finding out more information about some of the ethicists described in this book or delving a bit more deeply into their ideas. If so, the following works are highly recommended:

Ashby, Warren. *A Comprehensive History of Western Ethics: What Do We Believe?* Amherst, NY: Prometheus Books, 1997.

Becker, Lawrence and Charlotte. *A History of Western Ethics.* Hamden, CT: Garland, 1991.

Bourke, Vernon. *A History of Ethics.* Garden City, NY: Doubleday, 1968.

Fieser, James. *Moral Philosophy Through the Ages.* Mountain View, CA: Mayfield Publishing Company, 2001.

MacIntyre, Alasdair. *A Short History of Ethics.* New York: Macmillan, 1998.

Schneewind, J.B., ed. *Moral Philosophy from Montaigne to Kant.* 2 Vols. Cambridge: Cambridge University Press, 1990.

Wagner, Michael. *An Historical Introduction to Moral Philosophy.* Englewood Cliffs, NJ: Prentice Hall, 1990.

chapter 2

WHAT IS A MORAL ACT?

Case Study: Under the Influence

Johnny Santaniello was born into a poor family on Chicago's South Side. His father, who worked in construction, had a serious alcohol problem that led to his being fired from numerous jobs and eventually dying from liver cancer when Johnny was only 11. Johnny was raised by his mother, who was not able to provide him with much guidance or supervision, because she was working so many hours to support the family.

The neighborhood that Johnny grew up in was rough by any standards. Most of Johnny's friends were heavy drug users by the time they became teenagers and many spent considerable time in juvenile facilities, which only served to fuel their addictions to drugs. Although Johnny always tried to avoid using hard drugs, to fit in with his friends he would occasionally smoke pot. Unlike his friends, however, Johnny was eventually planning to go to college, anticipating that his decent performance as a varsity lacrosse player would get him an athletic scholarship at one of the colleges in his area.

During his senior year of high school, however, Johnny had a string of bad luck that pushed him over the edge. During a lacrosse game, he seriously damaged his knee, effectively ending his career as a lacrosse player. At the same time, Johnny's girlfriend of six years broke up with him because she became interested in another guy. The combination of these two events pushed Johnny into a state of depression and, to forget his problems, he began to abuse alcohol and assorted prescription drugs.

One night, when Johnny was driving home high from a combination of alcohol, pot, and pills, he accidentally drove over the dividing line on the road and crashed into a car occupied by an elderly couple. Although Johnny survived the crash, both occupants of the other car were killed. Johnny was arrested shortly after the accident.

During his trial, Johnny's attorney tried to plead that his client could not be held responsible for the accident because he was not fully in control of his actions due to his drug addiction. He also pleaded for leniency because of the hard life that Johnny had led. The prosecutor argued that Johnny deserved significant prison time because he was responsible for developing his addiction and freely chose to drive a car when he knew that he would be getting high.

FOR DISCUSSION

Do you think that Johnny is morally responsible for killing the elderly couple, or do you think that the specific circumstances of his life diminish, or even completely remove, his moral culpability? If you were a member of the jury selected to decide Johnny's fate, who would you side with: Johnny's defense lawyer or the prosecutor?

Voluntary and Involuntary Acts

On a daily basis, human beings perform a multitude of different acts. Some of these are fairly unimportant—deciding, for example, what clothes you will wear today or what you will have for dessert. Others may be incredibly significant—for instance, deciding whether you should seek out revenge for some insult or whether you should cheat on your income tax.

All of the acts we perform no matter how insignificant or monumental can be divided into two kinds: voluntary acts or involuntary acts. Voluntary acts are those acts we perform knowingly (i.e., consciously) and freely (i.e., with consent of the will), and for which we, therefore, are responsible. Voluntary acts can be further divided into two additional types: perfect voluntary acts or imperfect voluntary acts. A perfect voluntary act is one that is performed with full knowledge and full freedom. An imperfect voluntary act is one in which knowledge and/or freedom is either not full or lacking in some way.

Involuntary acts, on the other hand, are those performed either without knowledge or without freedom, and for which we cannot be held responsible. When a person commits an act without any foreknowledge or out of some necessity, we rarely, if ever, hold that person morally responsible for his acts, just as we would not hold a rock responsible when it falls through the force of its own weight onto someone's head.

As we continue on with this chapter and with the rest of this text, it will be extremely important to keep in mind the following principle: for an act to be moral in the true sense of the word, it must be a voluntary act. If an act is performed either without knowledge *or* without freedom, it usually is not considered within the realm of morality, since moral actions must involve some degree of conscious choice and deliberation. As we shall see, there are many factors that can affect the knowledge we possess and the freedom that we have to act in a particular situation.

Factors Affecting Knowledge

In general, a person is not considered responsible for acts done in ignorance. There are two kinds of ignorance: invincible ignorance and vincible ignorance. *Invincible ignorance* is ignorance that cannot be removed through effort or diligence. Because invincible ignorance destroys voluntariness, it also removes all responsibility from a person for the acts he performs. Imagine, for example, that a hunter in a remote part of the forest where there usually are no human beings sees something moving in the brush and believes it to be a deer. Only upon firing does he realize that he has killed another hunter, who chose not to wear the required orange safety vest that would have identified him to others. Such an individual would probably not be convicted of manslaughter, because he had no way of knowing that it was a human being in the brush.

Vincible ignorance, on the other hand, is ignorance that could have been removed through effort or greater diligence. Because it involves some degree of choice, it may lessen but does not free us from responsibility. Take, for example, the parents of a teenager, who have a sneaking suspicion that their son is having parties with his friends involving alcohol, but who prefer not to know too much about what is going on. In general, these parents would be responsible for the actions their child performs, because they had the ability to dispel their ignorance, but chose not to do so.

Factors Affecting Freedom

It is also a general principle of moral philosophy that a person can only be held responsible for actions committed freely. Whatever a person does out of necessity—whatever he cannot help doing—he is not responsible for. There are several factors that can affect human freedom:

Concupiscence has traditionally been defined as a movement of strong passion produced by the apprehension of some good or evil. The passions are love and hatred, desire and aversion, joy and sadness, hope and despair, courage and fear, and anger. These passions are neither good nor evil in and of themselves. They can be used by human beings for the purpose of self-preservation and great acts of compassion, but they can become evil if they are not regulated by reason.

Concupiscence can take either of two forms. In the case of antecedent concupiscence, a passion sweeps over a person without his intending it. Antecedent passion lessens freedom, and, in some cases may even remove it completely, because it hinders the reflection of reason. The classic example of antecedent concupiscence is the case of the wife who walks in on her husband in bed with another woman, and in a fit of rage kills them both. In such cases, many juries find defendants innocent by reason of temporary insanity caused by the influence of intense passion.

In general, the more intensive antecedent concupiscence is, the more it affects human freedom. However, unless concupiscence is so violent as to deprive one temporarily of the use of reason, it does not completely eliminate the power to refuse consent. When the will does consent, therefore, to the performance of wrongful acts, even though this consent may be reluctant, there is still freedom of choice and therefore responsibility for the act.

Another form of concupiscence is known as consequent concupiscence, in which strong emotions are freely admitted, consented to, or deliberately aroused, and therefore are completely voluntary. The best illustration of this sort of concupiscence would be the person who fuels her rage over some personal insult and then lashes out at the perpetrator later on. Since the anger in this case is deliberately aroused, this individual is said to be acting with full freedom of the will, and, therefore, is fully responsible for her actions.

Fear is a movement of passion formed by a threatened evil difficult to avoid. Fear can certainly affect freedom of the will to some degree. In the case of acts performed out of great fear, such fear can at times lessen, though not completely remove, responsibility, since human freedom is not destroyed completely. The only exception to this principle would be in the case of grave fear caused by the perception of some extreme evil, which one cannot easily avoid. In the standard plot of many action films, for example, a child is kidnapped and his parents are asked to perform a criminal activity in order to prevent their child from being killed. In an extreme situation like this one, one would have to acknowledge that the parents' extreme fear for their child's safety might very well exculpate them for certain immoral acts which they may have felt compelled to perform.

Coercion is usually defined as force, which compels a person to do something contrary to his will, brought to bear by some extrinsic agent. When someone is forced to perform an action which they otherwise wouldn't be inclined to do, we say that the person is being compelled to act through coercive means. If the coercion is irresistible, then an individual is not responsible for any acts that he may be compelled to perform. The caveat here is that to demonstrate that one was forced to act through coercive means, one must also demonstrate that he at least attempted some resistance. In some cases—for example, date rape—where a person is unable to offer any external resistance, internal resistance alone is usually considered adequate to eliminate responsibility.

In 1974 Patty Hearst, a wealthy heiress, was kidnapped from her Berkeley, California apartment by members of the Symbionese Liberation Army, a terrorist organization. Photographed wielding an assault rifle while robbing a bank, Hearst was later arrested in a San Francisco apartment with other SLA members. There were those at the time who claimed that Hearst was a willing participant in the criminal acts that she performed, and therefore, should be held responsible for them. Her attorney, F. Lee Bailey, argued that Hearst was compelled to act because of fear that her captors would kill her, and that her fear of death was so overwhelming that she was effectively brainwashed into acting as she did. Patty Hearst was eventually convicted of bank robbery and was sentenced to seven years in prison. Her sentence was eventually commuted by President Jimmy Carter and she served only 22 months in prison before she was released. To this day no one really knows for sure whether Hearst was truly coerced into joining the illegal activities of a terrorist organization or whether she was, to one degree or another, a consenting participant.

Habit is a readiness, borne of repeated acts, for doing certain things. If you perform certain acts long enough (e.g., smoking, drinking alcohol, etc.), these acts to a certain extent take on the form of necessity (i.e., you have a difficult time not doing them). It would seem at first glance that habit would eliminate responsibility, since acts done through habit appear almost involuntary. Deliberately admitted habits (e.g., smoking), however, are considered voluntary at least in their causes (e.g., the free choice to smoke that first cigarette) if not completely in their effects. In general, opposed habit lessens voluntariness, and sometimes precludes it completely.

Are We Really Free?

For an act to be a moral act in the true sense of the term, it must be performed voluntarily. This assumes that human beings are capable of acting freely. But is this necessarily the case?

As far back as ancient times, some philosophers came to question whether it is even possible to perform an act with complete freedom of the will. These philosophers, known as Determinists, argued that human beings are compelled by various factors—referred to as antecedent causes—to act in certain predetermined ways, and that, therefore, true freedom of the will is an illusion. The determinist argument is usually summarized in the following way:

> P1: An action is free only if a person could have chosen to do other than he did.
> P2: But all actions are determined by preceeding events (antecedent causes).
> C: Therefore, no action is free.

Determinist theory can take various forms. Biological determinists argue that basic human biology and our specific genetic make-ups determine what kinds of people we will ultimately become and even what kinds of actions we will perform. Biological determinists, for example, argue that things like sexual orientation are predetermined by our biological make-up. It makes no sense then to argue that gay men or women have some kind of choice in the matter or that they can "convert" if they make up their minds to.

Another common form of determinist theory is known as psychological determinism, which posits that deep-rooted psychic forces explain most of human behavior. Sigmund Freud, the father of psychoanalytic theory, in particular believed that human beings are determined by unconscious drives (e.g., the Oedipal complex) that society forces them to repress. He completely rejects the idea that simply because we feel that we are free that we actually are:

> As is known, many persons argue against the assumption of an absolute psychic determinism by referring to an intense feeling of conviction that there is a free will. The feeling of conviction exists, but it is not incompatible with the belief in determinism. Like all normal feelings, it must be justified by something. But,

so far as I can observe, it does not manifest itself in weighty and important decisions; on these occasions, one has much more the feeling of psychic compulsion and gladly falls back on it....

On the other hand, it is in trivial and indifferent decisions that one feels sure that he could just as easily have acted differently, that he acted of his own free will, and without any motives. From our analyses we therefore need not contest the right of the feeling of conviction that there is a free will (161-162).

Thus for Freud all of our significant decisions are determined by unconscious motives. Only the most trivial decisions—and what they are he does not explain—are free of such psychic conditioning.

Finally behaviorism is another psychological theory that argues that human behavior was determined not by unconscious drives, but rather by environmental factors. The most prominent of these behaviorist was B.F. Skinner, who in his works *Beyond Freedom and Dignity* and *Walden II*, argued that human beings are "conditioned" to act in specific ways by their environment, and that freedom, therefore, is an illusion. The only way to change a person's behavior according to Skinner is to change his environment. Skinner recommended the use of positive and negative reinforcement to alter human behavior, and believed that a perfect society could be created simply by figuring out how to condition people properly.

Responding to Determinism

In attempting to respond to the challenge of determinism, those who hold a belief in the existence of freedom of the will often begin by acknowledging that certain external factors can indeed affect human freedom. However, they dispute the fact that human beings have absolutely no freedom of decision-making. These theorists pose a number of objections to determinist theory:

Awareness of our personal freedom. As human agents our basic assumption is that the acts we perform are done freely, consciously, and deliberately. When you go to the mall to buy a pair of boots, for example, you don't think to yourself, "I have no choice in which pair of boots I buy." You automatically assume that you yourself decide what to buy, not some unconscious drives or behavior conditioning. The very act of weighing the pros and cons before we act demonstrates that, at least in our own minds, we assume that we are free. As Corliss Lamont puts it:

There is an unmistakable intuition of virtually every human being that he is free to make the choices he does and that the deliberations leading to those choices are also free flowing. The normal man feels too, after he has made a decision, that he could have decided differently. That is why regret or remorse for a past choice can be so disturbing (3).

Assumption of Moral Responsibility. In our society we frequently bestow praise on those who perform worthy or noble actions (e.g., the fireman who saves a child from a burning building) and assign blame to those who violate legal or moral norms (i.e., the neighbor who mows his lawn at 7am on a Saturday). But if no one does anything freely, then they are not responsible for their actions and neither deserving of praise nor blame.

Punishment of the Guilty. We believe that people who break the law should receive punishment for their crimes. But, if people are not free when they commit criminal activities, then they should not be punished for their actions. Drug dealers and rapists would undoubtedly appreciate this line of argumentation.

Controlling Desires. Psychological determinists argue that human beings are the victims of desires that they cannot control. And yet there are numerous instances of individuals who have overcome their deep-rooted desires and addictions through the force of their wills. They are capable, in other words, of overcoming their conditioning, which implies some degree of freedom.

The ultimate problem with determinism is that it ultimately renders morality impossible since, as we have already seen, freedom of the will is an essential characteristic of moral action. If you eliminate freedom, therefore, you eliminate morality (as most of us understand it, anyway). For this very reason most moral thinkers accept the existence of at least limited freedom of the will.

Certainly no one would argue that human behavior is not affected by various factors—aberrant mental states, the environment, our genetic makeup, etc. The question is whether these factors determine our behavior. Indeterminists—those who accept the existence of freedom of the will—believe that this is not the case. They argue that there is a fundamental difference between human beings and all other things in the natural world. Unlike all other entities, human beings are conscious of the operation of the natural and psychological laws that affect them. We can step back and reflect on these laws as more or less objective observers, and make our choices in light of these reflections. We are capable, in other words, of choosing to give in to our conditioning or not.

Take two people, for example, Willard and Mordecai. Willard grew up in a warm and loving household, with parents who took very good care of him, and who provided him with ample opportunities for personal and intellectual growth. Mordecai, on the other hand, grow up in a poor, abusive household in a neighborhood rampant with drugs and violent crime. All of us would agree that, given his background, Mordecai would have a much more difficult time than Willard in becoming a productive and responsible member of the society. But both these individuals ultimately have to choose how they are going to behave. Certainly it would take much more effort for Mordecai to resist the temptations to give in to drug use and criminal activity than it would for Willard. We would have to argue, however, that although it may be much harder for Mordecai to remain on the "straight and narrow" path, it is certainly not impossible. For an indeterminist the ability to break free of our conditioning is the "proof" that human beings are in fact free.

The determinist would argue that this belief in human freedom is simply an illusion—a pipe dream that we create in order to avoid the unpleasant fact that our actions are as determined as those of any other natural object in the universe. In the end, we have no way of knowing with utter certitude whether we are indeed free or not. The arguments of the determinist and the indeterminist are equally inconclusive. The moral enterprise, however, demands that we at least assume we are free, until it can be proven otherwise.

For Further Discussion

You are a representative on a college disciplinary tribunal set up to determine how students who have committed violations of school conduct codes should be punished. The following students have all argued that they are not responsible for the actions they committed for the reasons specified. Your job is to determine the degree of responsibility that each student has for the acts they committed and what sort of punishment, if any, would be most applicable:

- A sophomore from a financially strapped family steals $50 out of a wealthy student's dorm room. He maintains that he was driven to commit this action because he didn't have enough money to pay for the books he needed for class.

- In a heated exchange an African American student is called a racial slur by another student. In a fit of rage, he retaliates by hitting the student. He later claims that his anger over the insult drove him to respond in violence and that he shouldn't be held responsible for his actions.

- A freshman with a history of psychological problems is caught surreptitiously taking pictures with his cell phone of girls' bare feet as they sunbathe on the campus green. He claims that he has a foot fetish and can't control himself.

- A wealthy student is caught stealing a $1 folder from the campus bookstore. He maintains that he is being treated for kleptomania and was unable to stop himself from stealing. He also says that he never steals anything worth more than $2.

- Two students go on a date and when they return to campus begin to engage in consensual intimacies involving kissing and heavy petting. When the female student begins to feel uncomfortable and tells her partner that she wants to stop, he refuses. She reports him to the campus police, but he maintains that she was to blame for willingly arousing him to a point beyond which he could reasonably be expected to control himself.

- A senior goes out drinking with his fraternity buddies during graduation week and becomes extremely drunk. He arrives at his dorm room at 2am, but finds that he has been locked out. Unable to get anyone to open the door for him, he breaks a window to get in. When he is caught by the campus police, he maintains that he was too drunk to know what he was doing, and therefore was not responsible. This is the only time that he has gotten into trouble during his four years at college.

Sources and Further Reading

Double, Richard. *The Non-Reality of Free Will*. New York: Oxford University Press, 1991.

Dworkin, Gerald. *The Theory and Practice of Autonomy*. Cambridge: Cambridge University Press, 1988.

Ekstrom, Laura Waddell. *Agency and Responsibility*. Boulder, CO: Westview Press, 2001.

Freud, Sigmund. *Psychopathology of Everyday Life*. New York: Modern

Library, 1966.

Kane, Robert. *Free Will and Values*. Albany, NY: SUNY Press, 1985.

Lamont, Corliss. *Freedom of Choice Affirmed*. New York: Horizon, 1967.

Skinner, B.F. *Beyond Freedom and Dignity*. New York: Alfred A. Knopf, 1971.

—. *Walden II*. New York: Macmillan, 1976.

Watson, Gary. *Free Will*. Oxford: Oxford University Press, 1982.

Wolf, Susan. *Freedom Within Reason*. New York: Oxford University Press, 1990.

chapter 3

CHALLENGES TO ETHICAL THEORY

Case Study: Lucy and Elsie

Lucy Cappamezzo is a 35-year-old assistant vice-president at Chase Manhattan Bank. Since she graduated from college thirteen years ago, she has worked hard to move her way up the corporate ladder. She was particularly excited about becoming an executive at a prestigious organization like Chase, because there are not many women in this kind of upper level position. Her life right now is exactly what she wants it to be: she commands an extremely high salary. She owns a wonderful condo on the upper East Side of Manhattan facing the river, and she has been told that she has the potential to move to the top of her organization.

A few months ago Lucy met Brad Sullivan, a 37-year-old businessman, whose computer software company has really started to take off, generating millions of dollars each year. Brad is currently separated from his wife of five years and has a four-year-old daughter who he visits on occasion. From the moment that Brad and Lucy met at a local East Side bar, they were immediately attracted to one another, and started dating regularly. Neither of them, however, can afford to take time out of their busy schedules to make any kind of real commitment to a partner, but both would like to have a casual, noncommittal, sexual relationship. They meet about three times a week for dinner, companionship, and sexual intercourse.

When Lucy's mother Elsie Cappamezzo found out about this arrangement she became extremely agitated and told her daughter that her behavior was completely unacceptable. She said that there were rules about how people should behave sexually, and that Lucy was breaking all of them. Quoting both the Old and the New Testament as well as some recent pronouncements of the Pope, Elsie maintained that Lucy was putting her immortal soul in danger through her immoral and inde-cent behavior.

In reply, Lucy told her mother that the rules that she was talking about simply reflect her own opinions about sexual matters. Each person, Lucy said, has his or her own ideas about right and wrong, and that hers were just different (not any worse) than her mother's. In the end, Lucy told her mother, all a person can do in life is try to be faithful to her own heart, and follow it wherever it may lead.

The discussion quickly degenerated into a full-blown argument, with Lucy remaining firm in her belief that lifestyle choices like hers were simply matters of preference and her mother arguing that God has ex-pressly forbidden the sort of behavior in which Lucy was currently en-gaged. Because neither party could understand the other's position and because neither was willing to listen to views that contradicted her own, the two stormed off angrily, vowing not to speak again until the other started acting more sensibly.

FOR DISCUSSION

How would you characterize Lucy's and Elsie's approach to moral issues? Which approach makes the most sense to you personally? Why? Do you see any potential problems with either of these approaches to ethics? If so, what?

Before we begin to examine the essential characteristics of moral prin-ciples, it would be useful to take a look at two approaches to ethics that pose enormous challenges to the moral enterprise, because each is so seductive in their simplicity. These theories go by the names of subjec-tivism and dogmatism. Although neither theory holds up upon careful examination, it's fairly easy to fall into the trap of approaching ethics either subjectivistically or dogmatically. As we'll see, the danger with both these approaches is that each in its own unique way undermines the very foundations of ethics as a rational enterprise.

Subjectivism

In order to understand the philosophical roots of subjectivism, one must first recognize that for many modern philosophers scientific statements seem to be of a different sort altogether than moral statements. Let's start with a little experiment to help illustrate this point. Read the two following statements, and ask yourself if they are true or false:

1. Statement #1: "It is raining outside."
2. Statement #2: "The death penalty is morally wrong."

What specific criteria did you use to determine whether each of these statements was true or false? (In other words, how did you determine whether or not it is true that it is raining outside? And how did you determine whether or not it is true that the death penalty is morally wrong?) Do these statements appear to be of the same kind or are they different in some way? Which of these statements seems more objective to you? Why?

If you are like many students, you probably thought that the scientific statement ("It is raining out.") was more objective in nature than the moral statement ("The death penalty is morally wrong."). You may have thought that the second statement was more a matter of personal opinion than objective fact and perhaps less open to being verified as true or false than the first statement. If this sort of response reflects the way that you viewed these two sorts of statements, then, congratulations, you are a subjectivist!

Subjectivists believe that, whereas scientific statements can be judged to be true or false depending on whether or not they correspond with reality, moral statements seem to lack this kind of objective basis. It is clear that a scientific statement like "it is raining out" can be proved or disproved by a careful observation of the way the world operates. Look out the window. If it is, in fact, raining outside, you know that the statement is true; if it is not raining, you know the statement is false. The same is true with more complex sorts of scientific statements as well (e.g., "$E=mc^2$" or the law of gravity).

On the other hand, if I were to maintain that "the death penalty is morally wrong," such a statement would seem to preclude the kind of demonstration that one finds in science. What "proof" could I give that would absolutely convince any rational person that my statement is true?

This apparent difference between scientific and moral statements has led certain philosophers to question whether there is any objective basis for our moral claims. Subjectivists argue that such claims instead simply represent our personal preferences or our individual feelings about certain actions. One of the main proponents of this theory was David Hume (1711-1776), a British philosopher whose aim was to debunk those thinkers who believed that they could provide a foundation for ethics that is grounded in reason. In Book III of his *Treatise of Human Nature*, Hume presents one of the earliest and most influential defenses of a theory of subjectivism. He begins by arguing that it is the passions, not reason, that moves us to perform certain actions. It is futile, then, to look for a rational basis for our moral acts:

> Take any action allowed to be vicious: willful murder, for instance. Examine it in all lights and see if you can find that matter of fact or real existence, which you can call vice. In whichever way you take it, you find only certain passions, motives, volitions and thoughts. There is no other matter of fact in the case. The vice entirely escapes you, as long as you consider the object. You never can find it, till you turn reflection into your own breast and find a sentiment of disapprobation which arises in you towards this action. Here is a matter of fact; but it is the object of feeling, not of reason. It lies within yourself, not in the object (468).

Thus for Hume our judgments about whether certain actions are right or wrong simply reflect whether one approves or disapproves of the action being performed. Morality in this approach becomes nothing more than a matter of taste, not unlike a preference that one might have for hamburgers over pizza. For example, to say that abortion is wrong is to express nothing more than my distaste for the termination of the life of the fetus. It is simply to say, "I disapprove of this type of behavior." But such a judgment says nothing about the objective status of the act itself. The subjectivist would, in fact, argue that the statement says more about the attitude of the speaker than about the nature of the act being spoken about.

Taken to its logical conclusion, subjectivism inevitably leads to another "ism" that is equally controversial in ethics—relativism. If our moral judgments are simply a matter of preference, and there is no objective basis for determining whether one set of moral preferences are superior to any other, then we must hold that all moral perspectives are equally valid. In the end, if I believe something to be right, then it must be right—at least for me. Nor can our moral preferences be subject to dispute. Just as we wouldn't think of criticizing someone who prefers hamburgers to pizza, we also can't object to those whose lifestyles may seem morally wrong to us. The way a person chooses to live and the specific moral decisions he makes should not ultimately be viewed as better or worse than anyone else's. In the words of the Roman sage: "De gustibus non est disputandum" (Taste must not be disputed).

Believe it or not, many individuals in our society are probably subjectivists without even knowing it. For example, in the course of a heated argument over the death penalty, one of the debaters might throw up his or her hands in disgust, shouting, "Well, you're entitled to your perspective and I'm entitled to mine." Or after a 50 minute Ethics class in which the instructor believes that he has made a persuasive case that partial birth abortion is wrong, systematically refuting opposing arguments and successfully countering all objections, at least one student will inevitably come up with the following kind of retort: "That's just your opinion." Even in those situations where they may personally feel a specific type of behavior is morally repugnant, they feel extremely hesitant to argue that it is objectively wrong, lest they be accused of being moral absolutists. "Who am I to say," such students lament, "how other people ought to behave?"

Despite the popularity of subjectivism as a moral approach, there are some obvious problems with such an approach to ethics:

There are objective wrongs. Certain extreme acts—rape, torture and child abuse—seem to be wrong, not just because of one's personal distaste for them, but because of the immoral nature of the acts themselves. Other less extreme acts—neglect of one's children, disloyalty to one's friends, marital infidelity—also seem objectively wrong to us, but because of the complexity of these issues we might need to spend more time developing cogent arguments to explain exactly why they are wrong.

Real argumentation implies an objective basis for our moral claims. There seems to be something intuitively wrong with subjectivism as well. Although when many people argue for or against some moral position they clearly do so in a way that signifies that they are simply expressing their opinion or preference on the subject, others actually attempt to give some rational justification for their position. The man who argues against the death penalty, for example, by attempting to demonstrate that it does not reduce violent crime or that it is an unjust means of punishing criminals, clearly believes that there is an objective basis to his moral position. He knows that he is not simply expressing his own preference, but is in fact expressing, however partially and imperfectly, some higher truth about the subject. Insofar as he is open to the reasonable opposing arguments of others—willing to allow, that is, their more convincing arguments to change his position on the subject—he is certainly doing something more than simply expressing a feeling about the death penalty.

Subjectivism precludes criticizing repugnant behavior. If moral judgments are mere opinions, similar to a preference for hotdogs or hamburgers, it is extremely difficult to criticize anyone for their moral viewpoints or behavior, no matter how repugnant they might be. The following example will help to illustrate this problem: Ted Bundy, a serial killer who murdered many young women during his infamous killing spree in the 1990s, expressed his feelings about what he did by espousing an almost perfect philosophy of subjectivism. As Bundy himself recounted:

Then I learned that all moral judgments are 'value judgments,' that all value judgments are subjective, and that none can be proved to be either 'right' or 'wrong.' I even read somewhere that the Chief Justice of the United States had written that the American Constitution expresses nothing more than collective value judgments. Believe it or not, I figured out for myself—what apparently the Chief Justice couldn't figure out for himself—that if the rationality of one value judgment was zero, multiplying it by millions would not make it one whit more rational. Nor is there any 'reason' to obey the law for anyone, like myself, who has the boldness and daring—the strength of character—to throw off its shackles....I discovered that to become truly free, truly unfettered, I had to become truly uninhibited.

And I quickly discovered that the greatest obstacle to my freedom, the greatest block and limitation to it, consists in the insupportable 'value judgment' that I was bound to respect the rights of others. I asked myself, who were these 'others?' Other human beings, with human rights? Why is it more wrong to kill a human animal than any other animal, a pig or a sheep or a steer? Is your life more than a hog's life to a hog? Why should I be willing to sacrifice my pleasure more for the one than for the other? Surely, you would not, in this age of scientific enlightenment, declare that God or nature has marked some pleasures as 'moral' or 'good' and others as 'immoral' or 'bad'?

In any case, let me assure you, my dear young lady, that there is absolutely no comparison between the pleasure that I might take in eating ham and the pleasure I anticipate in raping and murdering you. This is the honest conclusion to which my education has led me—after the most conscientious examination of my spontaneous and uninhibited self (Pojman 30).

The problem that those who intentionally or unintentionally espouse a subjectivistic viewpoint face is how on earth is it possible to criticize someone like Ted Bundy if all moral judgments express nothing more than preferences or opinion? If he were consistent, the subjectivist would have to say that Bundy's moral opinions are as valid as anyone else's. Or he would have to drop his own subjectivism in extreme cases—rape, torture, etc—but then he would be inconsistent.

How would you respond to Ted Bundy's "rationale" for why there is basically nothing wrong with the killing spree that he undertook? Do you think that, if you were faced with the challenge of responding to an argument like his, you would resort to the old platitude, "Well, everyone has his own opinion"? Are you starting to feel a bit uncomfortable now about where subjectivist moral views can ultimately lead? Perhaps you can see why many philosophers argue that subjectivism as a moral approach is not only ill considered, but extremely dangerous as well.

If, after reflecting upon these objections, you agree that subjectivistic attitudes towards moral issues are problematic, perhaps you would be willing to take me up on a challenge: make it a point from now on when you are talking about ethical issues to avoid qualifying moral judgments with phrases like "in my opinion" or "I believe." Force yourself to take a stand on ethical issues, to argue your position strongly and persuasively, and to stand by your moral judgment. If in time you are persuaded by facts or arguments to modify or even contradict your prior moral judgment, that's okay too. It means that you are evolving as a moral thinker. Just recognize that the moral judgments you make should be grounded in something more objective than a mere whim or some shallow preference.

Moral Dogmatism

Another very problematic approach to ethics that I would like to examine can be called "dogmatism," for lack of a better name. A dogmatist is someone who is so absolutely convinced of the truth of his or her viewpoint that he or she is unwilling to accept any countervailing viewpoint no matter how reasonable it might be. Although there are many different breeds of dogmatists, most share certain common characteristics:

- Dogmatists are unshakable in their moral outlook. They have a "black and white" view of reality with no shades of gray. They are rarely, if ever, given to doubts, struggles, or uncertainty.
- Dogmatists believe that their view is the only possible right one,

and discount those who have contrary views as being in error or even immoral.

- Dogmatists are usually not willing to argue their position rationally with those who disagree. When asked to defend their positions, they typically will cite an authority figure or "sacred" text as providing all the justification they believe is needed.

At first glance, dogmatism might seem to be almost admirable in an age when so many are given to treating ethics as a matter of opinion. Unlike subjectivists, a dogmatist has no problem taking a moral stand. Dogmatists are also often quite good at living up to their own values and defending them forcefully when necessary.

Examples of dogmatism can be found in almost every domain of life. A political dogmatist, for example, might believe that whatever a pundit or politician who shares his political leanings says must be taken as the gospel truth. Whether such an individual's pronouncements are, at times, contradictory or even illogical does not matter in the least to a committed dogmatist. Dogmatists of various stripes can also be found in the fields of science, education, health care, and, not surprisingly, in religion as well.

In fact, one of the oldest approaches to ethics—Divine Command Theory—is also a good example of religious dogmatism. Although this approach to ethics has always had its adherents, in recent years, in the United States especially, more and more Americans seem to resort to some form of this position when discussing complex moral issues.

Divine Command Theory actually refers to a number of related ethical theories. What they all have in common is that they take God's will to be the foundation for ethics. According to this theory, an act is morally good if God wills or commands it and an act is morally bad if he prohibits or condemns it. Thus the statement, "Adultery is wrong," therefore, simply means, "adultery is forbidden by God." No other justification is needed to decide if an act is right or wrong other than God's command or condemnation. For example, an adherent of this position might maintain that homosexual activity is morally wrong because such actions have been condemned by God. He might go so far as to show the specific passages in scripture or the magisterial proclamations that express God's will, but he would probably not go any further than this to make his case. He certainly would have no need to argue his case based upon the impact that homosexual relations might have on the well being of the larger society, for example.

One philosophical difficulty with this position has been raised by an argument known as the "*Euthyphro* Dilemma." The argument is found in Plato's text of the same name and is named after Euthyphro, Socrates' antagonist in the text. In this ancient dialogue, Socrates asks Euthyprho a perplexing question: "Are morally good acts willed by God because they are morally good or are they morally good because they are willed by God?" Either way that Euthyphro answers the question raises its own set of difficulties.

If Euthyphro attempts to argue the first position—that morally good acts are willed by God because they are morally good—then he faces the independence problem. If morally good acts are willed by God because they are morally good, then they are morally good independently of God's willing them. But this basically is a complete repudiation of Divine Command Theory.

If Euthyphro attempts to argue the second position—that morally good acts are good because they are willed by God—then he faces the arbitrariness problem. In this case morality seems to be based upon little more than the whim of God. Consider this hypothetical case: what if God were to command one to perform abhorrent acts such as torturing a non-believer. Would this then make such acts morally correct? We would have to argue, yes. Although one could argue that God has chosen not to command such acts, there is no reason why he could not. Take God's command to Abraham to kill his son Issac, described in Genesis 22, for instance. What if God didn't stop Abraham from sacrificing his son in the end? Would this mean that such an abhorrent act is morally permissible simply because God willed it?

Besides the philosophical critique posed by the *Euthyphro* Dilemma, there are two other more practical problems with Divine Command Theory:

How do we know what God prohibits? In some cases—rape, murder, incest—there would probably be some agreement among believers about what God forbids. In other cases, there may be much more debate. Take, for instance, the case of divorce. Catholics and conservative Protestants would argue that God forbids divorce while more liberal Protestants might argue that he allows it in certain circumstances. We could consult a sacred text like the Bible but we would probably get conflicting views on just about any moral topic that we were examining. One could also use the Bible in order to justify horrendous acts such as genocide or slavery if one was predisposed to do so.

Finally, which sacred text do we consult to discover God's will: The Bible? The Koran? The Book of Mormon? Adherents to different faiths would argue that their sacred text is the revealed word of God and would reject the legitimacy of other sacred texts. So which sacred text do we look to for the answers to our moral questions and, even more important, what means do we use to interpret this text in order to uncover the will of God?

How are you going to convince an atheist? Not everyone believes in God, and so many people will never buy into the basic premise of Divine Command Theory. The problem is that many individuals who support this theory often are trying to persuade others of the merits of their position, especially when it comes to public policy issues. To argue, for example, that gay marriage is wrong because God has condemned homosexual activity would be completely unpersuasive to a non-believer. It probably would also fail to persuade a more rationally oriented believer who may have his or her own religious reasons for supporting gay marriage—for example, because they believe God wants them to practice compassion towards other human beings.

There are very few people who think of themselves as dogmatists, because to do so would imply a kind of rigid, unreflective personality that most people are unwilling to acknowledge in themselves. And yet dogmatists abound in our society. In fact, if you are prone to thinking in black and white terms about moral issues or if you often resort to arguing about issues based upon the teachings of whatever religion you currently practice, you might be a bit of a dogmatist yourself. If you think this might be the case, I'd like to offer you a challenge: try to discuss moral issues without so often appealing to your religious beliefs or to the teachings of religious authority figures. I'm not telling you to abandon either your religious beliefs or the moral convictions that spring out of them. Just try to make your case in a way that those who are outside your religious framework might be able to accept, rather than presuming that your own beliefs are gospel truth and that anyone who challenges them must automatically be wrong.

If you do this, you may just discover that you actually become more persuasive in making moral arguments, because you'll be speaking to others from their perspective rather than your own. And you might even find that your moral perspectives gain a certain amount of depth from taking a vacation from your own dogmatic sensibilities.

Digging Beneath the Surface

On one level subjectivism and dogmatism would seem to represent polar extremes in ethics. The subjectivist doesn't recognize any objective basis for moral claims, and treats such claims purely as matters of opinion or preference; the dogmatist is so absolute in his moral pronouncements that he refuses to recognize that contrary moral positions might have even the slightest validity. Subjectivists value tolerance and openness to diverse moral perspectives; dogmatists value moral certainty above all else and often view tolerance as a gateway to moral vice. There would seem to be very little that these two ethical approaches could possibly have in common.

And yet dogmatists have much more in common with subjectivists than they might care to acknowledge. Underlying the dogmatists claim to objectivity is always the idea that something is right or wrong because God wills it or forbids it. We've seen that conservative Catholics and liberal Protestants read the same Bible to discover the will of God and yet Catholics interpret the Bible in such a way as to prohibit the possibility of divorce or the use of birth control, while liberal Protestants acknowledge no such prohibitions. It's the same Bible that they are both reading, but the way each group chooses to interpret what they regard as God's will is very different.

Upon what basis, then, does the dogmatist choose to accept one interpretation of scripture over another? According to the views of some religious authority? But then we must ask, upon what basis are the views of one authority figure (the Pope, for example) chosen over the views of another (the Dalai Lama, for instance). In the end, we must acknowledge that the dogmatist's basis for his moral claims is just as subjective as any subjectivists.

Neither of these flawed approaches to ethics in the end is able to provide what we really need in a viable moral position—a rational and objective basis for our moral claims. It remains to be seen if another approach to ethics is possible: one that can provide the kind of solid foundation that can guide us as we navigate our way through the moral challenges that we will inevitably face in our daily lives.

For Further Discussion

The following exercises can either be done individually or in groups, with one group developing the pro position, a second developing the the con position, and the third acting as a kind of jury to see which team's arguments were the most persuasive:

1. Gay Marriage: One of the important moral questions currently being raised in our society is whether or not gay couples should have the right to get married and receive the same benefits as heterosexual

couples currently do. Far too often when discussing this issue, those for and against gay marriage base their views on opinions, beliefs, or emotions rather than facts or logic.

- Pro Position: Develop as many strong, persuasive arguments as you can in support of gay marriage.
- Con Position: Develop as many strong, persuasive arguments as you can in opposition to gay marriage.
- Evaluation: Based solely upon the strengths of the arguments that you have developed (and trying, as much as possible, to leave out any biases you have about this issue), explain which position seems the most persuasive to you.

2. The Legalization of Marijuana: Another contentious issue in our society is whether or not marijuana should be legalized. Once again there are passionate people on both sides of this issue, who believe that their position is correct, but who also may be swayed more by emotion than by rational arguments.

- Pro Position: Develop as many strong, persuasive arguments as you can in support of the legalization of marijuana.
- Con Position: Develop as many strong, persuasive arguments as you can in opposition to the legalization of marijuana.
- Evaluation: Based solely upon the strengths of the arguments that you have developed (and trying, as much as possible, to leave out any biases you have about this issue), explain which position seems the most persuasive to you.

Sources and Further Reading

Harman, Gilbert and Thompson, Judith Jarvis. *Moral Objectivity*. Oxford: Blackwell, 1996.

Hume, David. *Treatise of Human Nature*. L.A. Selby-Bigge, ed. Oxford: Clarendon Press, 1978.

Nielsen, Kai. *Why Be Moral?* Buffalo, NY: Prometheus, 1989.

Paul, Ellen Frankel. *Objectivism, Subjectivism, and Relativism in Ethics*. Cambridge: Cambridge University Press, 2008.

Pojman. *Ethics: Discovering Right and Wrong*. 5th ed. Belmont, CA: Wadsworth, 2005.

Rescher, Nicholas. *Objectivity: The Obligations of Impersonal Reason*. Notre Dame: Notre Dame University Press, 1977.

Rorty, Richard. *Objectivity, Relativism, and Truth.* Cambridge: Cambridge University Press, 1991.

Westermarch, Edward. *Ethical Relativity.* Patterson, NJ: Littlefield, 1960.

chapter 4

GETTING ETHICS RIGHT

Case Study: Thwarting a Terrorist Attack

Authorities in New York City have recently heard through an informer that a group of Islamic militants living in Brooklyn plan to detonate a "dirty bomb" somewhere in New York within the next two days. Although this bomb can fit into a briefcase, it has the potential to kill hundreds of New Yorkers if it is exploded in a crowded building. The informer who reported this to the police is known for being extremely reliable and information he provided in the past has helped law enforcement officials round up a number of high profile terror suspects.

Raiding an apartment in Williamsburg, where one of the suspected terrorists was said to frequent, police arrested one man, Sadam al Baradi and his wife Fatima. The couple's three children were also taken in the raid and placed in foster care until the case could be sorted out. Sadam, a native of Saudia Arabia, continued to proclaim his innocence, although traces of chemicals that could be used to make a bomb similar to the one described were found in his apartment. When confronted with this evidence, Sadam broke down and told police that in previous weeks, his cousin, Hakkim, a known sympathizer of the terrorist group, Islamic Jihad, had been meeting in the apartment with some of his friends during the day when the family was not around. Through hours of intense interrogation, Sadam continued to maintain that he didn't know anything about his cousin's plans or the whereabouts of those whom authorities suspected were plotting the attack.

The FBI counter-terrorism expert in charge of the case, Fred Dobbs, has come to believe that Sadam probably is not directly involved in the plot, but he also suspects that he has not been honest about his knowledge of his cousin's whereabouts. With only one day before the bomb is set to explode, Dobbs is left with a difficult dilemma: does he continue to use only legal means to interrogate Sadam and risk having hundreds of innocent people die, or should he resort to the use of torture on Sadam, and perhaps even his wife, to get them to reveal the information that he believes they might possess. The methods that he is considering are so extreme that they have been condemned by civilized nations around the world.

FOR DISCUSSION

Pretend that you are a fellow FBI agent, and that Dobbs has come to you to help him decide on how to proceed in this case. You are known for being a highly objective and rational agent, so Dobbs asks you to come up with the strongest possible arguments for and against torturing Sadam and his wife, and then to advise him on what to do.

The Right Way to Do Ethics: Socrates in the *Crito*

Plato's famous dialogue, the *Crito*, opens with Socrates awaiting his execution in a jail in Athens. He is visited by Crito, a wealthy young friend, who tried to convince him that he ought to flee from prison rather than face death. Socrates's friends, Crito reminds him, are more than willing to use their own considerable wealth to bribe the guards who are watching over Socrates and provide the means for him to escape to some other city. If Socrates chooses not to flee, it will look as though his friends were too cheap or cowardly to save him when they could have and Socrates' enemies will take delight in his downfall.

It would have been all too easy for Socrates to take Crito up on his offer and escape to another Greek city. But Socrates was simply not that kind of man. In his reply to Crito, Socrates lays the foundations for his own approach to moral issues, leaving no doubts that he will be persuaded by sound arguments and not by the opinions of those who do not know what they are talking about, even if they happen to be in the majority:

> Dear Crito, your zeal is invaluable, if a right one; but if wrong, the greater the zeal the greater the evil; and therefore we ought to consider whether these things shall be done or not. For I am and always have been one of those natures who must be guided by reason, whatever the reason may be which upon reflection appears to me to be the best; and now that this fortune has come upon

me, I cannot put away the reasons which I have before given: the principles which I have hitherto honored and revered I still honor, and unless we can find other and better principles on the instant, I am certain not to agree with you; no, not even if the power of the multitude could inflict many more imprisonments, confiscations, deaths, frightening us like children with hobgoblin terrors ....

[Instead we should examine] whether I ought or ought not to try to escape without the consent of the Athenians: and if I am clearly right in escaping, then I will make the attempt; but if not, I will abstain. The other considerations which you mention, of money and loss of character, and the duty of educating children, are, I fear, only the doctrines of the multitude, who would be as ready to call people to life, if they were able, as they are to put them to death—and with as little reason. But now, since the argument has thus far prevailed, the only question which remains to be considered is, whether we shall do rightly either in escaping or in suffering others to aid in our escape and paying them in money and thanks, or whether we shall not do rightly; and if the latter, then death or any other calamity which may ensue on my remaining here must not be allowed to enter into the calculation (*Crito*, 46b-c; 48c-d).

In this passage Socrates rejects the idea that we should rely on our emotion to help us determine the correct way to behave, but should rely instead on reason, logic, and argumentation to make decisions. He also clearly believes that opinions of others don't matter at all in this process, but that we must rely on our own innate wisdom to solve moral problems. In short, if Crito wants Socrates to escape from prison he is going to have to persuade him rationally to do so.

To give Crito some idea about how the process of rational argumentation in ethics might work, Socrates devises three clever arguments to support his own contention that it would be wrong for him to escape from prison. We can summarize these arguments in the following way:

One ought never to intentionally cause harm to anyone.
If Socrates escapes from prison, he will cause harm to the state of
   Athens.
Therefore Socrates ought not to escape from prison.

If one remains in a state when one had the opportunity to leave it,
   then one is making an implied promise to obey its laws (and,

of course, one ought always to keep one's promises).
If Socrates flees from prison then he is breaking the state's laws.
Therefore Socrates ought not to escape from prison.

One's state is like one's parent or teacher, and one ought to obey
    one's parent or teacher.
If Socrates flees from prison, then he is disobeying the state—i.e.,
    his parent and teacher.
Therefore Socrates ought not to escape from prison.

In the end, Crito is unable to persuade Socrates using rational arguments, and Socrates, based upon the force of his own arguments, determines that the morally correct course of action would be for him to remain in prison and face certain death. How many people do you know who would choose death rather than be swayed by a bad argument?

Criteria for Viable Ethical Theories

Socrates' approach to moral issues, as has already been noted, laid the foundation for the future development of the field of ethics. In general, the approach to ethics that Socrates advocates in the *Crito* is one that is characterized by five clear criteria:

1. Rationality

Ethics is more than a matter of feeling, belief, or preference. If an ethical theory is to have any weight at all, it must be grounded in reasons that most sensible people would be willing to accept. Of course, it helps to have other rational people with whom to discuss and debate moral issues; otherwise ethical discourse becomes extremely difficult.

What does it mean to engage in rational moral discourse? In general, there are three essential steps involved in developing a rational argument: (1) Start from reasonable principles; (2) Argue logically from those principles; (3) Strive to be factually accurate.

Start from reasonable principles. For example, we might start with a principle like, "It is morally wrong to kill an innocent human being." This principle, while certainly lofty, would probably be accepted by most reasonable people. In fact, the conviction that innocent human life must always be protected is the moral cornerstone of most religious traditions. It is only in rather extreme cases—for example, where a family decides to withdraw life support from a patient who has been comatose for many years—that we might have some debate about whether or not this principle should be accepted absolutely.

Argue logically from those principles. Starting from our basic principle, we might then argue the following:

- It is morally wrong to kill an innocent human being.
- Abortion is the killing of an innocent human being.
- Therefore abortion is morally wrong.

The argument used above is what is known as a valid argument. What this means is that the conclusion of the argument follows necessarily from the premises. If you accept the premises, you are obligated to accept the conclusion as well. Many people might also say that the argument is sound. A sound argument is one in which the conclusion follows necessarily from the premises and the premises are also true. There are perfectly rational people, however, who would dispute the truth of the claim that the fetus is actually a human being. In attacking the truth of the second premise, the basic soundness of the argument gets thrown into question. In ethical discourse it is extremely important to strive to use arguments that are both valid and sound. Failure to do so will almost inevitably mean that your moral position will not be taken seriously by other people no matter how worthy it might otherwise be.

Strive to be factually accurate. We also need to be sure that the facts, data, and statistics that we use in our moral arguments are true and accurate. Never use facts that are made up or which you know to be wrong just to score some debate points with an opponent. The following argument made by Rush Limbaugh on his radio show is a good illustration of how some individuals use false information in order to persuade others: "Liberal tree huggers," says Limbaugh, "want to prevent any kind of logging because they say that the country is becoming deforested. But there are more trees in the country today than there were 100 years ago. So what is the problem with allowing folks to do a little logging in federal lands?"

The problem with this argument is that Limbaugh is playing fast and loose with his facts. Most ecologists will tell you that it is certainly not the case that there are more trees in the United States today than there were one hundred years ago and that many of the new trees that have been planted in the country are not the "old growth" kind that can sustain wildlife. When we use erroneous facts like this to bolster our moral theory, we do an incredible injustice to that theory and ultimately undermine our ability to persuade others.

The Example of Socrates. Look at the arguments that Socrates makes in defending his position to remain in prison. Does he start from reasonable principles? If so, what are those principles? Does he argue logically from those principles? Check to see if the arguments that he uses are both valid and sound. Finally, is he attempting to be factually accurate in the specific statements that he uses in arguments? I think that we would have to say that Socrates meets the criteria for rational discourse rather nicely in the arguments that he presents to Crito. One could quibble about whether all of Socrates' premises are in fact true—for example, is the relationship of an individual to his state really like that between a child and his parent?—but the arguments as a whole have struck people throughout the centuries as being persuasive. If they weren't, most people would think of Socrates as a fanatic rather than a morally heroic individual whose example is worthy of emulation.

2. Openness

If the ethical theory that you espouse is truly rational, then you should be able to enter into moral arguments even with those who espouse views different from your own. You should also be open to the possibility that individuals with whom you are arguing may very well be able to persuade you of the merits of their theory and force you to abandon your own. Remember, our basic assumption is that other people are just as rational as you are. If we accept this assumption as true then we must acknowledge that we may be able to learn something about the moral life from our opponents. Even in those cases where someone else's moral theory may come into conflict with our own, at the very least, we must be open to the idea that his or her perspective can at least influence ours.

Unfortunately, most people enter into moral debates assuming that their own theory is perfect and that they will be the ones to persuade others to change their moral perspectives. How many times have you had an argument with someone only to realize that he was simply not listening to what you were saying because his mind had already been made up on the issue being discussed? This kind of rigid and dogmatic attitude makes doing ethics extremely difficult, if not impossible. It also prevents individuals from attaining moral maturity by preventing their own ethical perspective from evolving.

The Example of Socrates. In the selection from the *Crito* used above, it would seem that Socrates really isn't all that open to the numerous points that Crito raises about why Socrates should escape from prison (e.g., people will think that Crito is too cheap or cowardly to save

Socrates; Socrates' enemies would gloat at his misfortune; his family will suffer if he dies). The problem with Crito's arguments, and the very reason why Socrates dismisses them so quickly, is that they really aren't arguments (logoi) at all, but rather groundless opinions (doxa). Crito's opinions are appeals to Socrates' emotions rather than to reason, they are not backed-up by the persuasive force of logic and rationality, and they place far too much emphasis on the empty beliefs of the majority. But, as Socrates himself puts it, he is the kind of man "who must be guided by reason, whatever the reason may be which upon reflection appears to me to be the best." Like Socrates, we are called to be open to the rational arguments of other people, but we need not spend endless amounts of time weighing the thoughtless opinions of those who prefer to make empty rhetorical pronouncements rather than use rational argumentation.

3. Universality

Most ethicists would also maintain that a viable ethical theory should also be universal in scope. Ethical theories are almost always articulated in the form of general rules of behavior. These rules are usually expressed in the form of a statement like, "Everyone ought to do x." But as Robert Solomon points out, the question of universality does raise some difficulties. Does the everyone included in this statement mean "everyone in the world, or everyone in this society, or everyone 'like us,' or, the most trivial, everyone who is in the same relevant circumstance?" (11)

A cultural relativist, for example, would have serious problems with the idea that moral principles transcend cultural barriers. They would argue that, while we can say an act is right or wrong for individuals in our society, it is extremely arrogant to presume that this moral judgment holds true for people in other societies as well.

The Example of Socrates. Socrates, however, clearly believed that moral judgments were universal in scope and should apply to all people at all times. The arguments that he develops for Crito are as applicable to those of us living today as they were to people in ancient Athens. The idea that one ought never to intentionally cause harm to another human being, which is the major premise of Socrates first argument, has been accepted as a universal principle for ethics throughout the centuries. We may debate whether or not one should accept this principle absolutely, but there is no question of its universal application.

As Socrates realized, if one's moral theory only applies to oneself or to a small group of individuals, then one's moral system becomes fairly superficial. Thus, we have to, at least, start with the assumption that moral principles are absolute and apply to everyone. Practical application will show us whether or not this is, in fact, the case.

4. Impartiality

If a moral theory is truly universal, then it must apply impartially to everyone. The principle of impartiality forbids us from treating one person differently from another when there is no legitimate reason for doing so.

This principle has been stated by Henry Sidgwick in the following way: "It cannot be right for A to treat B in a manner in which it would be wrong for B to treat A, merely on the grounds that they are different individuals, and without there being any difference between the natures and circumstances of the two that can be stated as a reasonable ground for the difference" (380). Therefore, the same moral rules that we demand others follow should apply equally to ourselves and to those close to us.

There are those, however, who believe that the requirement for impartiality in ethics is unnatural and perhaps even immoral. To illustrate the problems inherent in treating people impartially, let's examine the following, admittedly extreme, situation: imagine that on his way home a man comes upon two individuals trapped in a burning building. One is his daughter, a simple cleaning woman by profession; the other is a Nobel prize-winning scientist who is working on a cure for cancer. If this individual was trying to be completely impartial, he would have to recognize that the scientist's life was worth more objectively than that of his daughter, and he ought to save him rather than her. John Cottingham has argued that the person who acts in an impartial manner in such a circumstance is nothing more than a "moral leper" ("Partiality" 357).

He goes on to question whether the attempt to be impartial in our moral decision making is even possible. "Personal bonds, ties of affection, family ties," he argues, "are like the intimate concern one necessarily has for one's own body, an unavoidable part of what it is to be a human being. To say that the moral outlook is one which should attempt to ignore or transcend these bonds is to propose a concept of morality which seems inconsistent with our very humanity" ("Ethics" 89). For Cottingham, then, it is perfectly natural and completely moral for us to treat those close to us differently than we would less intimate others or strangers.

The Example of Socrates. Although Cottingham's position seems intuitively correct, Socrates once again provides us with an alternative perspective on this issue. As we have already seen, Socrates clearly believes that the arguments that he develops for Crito are universal in scope.

Because they are universal, Socrates doesn't hesitate to apply them to himself first and foremost, and as a result could not justify escaping from prison. Nor does he allow the unenviable position of his family, who would be left to fend for themselves if he was executed, deter him from doing what he believed to be right.

We might be inclined to treat those we like with greater moral favoritism than other individuals or apply a different set of moral standards when dealing with each group, but Socrates' example shows that, if we are serious about the moral life, we will strive to treat others in much the same way that we would treat ourselves or intimate others. If it is wrong to lie, for example, then it is as wrong to lie in our business dealings as it would be to lie to our family members. This is not to say that our attempts at applying moral rules impartially will be easy or that we will always be successful. It simply means that the goal of treating all those we have dealings with impartially should guide our moral decision-making.

5. Practicality

A theory that is so rigid and extreme that it cannot be practically implemented by human beings is no good to anyone. This does not mean that our moral theories and principles can't be idealistic, challenging, and lofty; it only means that our moral idealism must always be balanced by a practical consideration: can real human beings actually live according to such principles?

For example, a theory of radical altruism that argues that one must always be concerned with the good of others with no regard for one's self is highly unrealistic (who could consistently live this way? And who would want to?). Such a theory could only frustrate the individuals attempting to live according to its principles. In the end, it would collapse under the weight of its own naive idealism.

When you are developing your own moral principles, then, it is extremely important to ask yourself one crucial question: can a person with the highest moral standards live according to this principle? If it would be difficult even for an ethical giant to follow your principles, then it is reasonable to assume that you will have difficulty living according to them.

The Example of Socrates. There are those who maintain that Socrates' own moral approach was too rigid, and that, if he had only been a bit more reasonable and realistic, he could have gone on living a comfortable life in some other Greek city-state rather than facing death though hemlock poisoning. The problem with this position is that it fails to recognize that

Socrates had already spent years thinking about the reasonability of his moral way of life in light of the possibility of being killed by members of his society who were incensed by his endless interrogations. He was convinced that, if he maintained his moral integrity, he had nothing at all to fear from death. Reflecting on the possibilities surrounding death in his *Apology* (his defense speech to the Athenian jury that was trying him), he spells out the options in the following way:

> Let us reflect in another way, and we shall see that there is great reason to hope that death is a good, for one of two things:—either death is a state of nothingness and utter unconsciousness, or, as men say, there is a change and migration of the soul from this world to another. Now if you suppose that there is no consciousness, but a sleep like the sleep of him who is undisturbed even by the sight of dreams, death will be an unspeakable gain. For if a person were to select the night in which his sleep was undisturbed even by dreams, and were to compare with this the other days and nights of his life, and then were to tell us how many days and nights he had passed in the course of his life better and more pleasantly than this one, I think that any man...will not find many such days or nights, when compared with the others. Now if death is like this, I say that death is a gain; for eternity is then only a single night. But if death is a journey to another place, and there, as men say, all the dead are, what good, O my friends and judges, can be greater than this?...What would not a man give if he might converse with Orpheus and Musaeus and Hesiod and Homer? Nay, if this be true, let me die again and again.
>
> Wherefore, O judges, be of good cheer about death, and know this of a truth—that no evil can happen to a good man either in this life or after death. He and his are not neglected by the gods....
>
> The hour of departure has arrived, and we go our ways—I to die, and you to live. Which is better God only knows (Apology 40c-42a).

Socrates clearly believed that, if he maintained his moral integrity in this life, he would reap the rewards in the next. Although he is not certain what awaits him after death (an eternal slumber or an afterlife with the gods and heroes of Greece), he was convinced that whatever happened was nothing to fear and that "the good man cannot be harmed" in this life or the next.

So when we consider Socrates' ethics in light of his views on death and the afterlife, his position seems eminently pragmatic. We might disagree once again about whether his views on this matter are sound, but we cannot deny that if death is nothing to be feared than it is not quite so unreasonable to maintain one's moral convictions, even if these convictions might cause one to be executed, as Socrates eventually was.

Another Challenge

In this chapter, I have laid out what many ethicists consider the essential characteristics of a viable moral theory. In the second part of this text, you will be given the opportunity to examine some of the most influential moral theories in Western ethics. You might find some of these persuasive and others completely unconvincing. As you examine each of these theories, I would ask you to consider whether it meets the characteristics for a viable moral theory described above.

Of course, if none of the theories presented in this text meets with your approval, you are more than welcome to try to develop your own moral theory. Just be sure that it meets the criteria that we have just discussed.

For Further Discussion

1. Examine the following moral arguments and explain whether or not they are logically sound:

    • Intentionally taking the life of a human being is morally wrong. But war by its very nature always involves the intentional taking of human life. Therefore, no war can ever be morally justified.

    • Whatever saves a human life is justified. Experimentation on animals saves human lives. Therefore experimentation on animals is morally justifiable.

    • Society has an obligation to prevent harm from occurring to its citizens. Citizens are harmed all the time from smoking. Therefore society has an obligation to ban smoking.

    • People ought to be free to do whatever the hell they want as long as they don't hurt other people. The free exchange of money for sex (prostitution) doesn't hurt anyone. Therefore prostitution should be permitted in our society.

    • Individuals have a right to determine when and how to end their lives. The state's prohibition against physician assisted suicide is an infringement upon this basic right. Therefore, the state's prohibition against physician-assisted suicide is wrong.

- God's will ought to be followed at all times by human beings. The Bible represents God's will as it has been revealed to human beings. Therefore the precepts and rules laid out in the Bible ought to be followed by all human beings.

2. A Moral Debate: Miranda, Susan, Todd, Cortney and Glen are philosophy majors at Sacramento State College. One night while they are hanging out in Todd's dorm room, they enter into a debate on the ethics of the death penalty. Read the following transcript of their discussion and explain which of our rules for a viable ethical theory are broken during the course of the discussion.

- Miranda: "In order for a society to function effectively, all of its members need to know that those who commit violent crimes will be punished swiftly and severely. The death penalty sends a message to would-be offenders that if you take an innocent human life, yours will be taken as well, and therefore acts as a potent deterrent to other would-be violent offenders. After all, if you know you would be strung up, you sure as hell wouldn't stab someone you were having an argument with, would you?"

- Susan: "Well, in general I agree with you that the state has the right to take the life of those convicted of first degree murder. My cousin Lupe, though, is in prison right now for poisoning her boyfriend. She found out that he was cheating on her with her best friend and served him an arsenic cocktail just to teach him a lesson. Poor Lupe. She has had such bad luck in her relationships with guys that you just can't blame her for what she did."

- Todd: "Well, I think that we ought to live in a society in which all human beings' fundamental rights are respected, and this includes those convicted of violent crimes like murder. I simply don't believe that it pays to punish violent offenders, because all this does is prove that we as a society are unable to rehabilitate them. Instead I think that we ought to house such individuals with nurturing families so that they can receive the love that they never received from their own families."

- Glen: "What is wrong with you, Todd! The Lord has said, 'An eye for an eye, a tooth for a tooth.' God wills that those who commit violent crimes suffer by having their lives taken. You are such a damn idealist; there is no use even listening to you!"

• Cortney: "Calm down, Glen. There is a compromise position available. The Catholic Church, for example, has argued that, while the death penalty is morally wrong, it can be used in those societies where there is not the means available to incarcerate those convicted of murder. So, while use of the death penalty wouldn't be acceptable in the U.S. or in Europe, it could be used in many other countries throughout the world."

3. Imagine that you were involved in the discussion. Do you think you could develop an argument for or against the death penalty that would satisfy all of the requirements described in this chapter for a viable ethical theory?

Sources and Further Reading

Cohen, Stephen. *The Nature of Moral Reasoning.* New York: Oxford University Press, 2004.

Cottingham, John. "Ethics and Impartiality." *Philosophical Studies* 43 (1983): 83-99

—. "Partiality, Favourtism, and Morality." *Philosophical Quarterly* 36 (1986): 357-373.

Plato. *The Republic and Other Works.* Trans. Benjamin Jowett. New York: Doubleday, 1989.

Sidgwick, Henry. The Methods of Ethics. Indianapolis, IN: Hackett, 1981.

Solomon, Robert. *On Ethics and Living Well.* Belmont, CA: Wadsworth, 2006.

Taylor, Paul. "On Taking the Moral Point of View." *Midwest Studies in Philosophy* 3 (1978): 35-61.

Wallace, Gerald and Walker, A.D.M., eds. *The Definition of Morality.* London: Metheun, 1970.

Williams, Bernard. *Ethics and the Limits of Philosophy.* Cambridge: Harvard University Press, 1985.

PART TWO

THE GREAT ETHICAL THEORIES

INTRODUCING THE GREAT ETHICAL THEORIES

Case Study: To Squeal or Not to Squeal

Rosario Dominguez is a mid-level manager in the Customer Services Division of Kidco, a nationally recognized company that manufactures high-end children's toys out of wood. Recently, however, the new CEO of Kidco has decided that in order to compete with chains such as Fischer-Price and Mattel, the company needs to cut its manufacturing costs dramatically. To accomplish this goal Kidco is now sending its toys to be painted in China instead of at its own U.S. plants, where labor costs are much higher.

About eight months after these new toys started appearing on toy store shelves, an article appeared in the New York Times stating that three employees at the company handed over documents showing that several popular Kidco toys were painted in China using lead-based paints, which are outlawed in the U.S. because of the health risks associated with lead. The company is facing potential fines and lawsuits that could cause it to lose millions of dollars and perhaps even force it to reduce much of its workforce in the U.S. In order to mount a successful public relations campaign, the company needs to find out who the whistle-blowers are and to discredit them publicly by showing that their actions are politically motivated.

Investigators for the company have reason to suspect three disgruntled employees in Customer Services and they approach Rosario, asking if she has any knowledge about whether these three leaked the story to the Times. In fact, one of these suspected workers, Lori Grunthal, had confided to Rosario that she and the two others are indeed the whistle-blowers that the company is looking for, but made Rosario promise not to tell anyone. Rosario knows that if she rats out her colleagues, she will probably be promoted by the company as a reward, but that her three co-workers will certainly pay a severe price for speaking out against the company. Although the management of Kidco could not directly re-taliate against these employees because of federal whistle-blower laws, Rosairo knows that they would use any opportunity the could to make life miserable for these workers and ultimate drive them from the company.

FOR DISCUSSION

Answer the following questions as succinctly as possible:

1. In this specific case the right thing for Rosario to do would be...
2. The reason why this is the right thing to do is because...

What Makes an Act Right or Wrong?

Obviously the case presented above is a difficult one because there are so many conflicting values and interests at stake. Different people will likely view the moral dimension of this case in radically different ways and perhaps come up with conflicting interpretations of how Rosario should behave.

How did you answer the questions posed above? You were asked to specify what you believed would be the right thing for Rosario to do in this case, and then to justify your position. To put this in more theoretical terms, you were asked to explain what makes a human act morally right or wrong. Clearly, this is no simple question and has been the source of considerable debate throughout the history of philosophy. In answering the question of what precisely makes an act right or wrong, you are, in fact, doing nothing less than establishing the basic moral principle that you believe should guide all moral action. You are engaged, in other words, in the great project of moral philosophers throughout the centuries.

Now that I've frightened you a bit with the complexity of this undertaking, it is your turn to establish the basic moral principle that you believe should guide all human action. As you consider your answer to this question, you may want to think through various moral acts that you have performed in your own life and what it was that made them right or wrong:

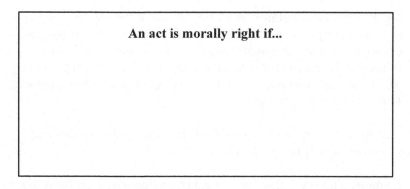

An act is morally right if...

Searching for Objective Criteria

We have seen that one of the problems with a moral system like subjectivism is that it provides no objective basis for determining which actions are right or wrong in different circumstances. If certain acts are right and others are wrong, then there must be some kind of objective basis for making such a determination.

Take the example of drug use, for instance. As we have seen, it is not enough simply to say that drug use is wrong simply because one may find the practice personally repugnant or that it is morally acceptable simply because one approves of the act. There has to be some kind of objective criteria that we can point to about the act that makes it right or wrong.

For illustrative purposes, let's take a look at two very different approaches to ethics:

A religious conservative might argue that drug use is morally wrong because God has condemned the use of such intoxicants. So the basic objective principle that he is operating under would be something like this:

"An act is morally right if, and only if, the act is consistent with what God commands."

While there are problems with this principle that were raised in Chapter 3, at least the advocate of religious conservatism can point to some more or less objective basis for maintaining that drug use is wrong. There might be some debate among believers about what God actually commands (the evidence from scripture is often ambiguous or inconclusive when it comes to many moral issues), but at least those who espouse this theory have a clear starting point for moral discussion.

Let's say we have a different objective basis for moral decision making. Perhaps we are ethical hedonists for whom the greatest good is to attain as much pleasure in life as possible. Naturally, there are some serious issues with this sort of approach to ethics as well, but, for now, let's just accept the possible validity of this approach. The hedonist may very well argue that drug use is morally acceptable because he is operating from the following principle:

> *"An act is morally right if, and only if, the act produces the greatest amount of pleasure for oneself."*

If you are a hedonist, then, any act which produces pleasure for yourself and avoids inflicting pain would be considered morally good. Of course, later on the hedonist may have to make some distinctions between immediate- and long-term pleasure, and decide which of these is the most important, but that is unimportant right now.

You are probably getting the point by now. When examining any ethical theory, it is important first to understand the basic objective criteria that the theory uses to determine in every imaginable circumstance which actions are right and which actions are wrong.

The Big Theories

For the remainder of this text we are going to be focusing on the five ethical theories that have had the greatest impact in Western moral thought: ethical egoism, utilitarianism, deontology, rights theory, and virtue ethics. Although there are many other theories we could also examine, these five are considered the "biggies" in the field of ethics. It is probably also the case that most people's own moral perspectives have been shaped and influenced by at least one of these main theories.

In a nutshell, here are the objective criteria that each of these theories fall back on:

> *Ethical Egoism:* "An act is morally right if, more than any other alternative available at the time, it brings about the greatest amount of good, or happiness, for oneself."

> *Utilitarianism:* "An act is morally right if, more than any other alternative available at the time, it brings about the greatest amount of good, or happiness, for all those who are affected by the act."

Deontology: "An act is morally right if it accords with a universal rule that all can follow."

Rights Theory: "An act is morally right if, in performing it, one does not violate the basic rights of others."

Virtue Ethics: "An act is morally right if it is performed by a person of virtuous moral character."

In general, we can fit all of these theories into two main categories: consequentialist theories and non-consequentialist theories. Consequentialist theories, such as ethical egoism and utilitarianism look to the consequences of an act to determine if that act is right or wrong. Non-consequentialist theories, such as deontology, rights theory and virtue ethics, maintain that the rightness or wrongness of an act have nothing to do with the consequences of the act, but rather have to do with something intrinsic to the act itself.

So now that you have an overview of the BIG ETHICAL THEORIES, we can examine each of them in detail. Although each of these theories has its benefits as well as its limitations, in the end you are the one who will have to determine which system makes the most sense for you.

For Further Discussion

1. The Bergmeier Case: The "Bergmeier Case," developed by John Keenan, is a notable one in contemporary Moral Theology. As you read the case, explain what you think would be the morally correct course of action for Mrs. Bergmeier. But more importantly, be prepared to justify your answer based upon some kind of moral principle you think people ought to follow:

   Mrs. Bergmeier is a married woman with several children and a husband who is ill. She has been arrested by the Nazis for assisting her Jewish neighbors and sentenced to six years without parole. After months in the camp, she learns that her husband's health is progressively declining due to his tending to the children, and that the children are not faring at all well due to their father's ailing state.

   She also learns something else: because of overcrowding, the camp releases pregnant women who are held for lesser crimes, like hers. Aware of one particular guard who regularly makes outrageous advances on her, Mrs. Bergmeier, for the sake of her family, submits herself to him. Three months later a pregnant Mrs. Bergmeier returns to her family to care for her husband and children.

2. Case Studies: Consider the following situations and explain whether or not you believe that the actions described are morally right or wrong in light of the basic moral principle that you selected earlier in this chapter.

• Marg Scherer and Walt Kaslow are competing for a managerial position at Kreskey's Department Store. Both are equally qualified and have been at the company the same number of years. Mr. Dellapisio, the store's general manger, decides that Kaslow should get the job because, based upon his experiences, he believes men in general are more dedicated to their jobs than women.

• Milton Barowski owns a failing cellophane production plant in Missouri. Because of poor business decisions that he has made, Milton has more debt than he can possibly repay. He realizes, however, that the fire insurance on his plant will be enough to repay all of his debts. One evening, when he is sure that no one is in the plant, he lights a fire in the plant, burning it to the ground.

• The State Environmental Protection Agency of Arkansas has mandated that hog farms treat pig waste in an environmentally sustainable manner. The approved methods of handling this waste typically cost hog farmers millions of dollars a year--costs which are normally passed on to the consumer. John Alfano owns a pig farm in Arkansas that employs 150 low-skilled workers. Because of rising costs, he is concerned that he will not be able to remain competitive if he follows the EPA's guidelines. Taking advantage of a loop-hole in the law, he allows the pig waste to seep into a nearby river. Although he believes that the quantities of pig waste he is allowing to enter the river will not be harmful to humans, he knows that it will have a negative impact on fish populations in the river.

• Marie Swaine is a physician in Delaware, where the use of marijuana, even for medical purposes, is illegal. Studies that she has read convince her that smoking marijuana can ease the severity of certain ill effects of cancer. She believes that several of her patients would profit from this treatment. She decides to make marijuana available to them, even though it is clearly against the law and could put her medical license in jeopardy.

Sources and Further Reading

Frankena, William. *Ethics.* Englewood Cliffs, NJ: Prentice Hall, 2001.

Keenan, James F. "Proposing Cardinal Virtues." *Theological Studies* 56 (1995).

Pojman, Louis. *Ethics: Discovering Right and Wrong.* Belmont, CA: Wadsworth, 2002.

Rachels, James. *The Elements of Moral Philosophy.* New York: McGraw-Hill, 2002.

Timmons, Mark. *Moral Theory.* Lanham, MD: Rowman and Littlefield, 2002.

Williams, Bernard. *Morality: An Introduction to Ethics.* New York: Harper & Row, 1972.

chapter 6

ETHICAL EGOISM

Case Study: A Matter of Choice

Denise Samos is a biology major at Monroe College in Rockland County, New York. For some time now she has had a crush on Matt Reich, a pre-med student at her college. Denise is not only physically attracted to Matt, but during conversations with him she has found him to be warm, funny, and very smart. In short, Matt is exactly the kind of guy that Denise would love to be dating if she had the choice. Unfortunately, just about every other girl at the college also finds Matt to be incredibly desirable, so Denise has been forced to resign herself to the fact that she and Matt will probably have to remain just friends.

One day during one of their bio labs, Matt casually mentions to Denise that he has managed to score two tickets to a Bob Dylan concert for the following evening, Thursday night, at Madison Square Garden—a real coup considering how hard these tickets are to come by. Matt knows from previous conversations that Denise, like himself, is a fanatical Dylan fan, and thought it might be fun if they went together. Needless to say, Denise was ecstatic about the offer, not just because she loves Dylan, but also because she thinks that this event might possibly lead to a more intimate relationship with Matt than she currently has.

There is one hitch, however. Denise has a very good friend named Marta, whom she has known since childhood and who also is a biology major at Monroe. Marta has been having a considerable amount of trouble with an Advanced Genetics course that she has been taking and is afraid that if she fails the midterm that is scheduled for this Friday, she will flunk out of the program. Marta's parents are hard-working immigrants from Colombia, who have little formal education of their own but who have managed to run a fairly profitable meat processing plant in upstate New York. They clearly don't think much of Marta's dreams of becoming a biology teacher and have told her that they will allow her to remain in college as long as she does well. Marta knows that if she fails out of the biology program her parents will use this as an excuse to insist that she leave college and come work in the family business—which she hates—as an assistant to her father.

Because Denise had already taken Advanced Biology and did very well in it, she had previously offered to spend Thursday afternoon and evening coaching Marta for the exam. Denise knows that with her knowledge of the subject matter, she can help Marta pass the exam and make it through the biology program.

Denise has to make a choice: help her dear friend study for this crucial exam or go with Matt to the Dylan concert and, perhaps, begin a relationship with him. Naturally she is torn by this decision and comes to you for your advice.

FOR DISCUSSION

What decision would you advise Denise to make? If Denise chooses to help her friend, Marta, do you think that this is evidence that she is behaving in a purely selfless way? Why or why not? If Denise decides to go with Matt to the concert, would there be anything morally wrong with this decision? If so, what?

In attempting to discern principles that can guide us in our ethical decision-making, we have already seen that we have numerous options from which to choose. The most intuitive place to start, I think, is with an approach to ethics that appeals to our basic human instinct to promote our own self-interest above and beyond all other concerns. The general term used for such theories is "egoism," but egoistic theories can come in either of two main forms—psychological egoism or ethical egoism. The differences between these two theories can be summed up in the following way:

- Psychological Egoism is a descriptive theory which states that human beings cannot help but behave selfishly, and, therefore, altruism is an illusion.

- Ethical Egoism is a normative theory which states that human beings ought to behave selfishly, and, therefore, altruism is foolish.

The main distinction, then, between these two theories lies in the fact that psychological egoism is a purely descriptive theory that describes how human beings presumably behave; ethical egoism, on the other hand, is a normative theory that prescribes how human beings ought to behave. One theory says that human beings are selfish; the other that human beings ought to be selfish. Psychological egoism is not a moral theory per se, but it does have interesting applications to ethics, which are definitely worth considering before we turn to our discussion of ethical egoism.

The Theory of Psychological Egoism

The basic premise of psychological egoism has a long history in Western ethics and has influenced a great many contemporary thinkers. What is this premise? It is that human beings always behave selfishly in everything that they do, and that it is impossible for them to behave otherwise. According to this theory, even when human beings appear to be acting out of altruistic—that is, selfless—motives, they are actually acting because of some advantage or benefit that they perceive for themselves. If you were to examine the supposedly altruistic acts of individuals carefully enough, according to the psychological egoist, you will inevitably uncover a selfish motive.

To illustrate the theory of psychological egoism more clearly, let's examine two actions that on the surface appear to be inspired by quite different motives. It is Thanksgiving Day and on the south side of Chicago there are two soup kitchens that will be serving dinner to the homeless. In one soup kitchen a politician who is running for high office has donned an apron and is carving turkey in front of cameras from two local television stations. In another soup kitchen a Sister of Mercy performs the same action out of her love for God's hungry children and with virtually no recognition. Most of us would probably argue that the politician is serving food to the homeless because of some advantage that he perceives for himself—most notably, a good photo-op that will help win greater support for his campaign. But what about the Sister of Mercy? We might be tempted to say that she is acting out of purely altruistic motives and that therefore her actions are much more laudable than the politicians'. But are they really? A psychological egoist would argue that in fact there is absolutely no difference between the actions of these two individuals: both are acting out of purely selfish motives. We know that the politician is engaged in a crass effort to convince his constituency that he is compassionate so that he will be reelected, but what are the selfish motives of the Sister of Mercy? The psychological egoist might argue that she derives pleasure from the act, and that this is her motivation for acting, not concern for those in need. Or he might suggest that there is some hidden motivation that inspires her: a desire to feel that she is noble or heroic, or perhaps to earn her reward in the next life. In any case, the psychological egoist would reject the idea that she is acting altruistically, since she obviously is deriving certain benefits from the act.

Psychological Egoism is actually quite an ancient theory. An early form of it was described by Plato in his dialogue, *The Republic,* where Plato has Glaucon, one of the participants in the dialogue, formulate a very persuasive argument in support of psychological egoism. In the second book of this work, Glaucon tells the story about Gyges, a shepherd, who came upon a magic ring in a fissure caused by an earthquake. Gyges quickly discovers that the ring he has found makes its wearer invisible, enabling him to go anywhere undetected. And what does Gyges do with this ring? Help the poor and suffering? Punish the wicked? Of course not! Putting the ring on his finger, he sneaks into the royal palace, violates the Queen, murders the king and seizes the throne for himself.

Glaucon goes on to ask us to imagine what would happen if there were two such rings—one given to a person of virtue and the other to a scoundrel. Would there be any difference in the way the two would behave? We would certainly expect the scoundrel to act horrendously in the absence of any social restraint. But would the virtuous man behave any better? Glaucon argues that, freed from the threat of punishment, the virtuous man would almost certainly behave just as badly as the scoundrel. At first he might be discrete in his use of the ring and try only to use it for good purposes, but after a while he would commit acts of injustice aimed at promoting his own selfish interest. Glaucon's argument in The Republic is that all human beings are naturally selfish and unjust. When we know that we can get away with something that is to our own advantage, we will do it, no matter how harmful it might be to others. The only reason, in fact, why most people behave decently is because of the threat of punishment. If we could somehow eliminate that threat there would be no limits to our selfishness.

Contemporary theories of psychological egoism are basically a new spin on this ancient idea. Examining human action, the advocates of this theory note that even apparently unselfish acts give the one performing them a sense of satisfaction, and that self-satisfaction produces a feeling of pleasure. They then go on to argue that the real object in performing "altruistic" actions is to have this feeling of pleasure, rather than to help others. This selfish motivation is as true for the student who gives up a night on the town to help her friend study for a calculus exam as it would be for Maximilian Kolbe, who sacrificed his life in a concentration camp for the sake of someone he barely knew. Neither can be said to be acting out of real concern for other human beings.

While psychological egoism is seductive in that it offers a simple and seemingly persuasive account of human action, it has been rejected on a number of different counts.

A major objection that can be raised against psychological egoism lies in the distinction between the causes and the effects of our actions. The psychological egoist, as we have seen, rejects the possibility of altruism because he looks at an apparently altruistic act and observes that one has received benefits from performing the act (i.e., feeling of pleasure). But just because someone receives benefits from an act doesn't mean that they necessarily performed the act for the sake of those benefits. The benefits, in other words, may very well be an effect rather than a cause of the good acts. Thus a woman who stays up all night caring for her sick child, depriving herself of comfort and sleep, naturally feels pleasure at the thought that she is acting the way a good mother should. While the psychological egoist would say that the feelings of pleasure that she receives from caring for her child are the cause of her actions, doesn't it make just as much sense to say that they are rather bi-products—or effects—of her selfless act? According to this view the goal of an altruistic person is not to attain pleasure, but simply to help someone in need. When we succeed in our goal, the result is pleasure. And there is absolutely nothing at all selfish about that.

Another problem with psychological egoism is that the theory fails to recognize the complexity of human motivations. If one takes the time to look carefully at the gamut of human activity, it is apparent that human beings actually act from a wide range of different, and sometimes even conflicting, motivations. Most acts are rarely so simple that they are performed out of one sole motivation. Take the example of the teenage boy who goes out of his way to help an elderly woman cross a busy street. He may be acting out of a "selfish" motivation to feel good about himself or have others think of him in a heroic light. But he may also be acting out of guilt, because the old lady reminds him of his dead grandmother; or he may simply be acting out of compassion for someone in need. It may very well be the case, however, that all three motivations are inspiring him at the same time.

It's also the case that a person can perform the exact same act at different times for quite different reasons. On my way to work on Monday, for example, I might pass a homeless woman asking for a handout, and give her $5.00 because I feel compassion for her. Then on the way home from work on Friday, I might see the same woman, and again give her $5.00. This time, though, my act is motivated purely out of a selfish desire not to be confronted by her humanity before the relaxing weekend that I have planned for myself. Finally, we have seen that the exact same act—serving Thanksgiving dinner—can be performed by two different people with very different motivations: the politician seeking self-promotion and the Sister of Mercy seeking to minister to individuals in need. The problem with psychological egoism is that it represents a shallow approach to understanding the complexity of human motivations. In reducing all motivation to selfishness, the psychological egoist turns all human actions to something banal and trite. And human actions, as we are all well aware, are anything but banal and trite.

All of these quite valid objections must inevitably make us conclude that, in its absolute form, psychological egoism is a fairly flawed theory of human motivation. Still, the theory does force us to reflect on what actually drives us to perform certain actions which might on the surface appear selfless. We certainly like to think that when we do something kind or generous for someone else we are acting out of purely altruistic motivations. But is this necessarily true? The psychological egoist would ask us to examine our deeper motivations to see what the real source of our actions is. While the psychological egoist may go a bit too far in rejecting even the possibility of a truly selfless act, certainly, as we have seen, our motivations for helping others is quite often mixed at best. It's also the case that quite often we deceive ourselves into thinking that we are doing something selfless, when in fact our true motivations might actually be much less noble than we'd care to believe. This is not to say that we can never be purely altruistic; just that we are probably motivated less by altruistic inclinations than we may think we are.

The Theory of Ethical Egoism

While psychological egoism can be discounted as a viable ethical theory, there is another type of egoistic theory that is much more useful in providing us with guidance in our human behavior. This is the normative theory of ethical egoism. Although there are not too many people who call themselves ethical egoists, the theory serves as the ethical underpinning for a political and economic theory that is highly influential in the United States—libertarianism. We'll return to discuss libertarianism in the third part of this text, but it should be kept in mind that much of our public policy in the United States has been shaped by that libertarian conviction that individuals should be allowed to maximize their own self-interest, a conviction which is essentially founded upon the principles of ethical egoism.

The basic principle that an ethical egoist would follow when determining how he should act would be something like this:

> Everyone ought to act so as to bring about the greatest amount of good, or happiness, for him or herself.

Every other theory that we examine in this text will maintain that the well-being of others is just as important as our own well-being (the radical altruist goes even further, arguing that the well-being of others is even more important than our own). Ethical egoism, on the other hand, argues that the well- being of others is an irrelevant consideration when we are determining how we ought to behave. Instead, we ought to pursue our own good with no thought to how it might benefit or harm others.

Moral Decision-Making Using Ethical Egoism

Step 1: Analyze all the possible consequences (short- and long-term, direct and indirect) of the action in terms of how they affect you alone.

Step 2: Determine if the action, more than any other alternative available at the time, will produce the greatest amount of good, or happiness, for you.

Step 3: If it does, then the act is morally right; if it doesn't, then the act is morally wrong.

Ethical egoism is above all a rational system for the promotion of one's own interests. This means that an intelligent ethical egoist would certainly not try to satisfy immediate desires at the expense of his long-term interests. For example, although it certainly might be pleasant to hang out at the beach instead of attending a boring ethics class, a true ethical egoist would know that his greater good is to be served by suffering through the class so that he can get a more fulfilling career later on in life.

This same rational approach to promoting one's own self-interest also means that an ethical egoist would probably not treat people indecently or unjustly. If he did treat people so callously, it might backfire on him, since the egoist's victims would either avoid him like the plague or work to undermine him. A sensible egoist, therefore, would probably want to treat at least some people well, but he would always do so only with the thought of what he can get back from them at a later date. In certain cases, in fact, he might even choose to sacrifice his own well-being when the long-term advantages of doing so outweighs the sacrifices he is forced to make.

Finally, although an ethical egoist wouldn't accept the idea that we have any moral obligations to our fellow human beings, he would not necessarily have any problem with individuals freely choosing to help the disadvantaged. He merely would argue that this should be done in the form of private charity, rather than through government programs involving the transfer of wealth in which the individual has no choice at all. If one were to raise the issue of what we should do to help starving children in Africa, for example, an ethical egoist would probably respond, "If you want to go help starving children in Africa, then go do it. Nothing is stopping you."

Several different sorts of arguments have been advanced by ethical egoists to support the truth of their theory:

The Natural Argument. In advancing his theory, the ethical egoist might point to nature to demonstrate that in the natural world various species selfishly pursue their goals with no thought to the well-being of other species or even members of their own species. In the end, the strong thrive and the weak perish, and the entire natural system benefits. What works for animals, argues the ethical egoist, would work equally well for human beings if we could just put aside our concern for the well-being of others and follow our natural (i.e., selfish) tendencies.

The Argument from Human Happiness. An interesting argument in favor of ethical egoism has been developed by Harry Browne that challenges the connection made by most of the world's religions between altruism and human happiness. We have seen that those who advocate an ideal of altruism argue that the world would be a better place if everyone were unselfish. Browne, however, uses an example to illustrate what the consequences would be if everyone sacrificed their own happiness for the sake of the happiness of others:

> Let's imagine that happiness is symbolized by a big red rubber ball. I have the ball in my hands, meaning that I hold the ability to be happy. But since I'm not going to be selfish, I quickly pass the ball to you. I have given up my happiness for you. What will you do? Since you're not selfish either, you won't keep the ball; you'll quickly pass it on to your next-door neighbor. But he doesn't want to be selfish either, so he passes it on to his wife, who likewise

gives it to her children. The children have been taught the virtue of unselfishness, so they pass it to playmates, who pass it to parents, who pass it to neighbors, and on and on and on.

To use a more realistic example, we might speculate what the world would be like if everyone acted like Mother Teresa, sacrificing their own happiness for others. According to Browne's argument, no one would be left to be the recipient of our generosity, and our attempts at altruism would be an exercise in futility. If we really are concerned about our own happiness, then we would be much better off hanging on to the big red ball (i.e., focusing on what makes us happy) than passing it on to others.

A related argument that Browne and other ethical egoists use is based upon the overall benefit of having each individual pursue his or her own self-interest. The argument goes like this: I know full well what makes me happy, but I really can't know what makes other people happy. If I spend my time trying to make others happy, therefore, I will probably fail in my attempt. But if I work on satisfying my own happiness, then I stand a very good chance of success.

The Economic Argument. The economic version of ethical egoism, which is known as libertarianism, supports a form of laissez-faire capitalism—that is, completely unregulated capitalism in which individuals are free to maximize their own wealth with limited government interference. The idea here is that if individuals are left alone to pursue their own economic self-interest everyone will benefit. This idea gained popularity during the Regan years under the name of "trickle-down economics." There are still a great many economists and political thinkers, however, who continue to argue that allowing individuals to focus on their own economic self-interests with limited government interference is the ideal way to maximize prosperity and happiness.

Political Ethical Egoism: Libertarianism

The political version of ethical egoism typically goes by the name of libertarianism. Although this political philosophy can take on many different, and often contradictory, forms—from radical anarchism to right-wing conservatism—all libertarians take as their starting point the basic premise of ethical egoism—namely, that the primary obligation that human beings have is to promote their own "rational self-interest" and happiness. Placing a strong emphasis on individual freedom and the right of self-determination, libertarians also argue that human beings have the absolute right to decide for themselves how they are going to live their lives without any undue interference from others.

Libertarians typically recognize three—and usually only three—basic rights: the rights to life, liberty and property. These rights are viewed as being absolute, and demand forbearance (restraint) on the part of others not to violate them:

The Right to Life. Each person has the right to dispose of his life as he sees fit. Anyone—and this includes the government—who attempts to take a person's life or injure him in any way through physical violence is violating that person's basic right to life. On the other hand, most libertarians would recognize the right of individuals to end their own lives if they see fit and therefore oppose laws prohibiting suicide and voluntary euthanasia.

The Right to Liberty. Libertarians place a great emphasis on individual liberty, which they view as the cornerstone of any civilized society. A person, they argue, has the right to live as he sees fit, as long as he doesn't interfere with anyone else's right to do the same. Libertarians object to any limitations placed upon freedom of speech, freedom of the press, freedom of assembly, and the right to own, manufacture, or sell weapons (including concealed weapons or assault weapons). They also believe that there should be no censorship of the media by the government. Although libertarians support the idea that every woman has the right to decide whether or not to have an abortion, they do not believe that taxpayers should be forced to pay for such procedures.

The Right to Property. Libertarians also emphasize the almost absolute right of individuals to use their property as they see fit, and object to any encroachments upon this right by individuals or governments (e.g., eminent domain laws, zoning ordinances, rent control, property taxes). Public lands such as national preserves and parks should be sold off for private ownership, since the government, they argue, has no business owning land.

In general, libertarians view government as a problem rather than as a solution (or, as John Hospers put it, "the most dangerous institution known to man"). Most governments, they argue, have an unfortunate history of violating human freedoms and enslaving their citizens. Therefore, the best government is the one that is most limited in scope and power. The sole role of government in libertarian political philosophy is to protect its citizens against violations of their basic rights to life, liberty, and property. Many libertarians, therefore, support taxation to provide for police protection and military defense. All other functions of government, they believe, should be privatized.

As we shall see later on in this text, libertarians reject the notion that government has any role to play in providing assistance to those who are poor or disadvantaged. As Hospers puts it:

> No one should be forced by law to help others, not even to tell them the time of day if requested, and certainly not to give them a portion of one's weekly paycheck. Governments, in the guise of humanitarianism, have given to some by taking from others ... And in doing so they have decreased incentive, violated the rights of individuals, and lowered the standards of living of almost everyone.
>
> All such laws constitute what libertarians call moral cannibalism. A cannibal in the physical sense is a person who lives off the flesh of other human beings. A *moral* cannibal is one who believes he has a right to live off the "spirit" of other human beings—who believes that he has a moral claim on the productive capacity, time, and effort expended by others (18).

Libertarians like Hospers believe that to tax the income of industrious citizens in order to help others less industrious than themselves is both immoral and unproductive. It is immoral because it confiscates the property (i.e., money) of one group of people and transfers their property to others who have no legitimate claim upon it. It is unproductive because it encourages the poor to become dependent and discourages others from working industriously to increase their own wealth.

Finally, libertarians also believe that government should not enact laws designed to prevent individuals from causing harm to themselves, rejecting the concept of "victimless crimes." Naturally, then, they oppose legal prohibitions on recreational drug use, prostitution, gambling, pornography or any kinds of sexual activities between consenting adults. They argue that government has no right to interfere in activity that harms no one else (see Libertarian National Committee).

Advantages of Ethical Egoism

Besides the philosophical arguments listed above—which are by no means inconsiderable—there are a few definite benefits that ethical egoism as a theory that make it extremely appealing to many people:

Self-interest is highly objective. Although it is extremely difficult for me to know what is in the best interest of others, I almost always know what is in my own self-interest. I am also in a much better position to determine how to satisfy my own self-interest than I would be trying to determine how to satisfy the interests of others. Ethical egoism, therefore, provides a highly objective criteria for moral action and makes it fairly easy to determine how one ought to behave in different circumstances. This is no small matter when we are confronted by serious moral dilemmas that require fairly quick moral deliberations.

Ethical egoism encourages personal responsibility. Many individuals in our society refuse to take responsibility for their own actions and look to government and their fellow citizens to lend them a helping hand when they fall on hard times. This is true even when such individuals are responsible for their own misfortunes because of bad choices that they have freely made. Ethical egoism, on the other hand, places full responsibility on the individual for maximizing their own happiness and well-being and recognizes the rights of others to do the same. Everyone, according to this theory, is completely responsible for their own success or failure in life.

Disadvantages of Ethical Egoism

Ethical egoism certainly is quite a seductive theory for many Americans. Our very way of life with its emphasis on "looking out for number one" seems to offer a practical justification for ethical egoism, as does our free-market economic system, which appears to be nothing more than ethical egoism on a national scale. But just as in the case of psychological egoism, the theory has some difficulties:

Ethical egoism is a self-defeating theory. The ethical egoist, as we have seen, advocates a theory which argues that everyone ought to promote his or her own interests regardless of the effect it has on others. It makes little sense, however, for the ethical egoist to advocate such a theory since the interests of others, if promoted, will eventually come into conflict with his own interests. Instead, a smart ethical egoist should advise others to be scrupulously virtuous, so that he will be able to promote his own interests without competition. To be consistent, he should actually be a champion of the purest form of altruism, rather than of ethical egoism.

Happiness is not a zero-sum game. Ethical egoists like Brown seem to think that there is just a limited amount of happiness to go around, and if one focuses on the needs of others, one will necessarily be depriving oneself. This argument ignores the fact that one's own happiness and the happiness of others are not necessarily incompatible. In fact, there are times when one's happiness is increased by focusing on the happiness of others (i.e., by passing on the big red ball).

Ethical egoism is too simplistic. Another objection to ethical egoism has been raised by James Rachels who argues that both the ethical
egoist and the radical altruist offer overly simplistic views of the moral
life. Rachels adopts what he calls the common sense view, namely that
one's own interests and the interests of others are both important and
must be balanced against one another. On certain occasions, according
to Rachels, it will appear that the best thing to do is to sacrifice my own
well-being for the sake of another; on other occasions it will be perfectly
acceptable for me to work to promote my own interest. There are times,
for example, when even the best mother has a right to ask her children
to leave her alone for a half hour so that she can enjoy a book that she is
reading, while at other times she may have to make extreme sacrifices to
promote their well-being. As Rachels correctly points out, the moral life
involves finding the right balance between the two extremes of ethical
egoism and radical altruism (Rachels 88).

*Our interests can also be served by promoting the well-being of oth-
ers.* Peter Singer, a contemporary utilitarian ethicist, offers a practical
argument against ethical egoism based upon the paradoxical idea that
sometimes it is more advantageous to be altruistic than selfish. In his
work, The Expanding Circle, he begins his argument with an interesting
example:

> Suppose two early humans are attacked by a sabertooth cat. If
> both flee, one will be picked off by the cat; if both stand their
> ground, there is a good chance that they can fight the cat off; if one
> flees and the other stands and fights, the fugitive will escape and
> the fighter will be killed (47-49).

Thus, if the two men in the example behaved altruistically, both would
benefit in the end, but if either of them behaved selfishly, the end result
would be tragedy for one of them (47-49). The implication of Singer's
example is that a group of rational individuals who were out to promote
their own interest will probably be better off in the long-run if they were
more altruistic and less selfish.

Evaluating the Theory

As you can see, there are some quite valid reasons why you might choose
to follow a moral theory like ethical egoism and some equally valid reason why this theory might be rejected. We'll encounter the same tension

in all the theories that we examine in this text. Unfortunately, there's no such thing as a flawless ethical theory. Each theory we will examine has its own unique strengths and weakness, its own advantages and limitations. The question that you need to ask yourselves is whether the theory that you are examining can provide the kind of sound guidance that will enable you to live out your life in an ethical way.

In the case of ethical egoism, the strict focus on maximizing one's own self-interest with little thought to the needs and interests of others is at the same time an advantage and a disadvantage of the theory. As we've seen, ethical egoism will certainly be one of the easiest moral theories to follow, because of its great simplicity. As long as you know what is going to make you happy—and assuming that you are not deluding yourself about this—then you also know how you ought to behave.

But if you think that an ethical system must necessarily take into consideration the needs and desires of others, then you will naturally find ethical egoism a deficient moral theory. And if you believe that the needs and desires of others are at least as important as your own when attempting to decide how you ought to behave, then you'll definitely want to look for another moral theory to follow.

For Further Discussion

1. Which of the following would a supporter of ethical egoism maintain is acting morally? Be prepared to justify your answers.

    *   A 37-year-old man, who is attractive enough that he is able to have sexual relations with his choice of women. After he gets tired of a woman, he simply discards her and finds another woman to take her place as his sexual partner.

    *   A 70-year-old multi-millionaire who has decided that, instead of leaving the bulk of his inheritance to his children, he will use the money to help find a cure for AIDS because he finds this a more meaningful use of his funds.

    *   A 27-year-old, who is currently unemployed and in treatment for substance abuse. This man grew up in dire poverty, in an extremely dysfunctional household, and in one of the most violent and crime-ridden communities in the country. He has been on public assistance for the past four years in order to get his life back on track.

    *   A 21-year-old college student who has decided that he would

rather spend his time at the beach than going to classes. He will probably fail out of college this semester, but doesn't really care.

• A 24-year-old woman who has given up her own life to care for her infirmed mother, because that is what she thinks is expected of her.

2. Ethical egoists argue that society as a whole would benefit if individuals consistently pursued their own self-interest exclusively with no thought about the interests of others.

    • Give some arguments to support this position.
    • Give some arguments in opposition to this position.
    • Do you think that the libertarian position on this issue is basically correct or not?

Sources and Further Reading

Bishop, Lloyd. *In Defense of Altruism: Inadequacies of Ayn Rand's Ethics and Psychological Egoism.* New Orleans: University Press of the South, 2001.

Broad, C.D., "Egoism as a Theory of Human Motives." *Ethics and the History of Philosophy.* New York: Humanities Press, 1952.

Brown, Harry. *How I Found Freedom in an Unfree World.* Liam Works, 1973.

Campbell, Richard. "A Short Refutation of Ethical Egoism." *Canadian Journal of Philosophy* 2 (1972): 249-254.

Feinberg, Joel. "Psychological Egoism." *Reason and Responsibility.* Ed. Joel Feinberg. Belmont, CA: Wadsworth, 1981.

Gautier, David, ed. *Morality and Rational Self-Interest.* Englewood Cliffs, NJ: Prentice Hall, 1970.

Kailin, Jesse. "On Ethical Egoism." *American Philosophical Quarterly, Monograph Series No. 1. Studies in Moral Philosophy* (1968): 26-41.

Krebs, Dennis. "Psychological Approaches to Altruism: An Evaluation." *Ethics* 92 (1982): 447-458.

Machan, Tibor. "Recent Works on Ethical Egoism." *American Philosophical Quarterly* 16, no. 1 (January, 1979): 1-15.

MacIntyre, Alasdair. "Egoism and Altruism." *Encyclopedia of Philosophy.* Paul Edwards, ed. New York: Macmillan, 1967.

Milo, Ronald D, ed. *Egoism and Altruism.* Belmont CA: Wadsworth, 1973.

Nagel, Thomas. *The Possibility of Altruism.* Oxford: Clarendon Press,

1986.

Plato. *The Republic*. Trans. Allan Bloom. New York: Basic Books, 1968.

Rachels, James. "Two Auguments Against Ethical Egoism." *Philosophia* 4 (1974): 297-314.

Rand, Ayn, ed. *The Virtue of Selfishness*. New York: Penguin, 1964.

Regis, Edward. "What is Ethical Egoism?" *Ethics* 91 (October 1980): 50-62.

Shaver, Robert William. *Rational Egoism*. New York: Cambridge University Press, 1998.

Singer, Peter. *The Expanding Circle*. New York: Ferrar, Straus and Giroux, 1981.

Sober, Elliot. "What is Psychological Egoism?" *Behaviorism* 17 (1989): 89-102.

chapter 7

UTILITARIANISM

Case Study: Hottie or Nottie

Mildred Schlossberg is a sophomore at Springfield University. For the past two years she has shared a dorm room with her best friend, Carmella Pio. The two have known each other since elementary school and are about as close as two people can get.

About six months ago, Carmella's boyfriend of two years, Vinny Cheramonte, broke up with her suddenly, saying that their relationship had been stale for some time. Because Vinny is considered a highly desirable boyfriend—"he's like sooo cool, has a great sense of humor and a really hot bod"—Carmella became extremely depressed after the breakup and has refused to talk about Vinny with anyone, even Mildred.

Two weeks ago Mildred bumped into Vinny in a local student bar and the two began an intense, highly passionate relationship. Mildred realized that she had always had strong feelings for Vinny, but could never act on them because he was in a relationship with her best friend. After several incredible dates, she is beginning to think that Vinny may in fact be her soul mate—the man she is meant to be with for the rest of her life.

Now Mildred is stuck in a dilemma. She has weighed three possible courses of action that she could now take, but can't decide which one would be the best moral choice: (1) She could tell Carmella the truth about her relationship with Vinny, but she knows that this will undoubtedly cause her pain, since she still has feelings for her former flame. Telling the truth might also cause Carmella to feel that Mildred has betrayed her, thus putting their relationship into jeopardy. (2) She could continue to sneak around with Vinny until Carmella has gotten over her feelings of rejection and then tell her the truth when she would be more receptive to hearing about it. The problem here is that Carmella might find out what is going on and really be devastated. (3) She could break off her relationship with Vinny in order not to cause her friend pain, but then she would be sacrificing what could potentially be one of the most meaningful relationships she has ever had.

FOR DISCUSSION

What would an ethical egoist advise Mildred to do? Imagine that Mildred was recommended by a friend to consider the impact that her decision would have on all those who are affected by her potential actions. Who are all the people involved in this case and what are the positive and negative consequences that each of the choices that she is considering would have on these people? Based upon this consideration, what is the right thing for Mildred to do?

Utilitarianism, like ethical egoism, is a consequentialist moral theory— that is, a theory in which the goodness or badness of an act is determined exclusively by the consequences of that act. The ethical egoist, as we've seen, is concerned only with producing the best possible outcome for him or herself. Utilitarians, however, broaden the sphere of moral concern to include **all** those who are affected by a given act. All utilitarians follow what has come to be known as the "principle of utility." This principle states that:

Everyone ought to act so as to bring about the greatest amount of good, or happiness, for all those who are affected by the act.

In utilitarianism, the good of everyone is considered equally important, and no one—oneself included—counts any more or less than anyone else. Thus when the good of the majority outweighs your own good, a utilitarian would argue that you are obligated to act in the majority's interest, even if this means sacrificing your own. In this sense utilitarianism avoids the pitfalls of ethical egoism, which gives exclusive concern to one's own good.

From the case study at the beginning of this chapter, you probably now realize that, if Mildred was simply concerned only with her own well-being when deciding whether or not to date Vinny, she would be operating out of an ethical egoist moral framework. But what if she decided to take others into consideration who might be affected by her actions? She'd still be a consequentialist, because all she's considering when determining whether her action is right or wrong are the consequences or effects of that action. But now she's moving from an ethical egoist moral framework to a more utilitarian one. Her own well-being would still be important in her moral calculations, but so too would be the well-being of other people who are affected by her actions.

Needless to say, utilitarianism is a somewhat more complex moral system than ethical egoism: it's always more difficult to think about the needs of others rather than simply looking out for one's own interests. There are those who believe, however, that utilitarianism provides a more nuanced and complete perspective on moral action than is possible using ethical egoist principles.

Before we can assess the worth of utilitarianism as a moral theory, however, the theory first has to be explained. And this requires a brief but necessary exploration of the historical development of utilitarian theory.

Classic Utilitarianism: Bentham and Mill

The origins of utilitarian theory can be found in the writing of the English social reformers, Jeremy Bentham (1748-1832) and John Stuart Mill (1806-1832). Bentham and Mill were determined to change what they perceived to be the corrupt laws and social practices of their day. British society in the late 18th century was already beginning to stratify into a world of have and have-nots. As Charles Dickens would later describe so well in novels such as *Oliver Twist,* conditions among the poor in English society were horrific, with harsh penalties for those who fell into debt and no child labor laws in existence.

Jeremy Bentham was dismayed by the plight of his fellow citizens and was motivated to develop a moral principle that, if applied, he believed would greatly help improve their lot in life. This principle— the principle of utility—would become the starting point for utilitarian ethics, with Bentham establishing as a "fundamental axiom" that "the greatest happiness of the greatest number that is the measure of right and wrong." (*Fragment*, preface).

In his major work, *Introduction to the Principles of Morals and Legislation,* Bentham defines happiness in a purely hedonistic way as the experience of a greater amount of pleasure than pain. Pleasure for Bentham is the only intrinsic good—that is the only thing that is good in itself. All other things we consider good (fame, fortune, freedom, etc.) are instrumental goods: they are useful, in other words, because they can help us to attain pleasure.

Being a product of his age, Bentham believed it possible to come up with a scientific way to measure quantities of pleasure and pain produced by a given act. In particular, he thought it necessary to measure each of the following features of the pleasure and pain produced:

1. *intensity*: how strong or weak is it?
2. *duration:* how long will it last?
3. *certainty*: what is the probability that it will occur?
4. *propinquity:* how soon will it be fulfilled?
5. *fecundity:* what is the probability that it will be followed by a similar pleasure or pain?
6. *purity*: what is the probability that it will be followed by the opposite sensation (e.g., pain after pleasure)?
7. *extent*: how many people will be affected?

Bentham believed that if we could just quantify the amount of pleasure produced by an act, the "hedonic calculus" that resulted would serve as an exact guide for moral reasoning.

Here's how Bentham thought his hedonic calculus would work: First, we sum up all the pleasures produced by a given act. The value of each pleasure would be determined by applying each of the seven features described above, and the sum of each would be added together. We would engage in the same process for each of the pains produced. The negatives would be subtracted from the positives to determine if the act was more pleasurable than painful for all those affected. If that's the case, the act would be considered morally correct and should be carried out; if not it would be considered morally wrong.

Bentham restricted his hedonic calculus only to the seven aspects of pleasure mentioned above. His concern therefore was purely about the quantity of pleasure produced, not the quality of the pleasure. No pleasure, he believed, was intrinsically higher or lower, better or worse, than any other: there was no qualitative difference between the pleasure produced by a night at the opera or that produced by drinking gin at a dingy bar. The reason for Bentham's hesitation to introduce the concept of qualitative differences between different pleasurable acts is that the idea of quality would introduce a subjective element into his system that would destroy his attempts to create a "moral arithmetic." As he was quoted as saying by Mill, "quality of pleasure being equal, pushpin [a simple English table game] is as good as poetry." (Mill, "Bentham" 123). It was statements like these the led critics like the historian Thomas Carlyle to derided Bentham's approach to ethics as "pig philosophy" because of its emphasis on bodily pleasures.

It was left to another generation of utilitarian thinkers to attempt to salvage Bentham's theory from criticisms like these. John Stuart Mill was actually Bentham's godson and raised by his father according to Benthamite principles. Like Bentham, Mill was an ardent social reformer, who wrote works in favor of personal liberty (*On Liberty*) and the right of women to vote (*On the Subjugation of Women*). Mill's aim was to take Bentham's utilitarian system and make it better suited to the "modern" world of 19th century England.

Mill completely accepted the starting point of Bentham's philosophy that "actions are right in proportion as they tend to promote happiness, wrong as they tend to produce the reverse of happiness. By happiness is intended pleasure, and the absence of pain; by unhappiness, pain, and the privation of pleasure."

Where Mill differed from Bentham was in the fact that he was more than willing to consider qualitative aspects of pleasure in his own approach to utilitarianism. Mill argued that there were higher and lower pleasures and the higher pleasures were preferable to the lower. As Mill puts it, "It is better to be a human being dissatisfied than a pig satisfied; better to be a Socrates dissatisfied than a fool satisfied. And if the fool or the pig, are of a different opinion, it is only because they only know their own side of the question" (*Utilitarianism*). For Mill, lower pleasures (pig pleasures) were sensual or bodily pleasures; higher pleasures (Socrates' pleasures) were pleasures of the intellect.

Mill then goes on to give his justification for the claim that higher pleasures are superior to lower ones, using what has come to be referred to as the "competent judge test." If we want to know, he says, the relative qualities of two different pleasures, we need to seek out those who are "competently acquainted with both" to rank them:

> Of two pleasures, if there be one to which all or almost all who have experienced both give a decided preference, irrespective of a feeling of moral obligation to prefer it, that is the more desirable pleasure. Now it is an unquestionable fact that those who are equally acquainted with and equally capable of appreciating and enjoying both [physical and intellectual pleasures] do give a most marked preference to the manner of existence which employs their higher faculties. Few human creatures would consent to be changed into any of the lower animals for a promise of the fullest allowance of a beast's pleasures; no intelligent human being would consent to be a fool, no instructed person would be an ignoramus, no person of feeling and conscience would be selfish and base, even though they should be persuaded that the fool, the dunce, or the rascal is better satisfied with his lot than they are with theirs (Utilitarianism).

Mill argues that those individuals of high mental ability who have experienced both pleasures of the physical and intellectual variety give the preference to intellectual pleasures, ranking them as superior. On the other hand, those of limited mental capacity are unable of experiencing the higher pleasures of the mind, and therefore are not capable of passing adequate judgment on the relative qualities of each.

There are numerous difficulties with Mill's position on the superiority of intellectual pleasure—not the least of which being that his reasoning is both circular and somewhat elitist. Certainly, the majority can often be wrong about many things (as Mill himself pointed out in *On Liberty*). There is also the problem of what constitutes a qualified judge. Finally, it isn't necessarily true that most people—or even highly refined people—would choose higher pleasures (going to an art gallery) over lower ones (having sex or eating a good meal) if they had the choice. It would seem that, in his attempt to save utilitarian theory from the criticism of being little more than "pig philosophy" by introducing the concept of higher and lower pleasures, Mill has unintentionally introduced even more difficulties into the theory.

Despite these criticisms, Mill's achievement was to recognize that an existence devoted simply to physical pleasure would be a greatly diminished sort of human life. It seems intuitively true that a complete life would include both lower and higher sorts of pleasures: sex, drink, and rock and roll—to be sure—but also poetry, art, great music, and philosophy. And a life devoid of the latter clearly would be a life that is less than fully human. Notwithstanding Mill's ability to offer a strong argument in defense of his addition of qualitative dimensions of pleasure, then, we still might agree with him that in the end it is indeed preferable to be a dissatisfied Socrates than a satisfied pig.

Act Utilitarianism

In the 20th century, utilitarian theory came to take on two main forms—act utilitarianism and rule utilitarianism. The basic difference between these two is that an act utilitarian would apply the principle of utility to specific actions, while the rule utilitarian applies this principle to moral rules.

The approach that Bentham and Mill took was clearly that of act utilitarianism. In this approach, for each individual act we are about to perform, we need to appeal directly to the principle of utility—that is, we must ask ourselves whether this specific act in this circumstance will produce the greatest amount of good (or the greatest happiness) for all those involved. We do this by weighing the positive and negative consequences of an action. If the act produces a greater amount of good than evil for all those who are affected by the act, then the act is good; if not, the act is bad.

Moral Decision-Making Using Act Utilitarianism

Step 1: Determine who will be affected by this action.

Step 2: Analyze all the possible consequences (short- and long-term, direct and indirect) of the action for all those who are affected.

Step 3: Determine if the action, more than any other alternative available at the time, will produce the greatest amount of good, or happiness, for all those affected by the action.

Step 4: If it does, then the act is morally right; if it doesn't then the act is morally wrong.

But what about moral rules that are commonly accepted, such as "don't lie"? Can't rules like these be used as a guide for one's actions? According to John Stuart Mill, such rules, while in general appropriate to follow, cannot be used as an absolute guide in moral decision-making. There are many instances when lying, in fact, may be perfectly acceptable—for example, when telling the truth will subject an innocent to a greater evil. The individual who lies to thugs about where their victim is hiding is also probably behaving properly even though he is forced to resort to a deception. Mill's point is that while relying on moral rules may be helpful at times, when following those rules causes more harm than good, we should not hesitate to discard them.

Advantages of Act Utilitarianism

As we have seen, the utilitarian approach is certainly to be credited for the attempt it makes to look beyond the individual's own interest in determining which actions are right and wrong. Any legitimate utilitarian must always be concerned with how his actions affect others, his own well-being weighing no more heavily than any other's in determining which actions he should or should not perform. "The happiness which forms the utilitarian standard of what is right in conduct, is not the agent's own happiness," writes Mill, "but that of all concerned. As between his own happiness and that of others, utilitarianism requires him to be as strictly impartial as a disinterested and benevolent spectator."

As we have seen, in certain circumstances a utilitarian may even be obligated to sacrifice his own happiness and well-being if doing so will help to promote the greater good. In this sense, utilitarianism represents a marked improvement over approaches which make self-interest the basis for ethical decision making, and is certainly preferable to moral subjectivism insofar as it provides some kind of objective standard of right and wrong.

Disadvantages of Act Utilitarianism

For all of its advantages as a moral system, there are some serious problems with act utilitarianism that must be considered:

Act utilitarianism is an impractical approach to decision-making. One obvious problem with act utilitarianism is that it seems like an impractical approach for helping to guide one in moral decision-making. For one thing, although a person may be able to gauge the direct and immediate effects of his action, it is considerably more difficult to gauge the indirect and long-term effects.   Indeed one might argue that it is in fact impossible to calculate every possible consequence of an action. An act might very well produce positive benefits initially, but in the long run might prove extremely harmful. A second problem with act utilitarianism is that when an individual is faced with a moral dilemma, he is often required to make instantaneous decisions. If he has to weigh the positive and negative effects of each action that he is about to perform, and also consider long-term effects, he will ultimately be paralyzed. Therefore if we are to be able to make useful moral decisions, we need to have some clear and concrete rules that can be appealed to in various circumstances.

Act utilitarianism can lead to violations of the rights of individuals and minority groups.   For example, suppose a utilitarian has to decide whether or not painful scientific studies on orphaned mentally retarded children ought to be performed. He is convinced that these experiments could realistically lead to a cure that could save thousands of "normal" children in the future. This kind of experimentation could easily be justified by engaging in a utilitarian calculus. The experiments would not cause mental pain to others because the children are orphaned, and their disability—assuming that it is severe enough—would prevent them from having the kind of mental anguish that many of us would have knowing we were about to be experimented on against our wills. If unfortunate accidents did occur as a result of the experimentation that cut short the lives of these children, at least the experimenters would have the satisfaction of knowing that the future prospects of these children were dim anyway, and, had they lived, they would only have been a drain on the resources of society. Consequently, our utilitarian researcher should have no qualms about performing these experiments, even though such practices would be rejected completely by most civilized people.

Peter Singer, a prominent utilitarian thinker, goes even further than this when he maintains that if we indeed had to perform such experiments, it would be preferable to do so on severely mentally handicapped orphans than on healthy rats. The rats, he says, would be "more intelligent, more aware of what is happening to them, more sensitive to pain, and so on, than many severely brain damaged humans barely surviving in hospital wards and other institutions." (*Practical Ethics*, 67-68).

Act utilitarianism can lead to violations of the basic principles of justice. An act utilitarian approach can also easily be used to violate the principles of justice. The most basic demands of justice state that we treat people fairly and reward or punish them based upon their own merits. As the following imaginary case illustrates, it is all too easy to violate this principle using a utilitarian approach:

> Suppose a utilitarian were visiting an area in which there was racial strife, and that, during his visit, a Negro rapes a white woman, and that race riots occur as a result of the crime, white mobs, with the connivance of the police, bashing and killing Negroes, etc. Suppose too that our utilitarian is in the area of the crime when it is committed such that his testimony would bring about the conviction of a particular Negro. If he knows that a quick arrest will stop the riots and lynching, surely, as a utilitarian, he must conclude that he has a duty to bear false witness in order to bring about the punishment of an innocent person (McCloskey, 239-255).

A utilitarian in this position would have to support the idea of bearing false witness against an innocent man. Weighing his options, he would certainly realize that the benefits of a return to public order far outweighs the need to protect the life of one innocent human being.

An Alternative: Rule Utilitarianism

The other form that utilitarian theory takes is known as rule utilitarianism. According to this approach, certain moral rules, if followed, will always produce the greatest amount of good over evil. Thus a rule utilitarian would maintain that, instead of each individual acting to bring about the greatest amount of good over evil, everyone should follow those rules which will tend to bring about the greatest amount of good. The basic principle that a rule utilitarian would follow, therefore, would be a slightly modified version of the principle of utility:

Everyone ought to act from those moral rules, the following of which would bring about greatest amount of good, or happiness, for all those affected by the action.

For example, instead of wondering in each and every moral situation whether one ought to tell the truth or not, one would establish a rule like the following: "one should always tell the truth because doing so will produce the greater good." Certainly it might be the case that in a specific situation telling the truth will not produce good consequences (for example, telling one's already depressed grandfather that he has only six months to live), but in general, the rule utilitarian would argue that it is in the best interest of society if everyone told the truth. Similarly, a rule utilitarian would argue that following a rule like "always keep your promises" would produce the greatest amount of good over evil within a society. Therefore, unless there is some legitimate reason for not keeping your promises (e.g., you are caught up in an emergency situation), you ought always to do so. Other rules that a rule utilitarian might support might be something like: "Do not kill except in self-defense" (or the similar rule: "Do not kill innocents"), "Do not cheat," and "Always protect innocent human life."

Moral Decision-Making Using Rule Utilitarianism

Preparation: Select a limited number of rules, which, if followed, will generally achieve the greatest amount of good, or happiness, for all those who are affected by the act. You may want to write these rules down, so you remember them.

Step 1: Determine who will be affected by this action.
Step 2: Assess what moral rules apply to the action that you are considering.
Step 3: Determine if the action being considered accords with these moral rules.
Step 4: If it does, then the act is morally right; if it doesn't then the act is morally wrong.

There are certain definite advantages that rule utilitarianism has over its counterpart. For one thing, rule utilitarianism makes moral decision-making less complex than act utilitarianism. Instead of having to decide in every specific circumstance whether an act is producing the greatest good for the greatest number, one only needs to appeal to a rule that will achieve this same result. This inevitably speeds up moral decision-making. It is also true that the theory manages to avoid the dubious sorts of moral difficulties associated with act utilitarianism that we have discussed above. By following rules like "Do not kill innocents," or "Do not cheat," it is unlikely that a rule utilitarian would engage in the kinds of odious practices that could be condoned using act utilitarianism.

Despite some of the advantages of rule utilitarianism, there are definite problems with the theory that are difficult to overcome. First, *it is not so easy to find rules that do not admit of any exceptions.* Thiroux uses the example of the rule, "Never kill except in self-defense," which would seem to be the kind of rule that would appeal to a rule utilitarian. But even this rule would seem to admit certain exceptions:

> can the rule never kill except in self-defense actually cover all situations human beings will become involved in? Will it cover abortion, for example? Many antiabortionists think so, stating that in no way can the unborn fetus be considered an aggressor; therefore, it cannot be aborted. Prochoice advocates, on the other hand, either don't consider the fetus a human being or argue for the precedence of the mother's life over the fetus's and believe that there are times when the fetus must be aborted. How, for example, would the rule utilitarian deal with aborting the fetus when the mother's life is endangered not specifically because she is pregnant but for some other reason? The fetus cannot be considered the aggressor, so how can it be aborted in self-defense? (51)

There is also the problem that *moral rules can often come into conflict with one another.* What happens for example when the rule, "Tell the truth," comes into conflict with the rule, "Protect innocent human life." Which rule should we follow? Unfortunately, rule utilitarianism has no way of deciding between conflicting rules, except by reverting back to act utilitarianism.

Finally, *rule utilitarianism seems to contradict itself* by at the same time seeming to both accept and reject the principle of utility—the bedrock of utilitarian theory. If the goal in our moral actions is to strive to produce a maximum balance of good over evil, as all utilitarians hold, then one may have to allow for the same kinds of problematic actions, including punishing the innocent, that made act utilitarianism seem so morally repugnant. If on the other hand, rules calling for truth telling at all times or protecting the innocent are followed, then it must be recognized that at times the principle of utility will have to be sacrificed.

For Further Discussion

1. Return to Exercise #1 on page 87 in the chapter on ethical egoism. Applying the principle of utility, assess whether the actions descibed would be considered right or wrong.

2. Utilitarianism and Public Policy: Very often public policy decisions in the United States are made by adopting a utilitarian calculus. When determining whether or not to adopt specific legislation, elected officials will often look to see if the greatest good for the greatest number will be achieved if the legislation is enacted. Imagine that you are a new member of Congress, and are trying to determine whether or not the following policies should be enacted. You are also a scrupulous utilitarian, so your decision should be based exclusively on the principle of utility:

    •   In order to stem the rising tide of teen crime, all individuals under the age of 21 will hereby be subject to a curfew that requires them to be off the streets by 10pm.

    •   In order to promote a healthy sense of citizenship, upon graduating from high school all Americans will hereby be obligated to perform two years of social service or one year of military service.

    •   In order to encourage voting, a law will be enacted fining American citizens $100 for failure to vote in any November election.

    •   In order to curb emissions that contribute to global-warming, a new tax will be placed upon gasoline, raising the price in the New York area to $7.00 a gallon.

    •   In order to reduce health care costs for everyone and to promote good health, it will now be permitted for insurance companies to charge cigarette smokers and obese individuals with an insurance premium significant enough to off-set the costs that such individuals add to health care because of their unhealthy lifestyles.

Sources and Further Reading

Albee, Ernest. *A History of English Utilitarianism*, New York: Routledge, 2004.

Bentham, Jeremy. "Fragment on Government." *The Works of Jeremy Bentham*. Vol. 1. Ed. John Bowering. Edinburgh:

—. *The Introduction to the Principles of Morals and Legislation*. Ed. J.H. Burns and H.L.A. Hart. London: Athline Press, 1970.

Crisp, Roger. *Routledge Philosophy Guidebook to Mill on Utilitarianism*. London: Routledge, 1997.

Feinberg, Joel. "The Forms and Limits of Utilitarianism." *Philosophical Review* 76 (1967): 368-381.

Glover, Jonathan. *Utilitarianism and Its Critics*. New York: Macmillan, 1990.

Lyons, David. "Utilitarianism." *Encyclopedia of Ethics*. Eds. Lawrence C. Becker and Charlotte B. Becker. New York: Garland, 1992.

McCloskey, H.J. "A Non-Utilitarian Approach to Punishment." *Inquiry* 8 (1965).

Mill, John Stuart. "Bentham." *Utilitarianism, On Liberty, and Essay on Bentham*. Ed. M. Warnock. New York: New American Library, 1974.

—. *Utilitarianism*. Indianapolis: Bobbs-Merrill, 1957.

Pettit, Philip. "Consequentialism." *A Companion to Ethics*. Ed. Peter Singer. Oxford Blackwell, 1991.

Scarre, Geoffrey. *Utilitarianism*. London: Routledge, 1996.

Scheffler, Samuel. *The Rejection of Consequentialism*. Oxford: Clarendon Press, 1982.

Sheng, C.L. *Defense of Utilitarianism*. Lanham, MD: University Press of America, 2004.

Singer, Peter. *The Expanding Circle*. New York: Ferrar, Straus and Giroux, 1981.

—. *Practical Ethics*. Cambridge: Cambridge University Press, 1993.

Smart, J.J.C. and Williams, Bernard. *Utilitarianism: For and Against.* Cambridge: Cambridge University Press, 1987.

Smith, James M. and Sosa, Ernest, eds. *Mill's Utilitarianism: Text and Criticism*. Belmont, CA: Wadsworth, 1969.

8

DEONTOLOGY

Case Study: Constructing a Moral Dilemma

Tony DeStefano is a part-time student majoring in political science at St. Ignatius College in Baltimore. Because his parents are fairly poor, Tony has to pay for college classes completely on his own. He eventually hopes to go to law school, but at the rate he is going, it will take him almost seven years just to graduate from college.

To help pay his tuition, Tony has been working during the day at Zaffuto Construction Company, one of the largest, most respected, and most profitable construction companies in Baltimore. Mr. Zaffuto, the owner of the company, is a major player in the world of Baltimore politics and, because of his connections, receives millions of dollars in construction contracts every year from the city.

Mr. Zaffuto, who thinks extremely highly of Tony, would like nothing more than to see him finish law school and make a success of his life. One day he calls Tony into his office and takes him into his confidence. Mr. Zaffuto tells Tony that building materials that are supposed to be used for city projects are often stolen at night and have to be replaced at the city's expenses. He says that this is not unusual in the construction profession and that no one in city government thinks twice about it. He then reveals to Tony that he in fact is the one taking these materials and using them for his own private construction projects—a scheme which nets him several million dollars a year. This has been going on for over twenty years, he says, and because most of the major politicians and law enforcement officials in Baltimore are on his "payroll," there is no danger of getting caught.

Mr. Zaffuto then tells Tony that he needs someone that he can trust to help load these materials onto his trucks at night, so that they can "disappear" from the construction site. He also tells Tony that he is willing to give him a cut of $30,000 for his labors, which is more than enough to pay for his full-time tuition at the college and still save a substantial *amount for law school. Best of all, he would only need to work one night a week, and so he can devote most of his time to his studies.*

FOR DISCUSSION

What would an ethical egoist advise Tony to do in this situation? A utilitarian? Imagine that it is true that Tony would never get caught moving the construction supplies and that this scheme would in fact solve all of his financial difficulties. Is it still wrong for Tony to take Mr. Zaffuto up on his offer? If so, why?

Having examined two consequentialist ethical theories—ethical egoism and utilitarianism—we can now turn our attention to a few notable non-consequentialist theories. As we have already seen, non-consequentialist theories reject the idea that the goodness or badness of an act can be determined by its consequences. Instead, they argue that there must be something intrinsic to the act itself which makes it right or wrong.

One of the most famous of these nonconsequentialist theories goes by the name deontology. The word deontology actually comes from the Greek, *deon*, meaning duty. If you do your duty, you are doing what is right for its own sake and not because of any benefit derived from it. Deontology, therefore, offers an interesting counterpoint to theories such as ethical egoism and utilitarianism, which are exclusively consequence-driven theories.

Let's use cheating to illustrate the differences between these two approaches. The utilitarian would argue that the act of cheating could be morally acceptable if this act produces a greater balance of good over evil. Most of us, however, intuitively recognize that there is something morally wrong with cheating no matter what kind of positive consequences such an act produces. But what is it about cheating that makes it wrong? The deontologist would argue that there is something inherent in the act itself that determines whether it is right or wrong, regardless of the consequences. For a deontologist

an act is right if, and only if, it accords with a rule that can be universalized.

Although there are several possible rules that a deontologist might cite as the basis for moral decision- making, two stand out as being the most common: the golden rule and the principle of respect for persons.

The Golden Rule

Imagine the following situation: As you approach a railroad crossing, you notice a car has stopped on the tracks and the occupant, an elderly woman, is unconscious in the car. A train is rapidly approaching and has no time to stop before it crashes into the car. You have to decide what to do. If you jump out of your own car and try to save the woman, you yourself might be killed. If you were an ethical egoist, you would consider it foolish to risk your own life to save this woman. If you were a utilitarian, you would also probably not help her, because the greater good is not served by risking your life for someone who may not have many years to live anyway.

With little hesitation, however, you rush to the car and pull out the woman with only a few seconds to spare before it is destroyed by the on-coming train. Later, when you are asked why you risked your own life to save a mere stranger, you cite a basic moral rule that you have spent your life attempting to follow: "Do unto others as you would have them do unto you." In risking your own life, you were following what has come to be known as "the golden rule." Although you may know this rule from its Christian form, in fact many of the major religious traditions of the world have some version or other of the golden rule.

Most parents raise their children to follow this basic rule without even realizing it. For example, when a child does something wrong, his parents will typically not ask him if his actions produced positive benefits for himself or others. They will usually say something along the lines of "how would you like it if someone did that to you?"

Moral Decision-Making Using the Golden Rule

Step 1: Identify the act being considered.
Step 2: Determine whether it accords with a rule that can be universalized—in this case, the golden rule.
Step 3: If it does, then the act is right; if it doesn't, then the act is wrong.

Kant's Categorical Imperative

The most important attempt to construct a deontological approach to ethics is found in the moral writing of Emmanual Kant (1724-1804). Kant was a professor at the University of Konigsberg in Prussia and is considered one of the "greats" in the history of philosophy. His *Groundwork of the Metaphysics of Morals*, though brief in length, is acknowledged to be one of the great achievements of enlightenment thought. It is to this work that we will now turn in order to consider Kant's unique contribution to moral thought.

In the *Groundwork*, Kant rejects the basic premise of utilitarianism—namely, that consequences alone determine whether an act is right or wrong. Kant believes that consequences, in fact, are irrelevant in determining the moral status of an action. For example, if we could save many lives by sacrificing one innocent person, the act would still be intrinsically wrong for Kant, despite any positive benefits that the act might produce.

Kant also rejects utilitarianism because he believes that the consequences of our actions are often beyond our control, and, therefore, we should not be held responsible for them. Imagine that you are walking down the street and you see someone dying of a heart attack. You stop to help the person using CPR, but accidentally kill him in the process. Kant would argue that in performing this beneficent act you did the right thing and should not be held responsible for the unintended outcome of your action. Though the results of your action may have been unfortunate, you did not behave immorally.

Kant argues that the truly moral person is one who acts solely for the sake of duty—that is, out of a concern and respect for the moral law. But how do we know where our duty lies? The answer, says Kant, is that our duty lies in obedience to a particular rule, principle, or law regardless of inclination, self-interest, or consequences. It lies, in other words, in following a command that must be obeyed for its own sake. Kant calls this supreme principle of all morality the *categorical imperative*.

An imperative is nothing more than a command. In order to understand what Kant means by a categorical imperative, it must be contrasted with what he refers to as a hypothetical imperative. A hypothetical imperative is conditional: it tells you what you ought to do if you want to achieve a certain result. This kind of imperative has the form, "Do X to achieve Y." For example: "If you want to do well in your college classes, then make sure you study every night." This specific hypothetical imperative tells you what to do if you want to succeed in college. Of course, if you have no interest in succeeding in college, you don't need to follow such an imperative.

Kant, however, believed that moral obligations take on a very different form than most of the other obligations we have in life. If there is something that I am morally obligated to do, then I ought to do it no matter what. All moral obligations, then, take on the form of categorical imperatives. They always take the form, "Do X" (e.g., "Tell the truth."). Such moral obligations are unconditional (they apply no matter what) and universally binding (they apply not just to me but to everyone).

We have already seen that for a utilitarian the principle of utility is the basic tool for determining in every situation whether an act is right or wrong. Kant uses the categorical imperative for a similar purpose. It is his yardstick for determining right and wrong. Although Kant developed at least four different formulations of the categorical imperative, we will focus on his two most famous versions of this principle—the principle of universalizability and the principle of respect for persons.

The Principle of Universalizability

The first formulation of this Categorical Imperative is: "I ought never to act except in such a way that my maxim should become a universal law" (Kant 70). For each act that I am planning to perform, then, I have to ask:

1. What is the rule authorizing this act that I am about to perform? and
2. Can it become a universal rule for all human beings to follow?

Thus an act would be considered immoral for Kant if the rule that would authorize it (the maxim) cannot be universalized—that is, turned into a general rule for all to follow. To put this in another way, if we cannot affirm that everyone ought to act in the same way that we have done, we know our action is wrong.

Two examples would help to illustrate how Kant's system works. In the first example, Johnny Scollazo borrows money from a friend and promises to pay it back, although he has no intention to do so. Having some conscience he wonders if such an act is morally correct. Remembering what he learned about Kant in his college ethics class, he turns this into a rule, "Whenever I am short of money, I will borrow money and promise to pay it back, although I know that I will never do so." He then turns his rule into a universal law to see if it is right. What would happen, he wonders, if everyone broke their promises to repay money? The answer is that no one would ever lend money to anyone else, because they would never trust anyone's promises to repay the money they borrowed. Johnny immediately realizes that his act cannot be universalized without contradiction, and therefore it is not right.

In the second example, Eddie Dougherty, a lazy fellow, who is not really interested in working, is thinking of stealing from others to get what he wants. The rule for the action he is considering would be something like the following: "I shall never work but steal from other human beings." If this rule were universalized it would become: "no human beings should ever work but should steal what they need from each other." The reason why this rule cannot be universalized is fairly apparent: if no one worked, there would be no one to steal from and nothing to steal. Thus Kant would say that the action that Eddie is contemplating is immoral because it cannot be universalized without contradiction.

The Principle of Respect for Persons

The second formulation of the categorical imperative goes as follows:

> Always treat humanity, whether in your own person or that of another, never merely as a means, but always at the same time as an end.

In the *Foundations of the Metaphysics of Morals*, Kant goes on to elaborate:

> Man regarded as a *person*…is exalted above any price; for as a person…he is not to be valued merely as a means to the ends of others…, but as an end in himself, that is, he possesses a *dignity* (an absolute inner worth) by which he exacts *respect* from himself and from all other rational beings in the world. He can measure himself with any other being of his kind and value himself on a footing of equality with them (230).

Unlike animals and other living things, human beings have a special status conferred upon them because they possess rationality. Kant's principle of respect for persons tells us to treat other human beings always *as ends in themselves*—that is, as persons having intrinsic worth. To treat someone as having intrinsic worth is to recognize in all of our dealings with them that they have value in themselves as rational agents.

Let's make things clear here: Kant is definitely not saying that we can never use another person as a means to achieve our own purposes. It would be extremely difficult to live in the world in which we do without using people as means at least some of the time. For example, every time we go to a store, we are using the cashier as a means to purchase products that we need. According to Kant, this is perfectly fine as long as the cashier is acting autonomously in serving us.

What the principle of respect for persons states is that we can never use another human being *merely* as a means to our own ends. When we use someone merely as a means we are involving them in a scheme of action to which they could not in principle give consent. When we manipulate, coerce or deceive someone into doing something for us, then we are using them merely as a means, and this, according to Kant, is always wrong.

Moral Decision-Making Using Kant's Categorical Imperative

Step 1: Identify the act being considered.
Step 2: Determine whether it accords with a rule that can be universalized.
Step 3: If it does, then the act is right; if it doesn't, then the act is wrong.

Putting Kant's theory of respect for persons into practice is at times more difficult than relying on egoist or utilitarian approaches, which focus solely on consequences. We must always recognize that other human beings have their own goals, aims, and projects and we must strive to respect these. This is the reason why Kant believes deceiving someone is morally wrong, even when we think that we are doing so for his or her own good. This can lead to some unpleasant situations with friends or coworkers who may not always appreciate the value of candor.

The principle of respect for persons also demands that we allow competent adults to make their own decisions in life, even when we may not agree with their decisions. This becomes particularly tricky when we are faced with a mentally competent adult who decides to commit suicide. While Kant himself thought suicide was wrong, the principle of respect for persons would seem to demand that we respect the autonomy of the rational person who seeks to end his or her own life for whatever reason.

Kant and The Problem of Lying

A close friend of yours who is "generously proportioned" has been trying to lose weight for several months with only modest success. When she sees you she asks if you can tell that she has lost weight. You, however, don't notice any difference at all in her size. Should you be perfectly honest with your friend, and tell her that she looks exactly the same to you? Or, in this particular case, might it not be acceptable for the sake of your friend's psychological well-being to misrepresent the truth just a little bit?

We know how a utilitarian in this situation might respond. Applying the principle of utility, he would ask which possible course of action would produce the best possible consequences for all those who are affected by the act. Those affected in this case only include himself and his overweight friend. A utilitarian might very well choose to lie to a friend, since it would serve his own good (avoid the unpleasant effects of a truthful comment) as well as that of his friend (who would be encouraged to continue her diet program).

But how would a deontologist deal with this same situation? Kant, as we would expect, has a fairly rigid position against lying. He uses one of the most extreme situations imaginable to make his case. Imagine, he says, that a man fleeing from a murderer asks to hide in your house. The murderer comes along and asks you where the man went. You know that if you tell the truth, the man hiding will likely be killed. What should you do? For Kant the answer is clear: You have to tell the truth in all circumstances, including this one. If we lie and tell the murderer that the man whom he is chasing is not in the house, because we are afraid of what the consequences might be for telling the truth, then we are responsible for all the consequences of our action. The man that we are trying to protect might have decided to escape form the house using the back door, and by telling the lie, we put him directly in the hand of his murderer. We become complicit then in his murder. On the other hand, if we acknowledge that we can never know the consequences of our actions and follow universal principles of action in all circumstances, then we are on much firmer ground morally speaking, according to Kant (see "The Supposed Right to Lie from Benevolent Motives" in Part 3 of this work).

This does not mean that Kant, following his principle of respect for persons, would have absolutely no recourse but to tell the murderer exactly where his victim is hiding. Michael Sandel makes the case that Kantian deontology would allow for "hairsplitting" in a situation like this one. Hairsplitting is using a technically true but misleading statement to avoid those situations in which the unvarnished truth would cause harm, embarrassment, or social awkwardness. In the case of the overweight friend described above, an outright lie—unacceptable from Kant's perspective—would be to claim to have noticed the weight loss; the complete truth, on the other hand, might wound your friend and perhaps derail her weight-loss efforts. But one could instead say something misleading, but technically true like, "I can see that you've been trying hard to lose weight, and I'm very proud of you." No lie has been told, and the requirements of truthfulness have been satisfied.

Sandel argues that it is perfectly in keeping with Kant's approach to ethics to hairsplit when the killer asks if his victim is in the house. Avoiding both the unvarnished truth, which could cause considerable harm, and a complete lie, which would violate the principle of respect for persons, one could simply say, "I saw him down the road an hour ago," or some equally misleading but truthful statement (132-134).

Advantages of Kantian Deontology

Kant's principle of respect for person has two major benefits that have made it attractive to many moral thinkers:

Kantian Deontology is extremely egalitarian (at least when it comes to human beings). Kant's categorical imperative applies equally for all rational beings and thus avoids the problem of treating some individuals differently from others. Unfortunately non-humans are not viewed as ends in themselves and therefore have no moral standing. Although Kant may think cruelty to animals would be a bad idea because it might eventually lead us to become callous to human beings, he allows animals to be used merely as means.

Kantian Deontology cannot be used to violate individual's rights. Unlike utilitarianism, the Kantian approach, in rejecting positive consequences as the basis for moral decision-making, has a much better chance of preserving the rights of individuals and minorities than the utilitarian approach does. Indeed Kant's second formulation of the Categorical Imperative, which states that one ought never to treat any individual merely as a means but only as an end in themselves, assures that the unjust treatment of any individual, for whatever reason, must be considered wrong.

Disadvantages of Kantian Deontology

Although Kant's moral system does have some advantages over consquentialist forms of ethics such as ethical egoism and utilitarianism, as you might imagine, there are problems as well with this approach:

Kantian deontology is too rigid. As we have seen, moral rules for Kant are always absolute, bearing no exceptions. This becomes particularly problematic, as we shall see, in the example of the duty of truthfulness. Whereas each of the other moral theories that we will examine in this text are flexible enough to allow for exceptions to this duty, Kantian deontology is not, leading to some potentially problematic consequences (of course, Kant would say that he doesn't give a hoot about consequences).

The problem of conflicting duties. The example of the inquiring murderer raises another difficulty with Kant's system: namely, what to do when our moral obligations conflict with one another. As James Rachels put it, "Suppose it is held to be absolutely wrong to do A in any circumstances. Then what about the case in which a person is faced with the choice between doing A and doing B, when he must do something and no other alternatives are available?" Rachels argues that this sort of dilemma is extremely difficult to resolve if we maintain, as Kant does, that all moral rules are absolute (128).

The neglect of consequences. As we have already seen, Kant is to be congratulated for recognizing the dangers of using consequences alone as the means to determine the moral status of an act. Where he may have gone too far was in discounting the importance of consequences all together. There are many ethicists who would argue that moral intentions often have to be balanced by a consideration of consequences in order to arrive at truly moral decisions.

Ross's Deontology

Criticisms of deontology, such as those described above, led Sir William Ross (1877-1940), a Scottish philosopher, to update deontology in such a way as to soften Kant's rigid absolutism. While agreeing with Kant that consequences did not make an act right or wrong, he believed that it was necessary to take consequences into consideration when making moral choices.

Unlike Kant, Ross felt that moral duties cannot be absolute because there are certain circumstances when these duties may conflict with one another. All moral duties, therefore, are prima facie or conditional. The term prima facie literally means "at first glance," and implies that such duties, while generally morally binding, may on occasion be overridden by stronger moral claims.

In his work, *The Right and the Good* (1930), Ross identified seven prima facie duties:

1. Duties of fidelity: telling the truth, keeping actual and implied promises, and keeping contractual agreements.
2. Duties of reparation: making up for the wrongs we have done to others.
3. Duties of gratitude: recognizing what others have done for us and extending our gratitude to them.
4. Duties of justice: preventing the improper distribution of good and bad that is not in keeping with what people merit or deserve.
5. Duties of beneficence: helping to improve the condition of others in the areas of virtue, intelligence, or happiness.
6. Duties of self-improvement: the obligation we have to improve our own virtue, intelligence, and happiness.
7. Duties of nonmaleficence: not injuring others and preventing injury to others. (Thiroux, 21-22)

While acknowledging that his list of prima facie duties may be incomplete, he also maintained that all rational people would agree that these are in fact moral duties. Arguing that these prima facie duties are self-evident, Ross writes:

I should make it plain at this stage that I am assuming the correctness of some of our main convictions as to prima facie duties, or, more strictly, am claiming that we know them to be true. To me it seems as self-evident as anything could be, that to make a promise, for instance, is to create a moral claim on us in someone else. Many readers will perhaps say that they do not know this to be true. If so, I certainly cannot prove it to them; I can only ask them to reflect again, in the hope that they will ultimately agree that they also know it to be true (22).

By acknowledging that moral duties are prima facie, Ross recognizes that they can at times come into conflict with one another. Ross attempts to solve this difficulty by providing two principles to follow in the event that prima facie duties conflict: (1) Always do that act which is in accord with the stronger prima facie duty, and (2) always do that act which has the greatest prima facie rightness over prima facie wrongness. For example, in the case of a conflict between duties of nonmaleficence and beneficence, it is obvious that our obligation not to cause harm to others outweighs any obligation to do them some positive good.

Moral Decision-Making Using Ross's Deontology

Step 1: Identify the act being considered.
Step 2: Determine whether it violates any prima facie duties.
Step 3: If it doesn't, then the act is right; if it does, then the act is wrong.

In the case where prima facie duties conflict with one another,

Step 1: Identify which duties are in conflict.
Step 2: Determine which is the stronger prima facie duty.
Step 3: An act is right if it satisfies the stronger prima facie duty; it is wrong if it satisfies the weaker duty at the expense of the stronger.

Unfortunately, Ross acknowledges that there is no set formula for determining how to apply these principles in specific circumstances. In the case of conflicting claims, he acknowledges that "while we can see with certainty that the claim exists, it becomes a matter of individual and fallible judgment to say which claim is in the circumstance the overriding one" (198). In the end we are forced to use our reason and creativity to make good moral judgments.

While Ross's version of deontology helps to correct some of the difficulties inherent in Kantian ethics, it too has some inherent difficulties. For one thing, Ross is incapable of telling us upon what basis prima facie duties are chosen. As we have seen, Ross provides a list of duties that he claims are prima facie, but provides no real justification for why these have been chosen. Most of his prima facie duties do seem intuitively valid, but this is no basis for establishing an objective moral system. Also, Ross cannot tell us what to do when prima facie duties come into conflict with one another. Although he provides two principles, which he claims would help us to decide what to do when our prima facie duties conflict, these principles are difficult to apply. How, for example, do we determine which duty is stronger than the other?

For Further Discussion

1. Apply Kant's principle of respect for persons to each of the following cases:

- Dr. Morty Pankoff, a highly regarded plastic surgeon, has developed a lucrative practice filling out the wrinkles in his wealthy patients faces—mainly around the lip area where facial wrinkles on middle-aged women tend to be most pronounced—using injections of fat cells. His patients think that these cells come from their own buttocks, but, in fact, Dr. Pankoff frequently uses fat cells from his own large buttock on a regular basis to save money and to spare his patients painful injections. Not realizing the source of the fat cells injected in their faces, Dr. Pankoff's patients rave about the low costs, painlessness, and wonderful results of his treatments. Based upon Kant's principle of respect for persons, what is it about this act that makes it morally wrong?

- Adam knows that when Julie has too much to drink she loses all sense of inhibition and does things that she normally would be averse to doing. Wanting to have sexual intercourse with her, but knowing that she is not interested in him physically, Adam plans to get Julie drunk so that she will give in to his sexual advances. Since she would be technically consenting, Adam sees nothing wrong with what he is planning. Based upon Kant's principle of respect for persons, what is it about this act that makes it morally wrong?

- You have a close friend named Mike who is extremely popular with women but also a chronic philander. In the past he has lied to numerous women about his intentions, used them for his own pleasure, and then discarded them. A few weeks ago, Mike began dating a really lovely and kind-hearted girl name Brittney, who thinks Mike really cares for her and is interested in a long-term relationship. Mike has made you promise not to reveal his history with women to any of the girls that he currently is dating, and this naturally includes Brittney. One day during a conversation, she says that she has heard some rumors about Mike's relationships with other women and asks you specifically about this. Based upon Kant's principle of respect for persons, how should you respond to Brittney's request for information about Mike?

- Sophia has been dating Brad who has a substance abuse problem. One day Sophia tells her friends that Brad has asked her to marry him. She tells her friends that she plans to marry him and says that she understands that this is risky given Brad's problems. Her friends, who believe that she is making the wrong decision and will eventually be hurt by Brad, want to convince her not to get married. Based upon the principle of respect for persons, should Sophia's friends attempt to dissuade Sophia from marrying Brad? Would your answer be the same if you applied the golden rule to this situation?

- Your four-year-old son, Eddy, is a big fan of the Christmas holidays and looks forward to that magical time when Santa delivers presents to all the good little boys and girls. In his preschool class, however, another child tells him that Santa isn't real. Eddy comes home to you extremely upset and tearfully asks you if there really is a Santa Claus. What do you think a Deontologist would advise you to do? What do you think the right thing to do in this case would be?

2.   What would an ethical egoist or a utilitarian say is the morally correct thing to do in each of these cases? Would the results be dramatically different from those of a deontologist like Kant? If so, how?

Sources and Further Reading

Acton, Harry. *Kant's Moral Philosophy*. London: Macmillan, 1970.

Aune, Bruce. *Kant's Theory of Morals*. Princeton, NJ: Princeton University Press, 1979.

Augustine. *Enchiridion*. Trans. J.F. Shaw. *Nicene and Post-Nicene Fathers*. Vol. 3. Ed. Philip Schaff. Buffalo, NY: Christian Literature Publishing Company, 1887.

Darwall, Stephen. *Impartial Reason*. Ithaca, NY: Cornell University Press, 1983.

Guyer, Paul. *The Cambridge Companion to Kant*. New York: Cambridge University Press, 1992.

Kant, Immanuel. *Foundations of the Metaphysics of Morals*. Trans. Lewis White Beck. New York: Cambridge University Press, 1991.

—. "On the Supposed Right to Lie from Altruistic Motives." *Critique of Practical Reason and Other Wtitings in Moral Philosophy*. Ed. Lewis White Beck. Chicago: University of Chicago Press, 1949.

Nagel, Thomas. *The View From Nowhere*. New York: Oxford University Press, 1986.

O'Neill, Onora. *Acting on Principle: An Essay on Kantian Ethics*. New York: Columbia University Press, 1975.

Paton, Herbet J. *The Categorical Imperative: A Study in Kant's Moral Philosophy*. Chicago: University of Chicago Press, 1948.

Rachels, James. *The Elements of Moral Philosophy*. Boston: McGraw Hill, 1999.

Ross, William D. *The Right and the Good*. New York: Oxford University Press, 1930.

Sandel, Michael. *Justice*. New York: Farrar, Straus and Giroux, 2009.

Sullivan, Roger J. *Immanuel Kant's Moral Theory*. Cambridge: Cambridge University Press, 1989.

Ward, Keith. *The Development of Kant's Views on Ethics*. Oxford: Blackwell, 1972.

Wolff, Robert P. *The Anatomy of Reason: A Commentary on Kant's Groundwork of the Metaphysics of Morals*. New York: Harper and Row, 1973.

chapter 9

RIGHTS THEORY

Case Study: Free Speech or Hate Speech?

Martin Henry is a junior at Sunshine State University in Southern California. In an attempt to broaden his intellectual horizons he began reading Hitler's Mein Kampf *and similar works that advanced the theory of white supremacy. Excited about the ideas about which he had been reading, Martin decided to attend a meeting of the local chapter of Aryan Nation and soon became an active member of this organization. The members of Aryan Nation were delighted that a college student like Martin would be so committed to their cause, and even more delighted when they discovered that he was attending a liberal college like Sunshine State.*

In March 2007, Martin, at the request of the Grand Master of Aryan Nation, began to distribute fliers on his campus that informed students about the treachery of the Jewish people and argued that the Holocaust was nothing more than a myth. Although the flier didn't go so far as to advocate violence against Jews, it did maintain that past violence against this group was morally justifiable. Naturally, many students were outraged by the distribution of this flier and lodged an official complaint against Martin with the Provost of the University. After reviewing this situation, the Provost expelled Martin from Sunshine State and forbade him from ever coming onto the campus again.

Outraged by this violation of his right to freedom of speech, Martin asked the American Civil Liberties Union to defend him. Although members of this organization were disgusted by Martin's gross anti-Semitism, they agreed that his rights had in fact been violated and sued the University for two million dollars.

During the trial, Martin's lawyers argued that other controversial groups on campus, such as the Islamic Brotherhood and the Federation of Gays and Lesbians, had in the past distributed provocative materials without any disciplinary action being taken against them. Martin, they argued, was being punished because he was expressing a position that

*some on campus found offensive. The First Amendment, they said, was
established precisely to protect people like Martin from the tyranny of
majority opinion. By attempting to restrict Martin's speech—however
odious it might seem—the University was posing a threat to the civil
liberties of all of its students.*

*The lawyers for the University countered by arguing that the ma-
terials Martin distributed could have provoked violence against Jewish
students and, therefore, his speech was not protected under the First
Amendment. Freedom of Speech, they maintained, was not an absolute
right and must be balanced by other equally compelling interests—in
this case, the rights of students on campus to be free from intimidation.
They also argued that a college community is a voluntary association,
and that by agreeing to attend Sunshine State, Martin also agreed to
abide by a certain set of rules—in this case, refraining from speech that
could provoke violence.*

FOR DISCUSSION

Whose position makes the most sense to you—that of Martin's lawyers or that of the lawyers for the University? Do you
think that Martin's lawyers are right in arguing that there are
potential dangers to limiting freedom of speech, even if that
speech is hurtful or offensive? Why or why not?

What is a Person?

In contemporary moral philosophy a debate has arisen about what exactly a person is. This question gets to the heart of ethics because most
moral philosophers argue that we have certain moral obligations towards
persons that we don't have towards non-persons. We have seen in our
discussion of deontology, for example, that Kant makes a distinction between persons and things, arguing that the former must always be treated
as ends in themselves, while the latter can be used merely as means.
The question of what exactly a person is, however, is not as obvious as
it might seem.

Some moral philosophers have argued that the term "person" should
be used synonymously with human being. If this is the case, we still
need to ask ourselves what a human being is. Is it simply a matter of

appearance? But then what about someone born with numerous physical defects? Are they still human beings even though they may not have all the characteristics we normally associate with human beings? Perhaps a human being is simply a matter of having a certain genetic make-up. The problem here is that creatures such as chimpanzees have a genetic code that is 98 percent identical to human beings, but we would probably not classify them as human.

Other philosophers like John Locke focus on self-consciousness as the essential quality that distinguishes persons from non-persons. Locke defined a person as "a thinking intelligent Being, that has reason and reflection, and can consider itself as itself, the same thinking thing in different places and times, which it does only by that consciousness, which is inseparable from thinking, and as it seems to me essential to it" (*Human Understanding* 2.27.9). Thus a person for Locke is a living being conscious of itself as persisting over time and therefore having preferences about its own future.

The problem with Locke's understanding of personhood, of course, is that, based on his criteria, there may be persons that are not humans and humans that are not persons. For example, some highly evolved animals such as great apes or dolphins would have to be considered persons, while an irreversibly comatose patient or a baby would not be. Similarly, it might be possible in the future to create an artificial life form that is capable of meeting Locke's criteria for personhood. Would such a "being" then be entitled to the same respect and consideration as any other person?

A similar problem arises when we apply this criterion to the status of the fetus, as those in favor of abortion argue that the fetus is not a person, because it is not self-conscious, while those opposed to abortion argue that the *potential* for self-conscious awareness should be enough to convey personhood. There are difficulties, of course, with both positions. Advocates for abortion have to explain why the fetus should not be considered a person, while a newborn baby, which is equally lacking in self-consciousness, should be; on the other hand opponents of abortion have a difficult time explaining how a single-cell organism with no mind to speak of could possibly be considered a person.

Other possible criteria for personhood proposed by moral theorists include the following:

- the ability to engage in rational thought.
- the ability to make free choices.
- the ability to have projects and plans.

- the ability to use language.
- the ability to experience pleasure and pain.
- the presence of a soul created by God.

Unfortunately, each of these criteria presents its own unique set of problems that must be addressed. If we accept the first three of these criteria, then fetuses, babies, and the severely mentally handicapped would not be considered persons. If we use sentience—the ability to experience pleasure and pain—as our criterion, then animals would also be persons. Finally, the equation of personhood with the presence of a soul may appeal to religious believers, but would certainly not satisfy agnostics or atheists.

In the discussion of rights theory, the definition of personhood becomes extremely important. As we shall see, proponents of this theory argue that the basic rights of all persons must be respected. Once we resolve what these basic rights are, however, we still need to return to the even more difficult question of what constitutes personhood.

What Are Rights?

As Americans we are inundated with talk about rights. We hear constantly about the right to life, the right to freedom of speech, about women's rights, gay rights, even about the right to die. Indeed most of our moral dilemmas are shaped and framed by rights talk in one form or another. But what exactly are human rights anyway?

Moral rights are claims or demands that individuals and groups can make upon other members of a society, and which therefore impose a duty or obligation on the actions of others in that society. For example, if one has the right to freedom of speech, this means that other members of the society do not have the right to interfere with this speech; if one has the right to a free public education, this right imposes an obligation on others in the society to pay the costs of that education. Moral rights also entail a certain obligation on the part of the rights holder about how that right is to be exercised. For example, even though one might have a right to freedom of speech, one also has an obligation to exercise that right in a responsible manner. According to rights theory, therefore,

an act is right if, in performing it, one does not violate the basic rights of others.

In the event that two or more rights are in conflict, we are obligated to act in such a way as to ensure that the most important rights will be respected.

Historical Background of Moral Rights Theory

The idea of moral rights became popular in political thought in the 17th and 18th centuries. John Locke, who is considered by many to be the father of moral rights theory, developed a concept of natural rights, which he believed to be derived from God. In his work, *Two Treatises of Government*, Locke identified three fundamental natural rights—life, liberty and property. Locke's position had a great impact on the faculty fathers of the United States. Thomas Jefferson, most notably, took many of the ideas found in the writings of Locke and used them as the basis for his "Declaration of Independence":

> We hold these truths to be self-evident; that all men are created equal, that they are endowed by their Creator with certain unalienable rights, that among these are Life, Liberty and the pursuit of Happiness—That to secure these Rights, Governments are instituted among Men, deriving their just powers from the Consent of the Governed, that whenever any Form of Government becomes destructive of these Ends, it is the Right of the People to alter or abolish it, and to institute new Government, laying its Foundations on such Principles, and organizing its Powers in such Form, as to them shall seem most likely to affect their Safety and Happiness.

According to classical rights theory, moral rights are bestowed by virtue of humanity and have nothing to do with who you are, your social status, your citizenship, or the laws of the state. Moral rights according to this tradition are also understood to be "unalienable." They can't, in other words, be given or taken away. A rights holder may at times choose not to exercise the rights he possesses (for example, refraining from speaking when he has the right to) or to allow someone else to exercise a right for him (as a parent would do for his child or a severely mentally handicapped adult relative).

Not long after the Declaration of Independence was written, the newly established United States of America became the first country to enumerate specific rights for all of its citizens. These rights were introduced in a series of amendments to the Constitution proposed by James

Madison. In 1791 ten of these amendments were ratified and became the Bill of Rights. Among the rights recognized by the Constitution of the United States are the following:

- the right to freedom of religion, speech, press, and assembly, as well as the right to petition the government (1st amendment).
- the right to keep and bear arms (2nd amendment).
- the right to protection from unreasonable search and seizure (4th amendment).
- the right to due process under the law, protection against self-incrimination, limits placed upon eminent domain (i.e., private property taken for public use) (5th amendment).
- the right to trial by jury and other rights of the accused (e.g., the right to receive information about the nature and cause of the accusation, the right to confront witnesses, the right to have a defense lawyer provided (6th amendment).
- the prohibition of excessive bail, as well as cruel and unusual punishment (8th amendment).

Rights theory advanced considerably when on December 10, 1948 the General Assembly of the United Nations adopted the Universal Declaration of Human Rights, declaring the rights contained therein as "a common standard of achievement for all peoples and all nations." Among the rights recognized by this document that go beyond those enumerated by the U.S. Constitution are:

- the right not to be held in slavery and servitude (Art. 4).
- the right not to be subjected to cruel, inhumane, or degrading treatment or punishment (Art. 5).
- the right to seek and enjoy in other countries asylum from persecution (Art. 14).
- the right to marry and found a family (Art. 16).
- the right to social security (Art. 22).
- the right to work, to choose one's own employment, to be protected against unfavorable work conditions, to be protected against unemployment, the right to equal pay for equal work and the right to join labor unions (Art. 23).
- the right to rest and leisure, including limitations placed upon working hours and periodic holidays with pay (Art. 24).
- the right to a standard of living adequate to support oneself and one's family (Art. 25).

- the right to education, including free primary education, and equal access to higher education (Art. 26).
- the right to freely participate in the cultural life of one's community, to enjoy the arts, and to share in the benefits of scientific achievement (Art. 27).

Moral Decision-Making Using Rights Theory

Preparatory Stage: Determine what specific rights human beings possess (feel free to use the U.S. Constitution and the U.N. Declaration of Rights as guides) and to whom these apply.

Step 1: Identify the action being considered.
Step 2: Determine if the action being considered violates anyone's basic rights.
Step 3: If it doesn't, then the act is morally right; if it does, then the act is morally wrong.

Human and Legal Rights

A distinction that should be kept in mind is the difference between human and legal rights. Legal rights refer to those rights found within existing legal codes. Such rights are dependent upon the passing of a law which grants these rights to individuals within a given society and protects them under the laws of that society. For example, the right to receive a high school education is a legal right granted by the laws of the United States, but which would not be recognized in some other societies. Human rights, on the other hand, are rights which transcend the particular laws of a given society. The UN Universal Declaration of Human Rights, for instance, claims that all human beings have the rights to life, liberty and the security of person (Article 3), the right not to be held in slavery or servitude (Article 4) and the right not to be subject to torture, inhumane or degrading treatment or punishment (Article 5). Each of these rights is considered by those who drafted this document to be a human right existing independently of any individual legal code.

It should be noted that there are some political thinkers, such as legal positivists, who believe that the only rights that truly exist are those that originate within a legal system, and that therefore, human rights are fictions. "No laws," they argue, "no rights." The problem with such a limited perspective on rights is that it would seem to prevent any redress to those living in societies with unjust laws. Legal positivists, for example, would have had a difficult time arguing against the existence of apartheid in South Africa, because the laws in that country clearly sanctioned discriminary treatment of black South Africans. In such cases it becomes necessary to appeal to rights which transcend the specific legal codes, in order to protect individuals being treated inhumanely within their own countries.

Negative and Positive Rights

In recent times a somewhat controversial distinction has been made between negative and positive rights. Negative rights are rights not to be interfered with by government or fellow citizens. The rights to freedom of speech, religion, and assembly, which are included in the Bill of Rights of the U.S. Constitution, are negative rights of noninterference because they prevent others from interfering with the actions protected by these rights. Such rights, however, do not obligate others to help us exercise our rights. Positive rights—also known as entitlements or welfare rights—are rights which impose obligations on others to provide goods or services to which the rights holder is entitled. Rights to health care, education or employment are examples of positive rights.

While liberal thinkers tend to support the idea of positive rights, other political thinkers, such as libertarians, argue that there are no such things as positive human rights. Although they are adamant in their defense of negative rights, libertarians believe that so-called positive rights are nothing more than infringements upon the rights of those who are expected to provide entitlements. As Ayn Rand, the philosophical guru of many in the libertarian movement, writes:

> Any alleged "right" of one man, which necessitates the violation of the rights of another, is not and cannot be a right.
>
> No man can have a right to impose an unchosen obligation, an unrewarded duty or an involuntary servitude on another man. There can be no such thing as "the right to enslave."
>
> A right does not include the material implementation of that right by other men; it includes only the freedom to earn that implementation by one's own effort.
>
> Observe, in this context, the intellectual precision of the Founding Fathers: they spoke of the rights to the pursuit of happiness—not the right to happiness. It means that a man has the right to take the actions he deems necessary to achieve his hap-

piness; it does not mean that others must make him happy....

The right to property means that a man has the right to take the economic actions necessary to earn property, to use it and dispose of it; it does not mean that others must provide him with property.

The right of free speech means that a man has the right to express his ideas without danger of suppression, interference or punitive action by the government. It does not mean that others must provide him with a lecture hall, a radio station or a printing press through which to express his ideas.

Any undertaking that involves more than one man, requires the voluntary consent of every participant. Every one of them has the right to make his own decision, but none has the right to force his decision on the others...(113-114).

As we have seen, libertarians believe that the only obligation that we have to others is that of forbearance or refraining from interfering with their rights. They argue that there are no other obligations that we have towards our fellow citizens.

Liberty and Its Limitations

The First Amendment to the Constitution enumerates certain basic liberties that all human beings possess and which are protected by law. Among these are the right to freedom of religion, speech, press, and assembly. The wording of this amendment might lead one to conclude that these liberties are absolute, but this has never been the case. Since the time that the Constitution was written, there have been numerous questions about the scope of individual liberty and its limitations.

In 1859, the English utilitarian philosopher, John Stuart Mill, attempted to address this question in his work, *On Liberty*, which has come to be viewed by many as the greatest treatise on human liberty ever written. Mill's basic premise in *On Liberty* is that government has the right to limit people's freedoms only when it is necessary to prevent them from causing harm to others. As Mill wrote,

The only purpose for which power can be rightly exercised over any member in a civilized community, against his will, is to prevent harm to others. His own good, either physical or moral, is not sufficient warrant. He cannot rightfully be compelled to do or to forbear because it will make him better to do so, because it will make him happier, because, in the opinion of others, to do so would be wise or even right. There are good reasons for remonstrating with him, or reasoning with him, or persuading him, or entreating him, but not for compelling him or visiting him with any evil in case he do otherwise. To justify that, the conduct from which it is desired to deter him must be calculated to produce evil to someone else. The only part of the conduct of anyone for which he is amenable to society is that which concerns others. In that part which merely concerns himself, his independence is, of right, absolute. Over himself, over his body or mind, the individual is sovereign (9).

Unless they are likely to harm others, Mill believes that people should have an absolute right to do whatever they want. He notes, however, that this principle applies only to competent adults. It does not apply to children or those suffering from serious psychological illnesses.

Mill's "harm principle," on the other hand, would allow for government interference in acts that cause harm to others or which have the potential to cause harm to others—acts such as theft, violence, rape, or drunk driving. Short of that, Mill believes that people have a right to do whatever they want with their lives, even if their actions might cause harm to themselves. Thus, while cigarette smoking, drinking to excess, sky-diving, or eating fatty foods might cause harm to the individual engaged in such behavior, the government does not have a right to interfere, unless it can be demonstrated that other members of the society have been harmed by the behavior. We might forewarn such individuals about the follies of their ways, but we should not interfere with their behavior, no matter how irresponsible it might seem to us.

Mill also believes that individuals need to be protected against, what he refers to as, "the tyranny of the majority." This sort of social tyranny occurs when the majority uses coercive means to compel individuals to conform to its norms of behavior, Mill believes that the majority has even more pernicious ways to control its members:

Society can and does execute its own mandates; and if it issues wrong mandates instead of right, or any mandate at all in things in which it ought not to meddle, it practices a social tyranny more formidable than many kinds of political oppression, since, though not usually upheld by such extreme penalties, it leaves fewer means of escape, penetrating much more deeply into the details of life, and enslaving the soul itself. Protection, therefore, against the tyranny of magistrates is not enough; there needs to be protection against the tyranny of prevailing opinion and feeling, against the tendency of society to impose, by other means than civil penalties, its own ideas and practices as rules of conduct on those who dissent from them; to fetter the development and, if possible, prevent the formation of any individuality not in harmony with its own ways, and compel all characters to fashion themselves upon the model of its own. There is a limit to the legitimate interference of collective opinion with individual independence; and to find that limit and to maintain it against encroachment is as indispensable to a good condition of human affairs as protection against political despotism (7).

In Mill's view the tyranny of the majority is much more dangerous than the tyranny of governments because it is more pervasive and harder to protect oneself against. He believes, therefore, that individuals need as much protection against social tyranny as they do against political tyranny.

Advantages of Rights Theory

Rights theory has a number of distinct advantages that make it one of the most practical and concrete of all the moral theories that we have examined so far. Among these advantages are the following:

Rights theory protects and promotes the value of individuals. Any advocate of rights theory must hold that human persons have intrinsic value and that their interests must be protected from the interference of others. The theory also treats human beings as moral equals, and, therefore, helps prevent discriminatory practices towards members of different races, genders, or sexual orientations. The emphasis on moral equality also makes it an ideal ethical system for democratic societies.

Rights are objective. When rights theory clearly spells out those fundamental rights, such as life, liberty, privacy, and property that must be respected, it provides a clear framework for moral-decision making. Although there may be debate over how to interpret and apply certain rights—for example, whether there should be any limitations placed upon rights such as freedom of speech or religion—at least rights theory gives us a clear starting point for our moral deliberations.

Disadvantages of Rights Theory

As is the case with all of the theories we have examined, there are certain inherent problems with rights theory that have been raised by critics:

There ain't no such thing as rights. Some moral thinkers, such as

Jeremy Bentham, have argued that while the idea of moral rights sounds nice, in reality any talk about human rights is nothing more than "nonsense on stilts." Such critics maintain that rights only exist once they have been established by a given society. The idea of natural human rights, therefore, is simply a myth that has no philosophical justification.

Which rights are right? Even if we grant that there are such things as human rights, agreeing on exactly what rights human beings possess is still somewhat difficult. We have seen that many liberals would include the rights to decent housing, employment, and adequate shelter as basic human rights, whereas libertarians would reject these outright. One major problem with rights theory is that its proponents typically do little more than present a list of basic rights without providing an adequate philosophical rationale for why certain rights are fundamental and others are not. Libertarians tend to be better at providing this sort of rationale than liberals, although the number of basic rights they recognized is, not surprisingly, fairly circumscribed.

What are we to do when rights come into conflict? Like duties, rights are prima facie, and therefore may come into conflict with one another. The most famous illustration of this sort of conflict is between the woman's right to privacy and the fetus' right to life. In such cases it is often difficult to determine which right should take priority, and the result has been decades of political battles between abortion rights advocates and their opponents with no real resolution of this question.

For Further Discussion

1. Based on our discussion of moral rights theory in this chapter, answer the following questions concerning the scope of moral rights:

   - Should individuals have a right to health care even if they can't afford to pay for it? If so, who should be forced the bear the large costs necessary for ensuring this right?

   - Should people have the right to smoke in enclosed public spaces if they so choose?

   - Do only human beings have rights? Or do you think that animals have certain rights as well? If so, what would some of these rights be?

   - Should minors have the right to have an abortion without notifying their parents?

   - Do future generations have any rights? If so, what are they?

- Should individuals have the right to put whatever information they want on the Internet, even if such information might be a potential threat to public safety?

- During wartime or other times of great emergency, should people be allowed to criticize the actions of the government or, in such specific cases, should limitations be placed upon freedom of speech?

- Is there a right to privacy, and if so, is this right absolute?

- Do indivdiuals of the same sex have the right to get married?

2. The "establishment clause" in the first amendment of the U.S. Constitution specifically states that "Congress shall make no law respecting an establishment of religion or prohibiting the free exercise thereof." Do you think that this clause allows for the following:

- organized prayer during school hours (those students who feel uncomfortable with this practice are permitted to opt out)?

- voluntary Bible study and prayer after school on school grounds?

- the placing of art works or sculptures depicting the Ten Commandments in courthouses?

- the placing of a nativity scene on town or state property?

- government funds given to religious organizations to provide services for at-risk populations?

3. The second amendment of the Constitution states the following: "A well-regulated Militia, being necessary to the security of a free State, and the right of the People to keep and bear Arms, shall not be infringed."

- Do you think that the framers of the Constitution meant this amendment to allow anyone to own weapons?

- Is this right absolute?

- Does this right also allow people to own assault weapons, as the National Rifle Association maintains?

4. The eighth amendment prohibits the use of "cruel and unusual punishment." Does this mean that extreme methods of interrogation

(i.e., waterboarding, excessive sleep or food deprivation, etc.) cannot be used against terrorism suspects?

5. Liberty and Its Limitations: According to Mill's "harm principle," which of the following actions would be a legitimate use of government power to regulate the behavior of individuals?

    *   laws mandating the use of seatbelts in cars.

    *   laws preventing teens from drinking alcohol.

    *   laws requiring individuals to drive at certain speed limits.

    *   laws preventing adults from using drugs such as marijuana or hashish.

    *   laws preventing adults from using hard drugs such as heroin and cocaine.

    *   laws preventing access to certain sites on the Internet deemed dangerous

Sources and Further Reading

Donnelly, Jack. *Universal Human Rights in Theory and Practice.* Ithaca, NY: Cornell University Press, 1987.

Feinberg, Joel. *Rights, Justice, and the Bounds of Liberty.* Princteon, NJ: Princeton University Press, 1980.

Harpham, Edward, ed. *John Locke's Two Treatises of Government: New Interpretations.* Lawrence, KS: University Press of Kansas, 1992.

Locke, John. *On Human Understanding.*

—. *Two Treatises of Government.* New York: New American Library, 1965.

Libertarian National Committee. *National Platform of the Libertarian Party.* Adopted: July 2, 2006.

Luytgaarden, Eric van de. *Introduction to the Theory of Human Rights.* Utrecht: Utrecht University, 1993.

Lyons, David. *Rights.* Belmont, CA: Wadsworth, 1979.

Machan, Tibor. *Individuals and Their Rights.* LaSalle, IL: Open Court, 1989.

Meldon, A.I. *Human Rights.* Belmont, CA: Wadsworth, 1970.

Mill, John Stuart. *On Liberty.* Indianapolis, IN: Hackett, 1978.

Nickel, James. *Making Sense of Human Rights.* Berkeley: University of California Press, 1987.

Rand, Ayn. "Man's Rights." *Capitalism: The Unknown Ideal.* New York: Penguin, 1966.

Shue, Henry. *Basic Rights*. Princeton, NJ. Princeton University Press, 1980.

Simmons, *The Lockean Theory of Rights*. Princeton, NJ: Princeton University Press, 1992.

Waldron, Jeremy. *Theories of Rights*. New York: Oxford University Press, 1984.

chapter **10**

VIRTUE ETHICS

Case Study: An Attempt at Self Improvement

Valerie Carolan has come to an impasse in her life. She is currently a sophomore at Michigan State University and is enrolled in the university's rigorous pre-law program. One day she wakes up in her dorm room and realizes that her life is a mess: sprawled out in the bed next to her is some guy that she doesn't even know who smells really bad. Her head is pounding like a jackhammer from all the drinking she did the previous night and she realizes that she too must look (and smell) absolutely horrible from her wild night on the town.

As she gets out of her bed, she recalls the events of the previous evening—how she chose to go out partying instead of studying for the philosophy exam that she will have to take in one hour; how she drank to excess, and in a state of intoxication flirted outrageously with a dumb jock she met in a bar; how she fought with her roommates, who objected to her bringing a strange guy into their dorm room. She is pretty sure that she had some kind of physical intimacy with the jock in bed with her, but can't remember if they had sexual intercourse, and, if they had, whether they had used any kind of protection.

Getting out of bed quietly, she quickly puts back on the clothes from the previous evening that are scattered on the floor around her and slips out into the common area of her dorm room. Sitting there in the living room are Valerie's roommates who clearly are enraged with her. Her roommates tell Valerie that they have had it with her. They say that lately she has been ignoring all of her responsibilities and spending most of her time partying and picking up guys. If she continues in this way, they warn her, she will probably fail out of college and ruin her life. They also are tired of her explosive anger, her laziness and her sloppiness around the dorm. They tell her that, unless she makes a conscious effort to work on some of these character defects, they will have no option but to ask for her to be kicked out of the dorm.

Upon hearing this, Valerie explodes in a fit of rage and storms out of the living room. Walking through the campus, her head still pounding severely, Valerie reflects back on her life, acknowledging that for some time now her life has been spinning out of control. Although she is still angry at her roommates for their lack of support, she admits to herself that she needs to radically transform her character if she is going to make it through the next two-and-a-half years of college.

FOR DISCUSSION

What are some of the qualities of her character that Valerie needs to change if she wants to live a happy and productive life? What kind of program of character transformation would you recommend Valerie undertake in order to turn her life around? Be specific in your recommendations.

Imagine that Valerie has decided not to work on her character flaws, but rather chose to move into a single dorm room so that her behavior would not affect anyone else. Would her behavior in this case still be morally problematic? Why or why not? What would a utilitarian or a deontologist have to say about this?

Doing and Being

Most of the ethical theories that we have examined have focused on the rightness or wrongness of specific actions. The basic moral question for a utilitarian or deontologist would be the same: "What should I do?" In answering this question, the utilitarian or deontologist would point to specific rules or principles that ought to be used to guide moral action.

In opposition to these approaches, virtue ethics focuses on the character of the moral agent, and asks a more difficult—and perhaps more profound—question: "What kind of person should I become?" Instead of providing rules or principles, the virtue ethicist would focus instead on specific qualities of character—or virtues—that a good person ought to possess. "Be truthful, be compassionate, be generous," the virtue ethicist would respond, and you will probably behave the correct way in most circumstances. We do good, in other words, because we are good.

Virtue ethicists, therefore, argue that moral action has nothing to do with the rightness or wrongness of specific acts, but rather with the character of the person who performs the act. Thus the position of virtue ethics maintains that *an act is right if it is performed by a person of virtuous moral character.*

To help illustrate this point, let's imagine that you have a grandfather who is universally acknowledged to be an exemplary human being. In all the years that you have known him, you have never heard him utter an unkind word or perform an unjust action. In fact, he always goes out of his way to treat everyone he meets with charity, benevolence, and sensitivity. He is, in other words, a person of the highest moral caliber.

One day, however, the police come to your door and tell you that your grandfather has been accused of murdering an acquaintance and that the weapon used in the crime was found in your grandfather's possession. What would you think about hearing this from the police? Your natural reaction would be to think that there is some kind of mistake—that your grandfather couldn't have committed the act described or that, if he did, he must have had a very good justification. In the end, your views are proven to be correct. In fact, what actually happened was that your grandfather was helping a friend move his gun collection and, while he was removing a handgun, it accidentally discharged, killing his friend. You knew that your grandfather must have been innocent, because you knew what kind of character he had, and you also knew that a person with that kind of character would never kill anyone intentionally.

Thus, rather than spending time trying to figure out what kinds of actions are right or wrong, the virtue ethicist looks to exemplary individuals like grandpa—or perhaps even more saintly individuals, like St. Francis, Mother Teresa, Gandhi, or Martin Luther King—and tells us instead to develop the specific qualities of character that these kinds of people possess.

Aristotle's Virtue Ethics

Like utilitarianism and deontology, virtue ethics has taken on many different forms in recent times. Almost all contemporary virtue ethics approaches, however, owe a considerable debt to the theory of the virtues that was developed by Aristotle over 2,300 years ago. Aristotle was born in Stagira, Macedonia in 384 BC. After studying with Plato at his Academy he returned to Macedonia to act as a tutor for Alexander the Great. In 335 B.C. he went to Athens for a second time to found his own school, the Lyceum, and taught there for the next twelve years. After the death of Alexander, Athens rebelled against Macedonia, and Aristotle was forced to flee Athens to avoid being put to death. He died one year later in 322 B.C.

Aristotle certainly was one of the greatest thinkers in Western Civilization and wrote on almost every topic imaginable: biology, logic, poetics, rhetoric, politics, physics, and metaphysics. We know that he also wrote at least two, and perhaps three, different works on ethics. For our purposes the most relevant of these works is the *Nicomachean Ethics*, which contains his most complete treatment of the virtues. Because the work was written in the form of lecture notes and reflects the Athenian culture in which he was living, Aristotle's *Ethics* seems at first like a rather dubious vehicle for developing a virtue ethics for the 21st century. And yet, if we can get beyond his archaic language, we will find a work that is surprisingly engaging and extremely relevant to our own times.

Human Happiness

Aristotle's approach to ethics has been described as teleological in nature. A teleological approach is one that looks to the end, goal or purpose (*telos*) of human existence in order to determine how we ought to act. For Aristotle, everything in the universe had a purpose, so it is hardly surprising that he would think that human action would have some kind of purpose as well. Because Aristotle, like most of his Greek contemporaries, believed that this purpose was somehow directed towards the attainment of happiness, he begins his investigation of ethics with an examination of the nature of human happiness.

The highest good for human beings, Aristotle believes, is the attainment of happiness (*eudaimonia*) and it is the attainment of happiness that is the goal of everything we do in life. Aristotle goes on to define happiness as "activity of the soul in accordance with virtue (*arête*)." It is the life of virtue, in other words, that leads human beings to the happiness they ultimately seek. Although Aristotle speaks of different types of virtue—physical, intellectual and moral—it seems clear that he believes moral virtue is that human excellence that most directly contributes to happiness.

The Golden Mean

So if happiness is attained through the acquisition of moral virtue, the next logical question becomes: how is this virtue to be attained? Most moral action, Aristotle says, concerns itself in one form or another with the emotions. "By emotions," he specifies, "I mean appetite, anger, fear, confidence, envy, joy, affection, hatred, longing, emulation, [and] pity" (*Ethics* 1105b 20-22). For Aristotle there is nothing either good or bad about the emotions themselves; what is good or bad is how we choose to act upon them in a particular situation. The role of reason, therefore, is not to eliminate the emotions, but rather to regulate them, so that they do not get out of hand or lead us into trouble.

But what exactly is the right way for reason to control the emotions? Aristotle uses the analogy of a good work of art. For a Greek, the perfect work of art is one in which nothing can be added to or taken away from it. Think of a great work of art such as Michelangelo's David or Beethoven's Ninth Symphony, for example: there is a harmony to these kinds of works that makes them seem totally complete in themselves. We wouldn't want the artist to add or take away anything from them for fear of ruining their perfection. This kind of excellence in a work of art, then, would be destroyed through excess or defect. Excess and defect are also possible in the realm of human action: we can get too much or too little food, too much or too little exercise—both of which would prove harmful to a human being. In the realm of human action, then, Aristotle thinks that we ought always to strive for what the Latins called the "golden mean" (*aurea mediocritas*) or, to put it in his own language, a mean state between two extremes, excess and defect, with respect to action and emotion:

> Virtue, then, is a state of character concerned with choice, lying in a mean, i.e., the mean relative to use, this being determined by a rational principle by which the man of practical wisdom would determine it. Now it is a mean between two vices, that which depends on excess and that which depends on defect; and again it is a mean because the vices respectively fall short of or exceed what is right in both passions and actions, while virtue finds and chooses that which is intermediate (*Ethics* 1107a)

To put this in simpler terms, virtue for Aristotle is nothing more than a means between two extremes (an excess and a defect) with respect to a particular action or emotion.

Illustrating the Virtues

A few examples will help to illustrate Aristotle's theory of the virtues. Let's take the virtue of courage as our first example. Aristotle defines courage as a mean state between the two extremes of cowardice and recklessness with respect to the emotion of fear. A courageous person in this view feels just the right amount of fear when confronted by a dangerous situation; the cowardly person feels much more fear than he should; the reckless feels much less. Aristotle's treatment of courage might strike some as a bit dubious since many of us have been led to believe that a courageous person is someone who actually feels no fear at all. But if we take time to analyze the nature of courage we shall see that Aristotle's view actually makes much more sense than our popular notion of courage.

Imagine for instance that you and a friend are passing a building that is on fire. The building is being rapidly consumed by flames, but the local fire department is not yet on the scene. On the second floor of the building a child is crying out for help from an open window. How would a courageous person respond in such a situation? We know that a cowardly person would probably avoid getting involved for fear of being burnt alive. If you were a coward, you would probably argue that it is best to wait for the fire department to arrive, since they are trained to handle this kind of emergency. In the meanwhile, however, the trapped child will have been burnt alive. Another option is for you to rush into the burning building without a moment's hesitation or forethought, battle the smoke and flames, and try to climb up to the second floor to rescue the trapped child. Even if you managed to reach the child under these conditions, it is not certain that you would be able to carry him out of the house before the roof or stairway collapsed. Both you and the child would end up dead, and all of your heroic efforts would have been in vain. While some might describe your actions as courageous, Aristotle would correctly observe that you were in fact foolhardy rather than courageous—that is, that you didn't have the right amount of fear that you should have had in such a life-threatening situation.

So if you were a truly courageous person what would you do in this kind of situation? First, you would quickly size up the extent to which the house is being burned, the location of the child, and the resources that are available. If the child could in fact be saved by rushing into the house, you might risk it even though there was a chance that you yourself might be trapped; if there is no chance of saving the child that way, you would look for another option. If the child was small enough, for example, you might have him jump out the window into your arms, or if a neighbor was at hand (and there was enough time) you might have the neighbor get a sheet to use as a safety net. Whatever option you chose, it is certain that you would still feel some degree of fear—at the very least for the child whose life is in danger. Aristotle is certainly correct then, when he maintains that a courageous person, unlike a foolhardy one, feels fear. He just isn't crippled by it the way a coward would be.

Another important virtue for Aristotle is that of generosity, which he describes as a mean between the extremes of extravagance and stinginess with respect to the giving and taking of money. A stingy person is someone who exceeds in taking but is defective in giving. We can think of a miserly old person—Dickens' Scrooge, for example—who is excellent at making money from his dealings with other people, but who is horrible at giving it away, even for a good cause.   Once again, we might be tempted to think of a generous person as one who gives without thought to anyone in need, but for Aristotle this would be an extravagant person, not a generous one. This kind of person, he says, exceeds in giving but is defective in taking. I have known people, for example, who, filled with the spirit of Christian charity, have given away much of their money to worthy causes or individuals in need. Unfortunately, many end up not having enough left to pay their monthly bills, and are forced to borrow money from friends or family to survive. This kind of person, while appearing to practice the virtue of generosity is actually not virtuous at all, since he gives from other people's pockets rather than his own.

Finally, for Aristotle, even-temperedness is a means between the extremes of short-temperedness and apathy with respect to the emotion of anger. The even-tempered person is not that individual who never gets angry under any circumstance. There are certainly occasions when even the most mild-mannered person would demonstrate extreme anger—when a great injustice has been committed, for example. If he was protecting the life of someone he loved his anger might even compel him to lash out with great violence. At all times, however, he directs the correct amount of anger towards precisely the right object in order to accomplish his goals. The short-tempered person on the other hand responds to many of life's adversities with an excessive degree of anger and often directs it at the wrong object. He might, for example, be humiliated at work by his boss. Instead of directing his anger at the appropriate source (his boss), in the right way (preferably in private) and to the right degree (firmly but not in a shrill or volatile manner), he takes his hostility out on his wife and children, towards whom his anger should not be directed at all.

In the *Nicomachean Ethics*, Aristotle provides an extensive list of virtues that he believes are essential for morally good persons to possess. Each of these virtues basically follows the same format described above. They are understood to be means between two extremes, an excess and a defect with respect to a particular emotion.

Acquiring Virtue

We have seen that for Aristotle all human action aims at happiness and that happiness is connected to a life of virtue. If we accept this starting point of Aristotelian ethics, the next question that should automatically be asked is: how do we learn to become virtuous men and women? In answering this question Aristotle begins by making the distinction between intellectual virtues, such as practical wisdom, and moral virtues, such as courage, generosity, and the like. Intellectual virtues, he believes, are acquired by education; moral virtues by habit. In other words, Aristotle rejects the notion that a child—or even an adult for that matter—can be taught to be good:

> Argument and teaching, I am afraid, are not effective in all cases: the soul of the listener must first have been conditioned by habits to the right kind of likes and dislikes, just as land must be cultivated before it is able to foster the seed. For a man whose life is guided by emotion will not listen to an argument that dissuades him, nor will he understand it. How can we possibly persuade a man like that to change his ways? And in general it seems that emotion does not yield to argument but only to force. Therefore, there must first be a character that somehow has an affinity for excellence or virtue, a character that loves what is noble and feels disgust at what is base (*Ethics* 1179b 23-31).

The problem as Aristotle sees it is that if a person does not already have a virtuous disposition, then he will not be open to moral education, and if he already has a virtuous disposition then he really doesn't need it.

All human beings, Aristotle believes, are born as blank slates, without either good or bad characters. The character that we ultimately develop is a result of upbringing, and this character can get better or worse depending on the specific kind of training that we receive growing up. Parents, therefore, need to mold the characters of young people in the right way to help them become virtuous adults. Aristotle uses the example of learning to play a musical instrument to demonstrate the right way to go about training young people to be moral. Certainly no one believes that he can simply teach a child to become the next George Gershwin. To learn to play the piano well, a child must constantly practice, starting with the most basic notes and working his way to the most complex scales. At first the child will inevitably stumble over the notes he is learning to play, but eventually, if he is diligent enough and practices every day, he will be able to play the piano as though it was second nature to him. According to Aristotle, a similar process is involved in training a child to behave virtuously. When a child is first being trained, he finds it difficult and often has trouble doing what his parents expect of him. As he constantly practices specific virtues, such as honesty and generosity, he will eventually find it easier and easier to behave virtuously, until it becomes extremely difficult for him to even conceive of engaging in any kind of vicious behavior.

ARISTOTLE'S VIRTUES

Virtue	Excess	Defect	Emotion
Courage	Cowardice	Foolhardiness	Fear
Temperance	Self-Indulgence	Insensibility	Desire for pleasure of the body (eating, drinking, sex)
Generosity	Extravagance	Stinginess	Desire to give money to those who need it
Proper Pride	Vanity	Humility	Desire to receive great honors
Good Temper	Irascibility	Apathy	Proneness to anger
Wittiness	Buffoonery	Boorishness	Desire to amuse others
Modesty	Bashfulness	Shamelessness	Susceptibility to shame

A Program of Moral Perfection: Benjamin Franklin

In his *Autobiography*, American writer, inventor, and diplomat, Benjamin Franklin offers a description of his rise from a poor tradesman to a giant in the pantheon of American history. Franklin was encouraged to write his autobiography in order to inspire young men to strive to rise above the limitations of their social condition and achieve the kind of success that he had in his own life. The work itself became so famous that it has served as a kind of bible of self-improvement for generations of Americans.

An important part of Franklin's program of self-improvement was an attempt he made at a fairly early age to become morally perfect. Describing his motivations for this project, Franklin writes:

> ...I conceived the bold and arduous project of arriving at moral perfection. I wished to live without committing any fault at any time; I would conquer all that either natural inclination, custom, or company might lead me into. As I knew, or thought I knew, what was right and wrong, I did not see why I might not always do the one and avoid the other (120).

Franklin soon discovered that it was easier to desire to live a moral life than it was to live one. Like all individuals who make resolutions to improve their lives, Franklin realized that the habits of a lifetime were not soon broken, and that the vices that he had cultivated often proved too strong to overcome. He concluded that "the mere speculative conviction that it was in our interest to be completely virtuous was not sufficient to prevent our slipping; and that the contrary habits must be broken, and the good ones acquired and established, before we can have any dependence on a steady, uniform rectitude of conduct" (121).

The way he set about to achieve moral perfection was to examine the ideas of the great moral theorists throughout the ages to see what specific virtues they advocated practicing. Putting his own distinctly American spin on the project, Franklin soon devised a list of 13 virtues that he deemed most applicable to his project of moral self-improvement: temperence, silence, order, resolution, frugality, industry, sincerity, justice, moderation, cleanliness, tranquillity, chastity, and humility.

Because Franklin believes that it would be too arduous an undertaking to attempt to master all these virtues at once, he resolved to fix upon one of them at a time. Once he mastered one of the virtues, he would then move on to the next, until he acquired all 13.

But Franklin also determined that he needed a method for determining that he was progressing in mastering each virtue. And so he created what might be called a virtue log:

> I made a little book to which I allotted a page for each of the
> virtues. I rul'd each page with red ink, so as to have seven
> columns, one for each day of the week, marking each column
> with a letter for the day. I cross'd these columns with thirteen
> red lines, marking the beginning of each line with the first letter
> of one of the virtues, on which line, and in its proper column, I
> might mark, by a little black spot, every fault I had found upon
> examination to have been committed respecting the virtue upon
> that day.
>   I determined to give a week's strict attention to each of the
> virtues successively. Thus in my first week, my great guard was
> to avoid even the least offense against Temperance, leaving the
> other virtues to their ordinary chance, only marking every eve-
> ning the faults of the day (124-125).

Thus Franklin turned his attention week by week to each of his thirteen
virtues, determined to have no black marks in the column devoted to that
week's specific virtue. If he could succeed in this endeavor, he thought,
he would have strengthened that virtue and weakened its opposing vice.

Benjamin Franklin doesn't usually get recognized as a great moral
theorist, and this is perhaps justified given that his account of his own
program of moral improvement only takes up about seven pages of an
autobiography otherwise devoted to his business practices. And yet
Franklin offers us a unique step-by-step method for moral improvement
that is unique in Western thought. His method, in fact, is perfectly applicable to anyone seeking to improve his or her moral character.

Developing Your Own Core Virtues

All virtues can be divided into two different kinds: those that pertain to
other people (other-regarding virtues) and those that pertain to oneself
(self-regarding virtues). The former help to make social life possible;
the latter enable us to develop character traits that lead to personal integrity and moral wholeness.

The following is a typical list of both kinds of virtues:

Other-Regarding Virtues	**Self-Regarding Virtues**
Benevolence	Courage
Civility	Industriousness
Compassion	Moderation

Kindness	Self-Control
Dependability	Self-Discipline
Justice	Self-Reliance
Generosity	Cleanliness
Honesty	Pride
Loyalty	Self-Respect
Tolerance	Humility
Sensitivity	Dignity/Honor
Friendliness	Prudence
Discretion	Modesty
Reliability	

According to virtue ethics, part of the moral maturation process that human beings go through involves identifying—as both Aristotle and Franklin did—core virtues that one voluntarily chooses to practice. Some of these virtues may have been imposed upon us as children or by the particular cultures in which we live, but most virtue ethicists believe we have some control over whether or not we choose to continue to embrace these virtues as we mature.

One way of identifying those virtues that are important to you is to ask the following question: If you were a parent, which of the above virtues would you want your children to possess? Focusing on your actual or future children is a good way to develop a list of virtues that is personally significant, because it offers the opportunity for you to step back and think about this question in a slightly more objective way than if you focused on your own character.

Once you've approached the issue in this way, you can then put the spotlight more directly upon yourself. You've come up with five or ten virtues that you'd want your children to possess. Are these the same set of virtues that you would have selected if asked to choose for yourself? Not surprisingly, most people normally tend to answer this question in the affirmative. If that's also the case for you, then the next obvious question would be: what are you doing to strengthen these virtues in your own life?

As we saw from our discussion of Aristotle, moral virtue is all about practice, practice, practice. Once your core virtues have become habitual and no longer represent a struggle for you, morality in this system basically takes care of itself. The person of good moral character doesn't have to agonize over specific moral decisions, because he or she is now flying on a kind of ethical auto-pilot. It's not a matter of knowing what the right thing to do is in a specific situation, but rather allowing your character to guide you into being the kind of person—kind, compassionate, discreet, loyal, just, etc—that you've always wanted to be.

Moral Decision-Making Using Virtue Ethics

Preparatory Stage: Make a list of those virtues which you be-lieve contribute to human excellence. You may want to make use of the lists on the previous page to assist you in this effort.

Step 1: Practice each of these virtues regularly until they be-come habitual (i.e., second nature).
Step 2: Add more virtues as needed until you develop the kind of optimal moral character to which you aspire.
Step 3: There's no need to worry about specific moral actions, since a person with good moral character will automatically act in the right way without great effort.

Contemporary Virtue Ethics Theory

One of the most interesting attempts in recent times to revive a theory of the virtues has been carried out by Alasdair MacIntyre in his provocative work, *After Virtue*. In this work, MacIntyre offers an extremely per-suasive critique of the state of contemporary moral philosophy and an impassioned argument in favor of the return to a more classical approach to ethics with an emphasis on the virtues.

MacIntyre begins his account by describing human life as a "narra-tive quest." This quest, he maintains, represents a search for self-fulfill-ment—that is, for our own good as human beings—and it is the virtues that support us in this quest. Our understanding of the virtues, however, is not shaped by ourselves but by the particular tradition to which we belong. Thus MacIntyre points out that in Homeric culture, in which the paradigm of excellence was the warrior, the virtue of courage would be paramount, while in Aristotle's own time the paradigm was the Athenian gentleman, and, therefore, the virtue prudence would take priority. He goes on to demonstrate that the specific virtues that were considered im-portant in first century Christian circles, in Jane Austen's England, and in Benjamin Franklin's America likewise prove to be fairly distinct from one another.   Each tradition, according to MacIntyre, will have its own catalogue of the virtues and these catalogues will often be in conflict with one another:

Homer, Sophocles, Aristotle, the New Testament and medieval thinkers differ from each other in too many ways. They offer us different and incompatible lists of the virtues; they give a different rank order of importance to different virtues; and they have different and incompatible theories of the virtues. If we were to consider later Western writers on the virtues, the list of divergences and incompatibilities would be enlarged still further; and if we extended our inquiry to Japanese, say, or American Indian cultures, the difference would become greater still. It would be all too easy to conclude that there were a number of rival and alternative conceptions of the virtues, but, even within the traditions which I have been delineating, no single core conception (181).

MacIntyre's conclusion is that there are no universal set of virtues that can be applied to all people at all times. Each culture or tradition's set of virtues will be unique to that tradition, and fully understandable only from within that particular tradition.

The analysis of the virtues developed by MacIntyre points to a significant problem that must be addressed before we can continue any further. MacIntyre suggests that any attempt to develop an ethics of virtue would necessitate an acceptance of cultural relativism, and that the terms "virtue" and "universal" must be understood to be mutually incompatible. This sort of tradition- or context-bound account of the virtues has consequently been criticized by those who are looking for a more universal ethic that can transcend cultural boundaries. Martha Nussbaum, summing up these objections, writes,

> For this reason it is easy for those who are interested in supporting the rational criticisms of local traditions and in articulating an idea of ethical progress to feel that the ethics of virtue can give them little help. If the position of women, as established by local traditions in many parts of the world, is to be improved, if the traditions of slave holding and racial inequality, if religious intolerance, if aggressive and warlike conceptions of manliness, if unequal norms of material distribution are to be criticized in the name of practice reason, this criticizing (one might easily suppose) will have to be done from a Kantian or Utilitarian viewpoint, not through an Aristotelian approach (33).

James Gustafson goes even further when he accuses thinkers like MacIntyre of adopting an anti-rational and sectarian approach to ethics that ultimately forfeits any relevance beyond the particular tradition of the moral theorist (92).

In an effort to respond to some of these objections, attempts have been made in recent times to demonstrate the universality of certain virtues. Jean Porter, for example, argues that there are certain virtues, such as practical wisdom, courage, and temperance, that are "perennial" and which would be recognized as virtues in every culture. "They are perennials," she writes, "because they are integrally related to the human capacity to sustain a course of action, based on overarching principles, ideas, plans or goals" (61).

Similarly, Martha Nussbaum attempts to refute the claim that Aristotelian virtues are essentially relativistic. She argues rather that Aristotle presents a single objective account of the human good, which is derived, not from a local tradition, but from something shared in common by all human beings. That which we all share in common are "spheres of experience" that are perfected by virtue. She selects eleven spheres from Aristotle and says that each of these spheres is essential for human living. Nussbuam thus argues that Aristotle's account of the virtues actually transcends cultural boundaries (36).

Advantages of Virtue Ethics

Among the strengths of virtue ethics as a moral theory are the following:

Virtue Ethics places an emphasis on creating good human beings. People typically do not behave morally simply because they have accepted certain rules or principles of moral behavior, but rather because they are good human beings. The basic premise of virtue ethics is that if we can work to transform our characters—to become, in other words, virtuous individuals—then we will consistently act in a morally good manner. On the other hand, all the rules and principles in the world will not help us if we have morally defective characters.

Virtue Ethics places an emphasis on human motivation. In recent years many moral philosophers have begun to reexamine virtue ethics as a preferable alternative to modern moral theories. One of the greatest strengths of virtue ethics is that, unlike some of the other moral theories that we have examined, it focuses not just on actions, but on motivation as well, and therefore, provides a richer account of moral action.

Consider the following example used by James Rachels:

> You are in a hospital recovering from a long illness. You are bored and restless, and so you are delighted when Smith arrives to visit. You have a good time chatting with him; his visit is just the tonic you needed. After a while you tell Smith how much you appreciate his coming—he really is a fine fellow and a good

friend to take the trouble to come all the way across town to see you. But Smith demurs; he protests that he is merely doing his duty. At first you think that he is only being modest, but the more you talk, the clearer it becomes that he is speaking the literal truth. He is not visiting you because he wants to, or because he likes you, but only because he thinks that it is his duty to "do the right thing," and on this occasion he has decided it is his duty to visit you—perhaps because he knows of no one else who is more in need of cheering up or no one easier to get to (Rachels, 187; adapted from Stoker).

The point of this example is that, while there is nothing wrong with Smith's actions, we would rightly be disappointed with his motives. We would much rather have a friend act out of loyalty or devotion—out of virtue, in other words—than simply out of a cold, calculating, rational sense of duty.

Disadvantages of Virtue Ethics

Although a character-based approach to ethics has some distinct advantages over the rule-based approaches that we have examined in this text, it also has some distinct disadvantages as well. Among the most notable weaknesses of virtue ethics are the following:

Virtue Ethics fails to provide adequate moral guidance. Let's imagine that you are faced with a moral dilemma about whether or not to end life support for your ailing parent. The best advice that virtue ethics could offer you would be to do what a person of good moral character would do in this situation, which doesn't provide much concrete guidance in these kinds of crisis situations. It doesn't tell us which acts are virtuous and therefore ought to be performed in this specific circumstance.

What virtues should we adopt? In his work, After Virtue, Alasdair MacIntyre argues that all virtues are relative to the specific cultures in which they exist. Aristotle's list of virtues, Macintyre maintains, would look very different from that of Thomas Aquinas, Benjamin Franklin or Jane Austin. It would appear then that there is no universal set of virtues that would apply to all individuals. We are left to wonder which virtues we ought to adopt when deciding on how best to improve our moral characters. In the end, there could be as many different sets of possible virtues as there are different cultures—or even individuals—in the world.

For Further Discussion

1. Case Studies in Virtue Ethics

   a. Cheating in Chemistry

      Nakeem and Alex are two college students who are also star players on their college basketball team. Because they are teammates they have spent a great deal of time together at practice and at games. Occasionally they socialize together, though usually as part of a larger group of friends.

      The two also happen to be taking advanced chemistry together, because they are both Pre-Med majors. Doing well in the course is considered essential for admission into a decent Medical School—a goal to which both Nakeen and Alex aspire. During their final exam for the class Nakeem spots Alex cheating. He wonders whether he should report Alex to the professor.

      What virtues or vices would be manifested if Nakeem reports Alex for cheating? What do you think Nakeem should do?

   b. Paying for an Abortion

      Park City, Utah. 1957. Midge and Sara are high school juniors who have been best friends since the second grade. Last year Sara became involved in a sexual relationship with Lou, a senior. Midge has never fully approved of the relationship, because she finds Lou untrustworthy. Being a supportive friend, however, she has kept her criticisms of the relationship to herself.

      One day Sara comes to Midge in tears, telling her that she is pregnant and that her boyfriend will leave her if she doesn't have an abortion. Because abortion is illegal, Sara has to go to a "special" doctor, who, she has been told, will perform the procedure in secret for $200. Neither Sara nor Lou have that kind of money themselves, but Sara knows that Midge can get the money from her father if she lies to him about what it will be used for. She implores Midge to help her. If she doesn't have the abortion, Sara tells Midge, her reputation will be ruined, her parents will disown her, and she will be abandoned by her boyfriend.

      What virtues or vices would be manifested by Midge getting the money for Sara? What do you think Midge should do?

c.   Squealing on Your Brother

For some time now, Kurt Zimmer has been aware that his brother, Gunther, has been hanging out with a crowd of friends who may be involved in illegal activities. Recently, there has been a rash of break-ins in the neighborhood, and thousands of dollars worth of personal property has been stolen. Police suspect that the culprits may be a gang of local youths.

One day, while Kurt is looking in his brother's dresser for an item of clothing that he lent him, he opens the bottom drawer and discovers several items of expensive jewelry that he knows Gunther could never afford. Kurt quickly closes the drawer and leaves the room, extremely disturbed by what he has seen.

Not knowing what to do, Kurt confides in the most virtuous person he knows, his good friend, Norbert Dressner. Norbert tells Kurt that he has a duty to report his brother and his friends to the police to prevent any more households from being robbed. The situation comes to a climax, when police come to the house and directly ask Kurt if he knows anything that could help them solve the case of the break-ins.

What virtues or vices would be manifested if Kurt decides squeal on his brother to the police? What do you think Kurt should do?

2. Dilemmas in Virtue

a.   In the Gospels, Jesus espouses a radical ethic of selfless love (*agape*) that involves sacrificing your own well-being at times to care for those in need. This ethic is reflected quite clearly in the Sermon on the Mount and the parable of "The Good Samaritan." Do you think it makes sense to practice the virtue of selfless love, particularly if it leads to sacrifice and suffering for yourself? Since this virtue is so central to the teachings of Jesus, does a rejection of the importance of selfless love also imply a rejection of Jesus' teachings?

b.   In liberal societies, tolerance is a fairly important virtue, since it allows individuals to pursue their own good without interference from others. Do you think tolerance is a virtue worth practicing? If so, does this mean you shoudn't criticize or interfere with behavior you find morally repulsive?

c.   Aristotle argues that true happiness comes from a life of virtue. And yet some of the most virtuous people in history have met fairly tragic ends—e.g., Socrates, Thomas More, Gandhi, Martin Luther King...The list goes on and on—while many extremely vicious people seem to lead perfectly delightful lives. Do you think there is a valid connection between happiness and virtue?

d. Many commentators have in recent years been bemoaning the death of civility among younger generations. Using expressions like "please" and "thank you," holding the door open for people behind you, and saying excuse me when you burp at the table may seem unimportant, they argue, but, in fact, the loss of such common courtesies is symptomatic of a basic lack of repect and concern for other human beings, and, therefore, is an important moral issue. Do you think a lack of basic courtesy and civility is simply a sign of changing cultural norms or do you agree that it represents a serious character defect?

e. To gossip is to say something negative about someone else behind their back. Gossiping is also something that just about everyone does to make social interaction much more pleasant. And yet, the fact that most people would never want the content of their gossiping to get back to the object of their gossip suggsts that most people intuitively recognize that there is something at least morally problematic about gossiping. Do you think gossiping is simply a neutral cultural practice or do you think it's a vice? If a vice, do you think that you could ever completely stop gossiping?

3. On the Virtue's Committee. This exercise is best done in a group. The aim is to see whether you and your fellow "committee members" can arrive at a consensus on a set of universal virtues:

You are the parent of a seven-year-old child, who has been selected to enter a new experimental school that is opening in your community. The three hundred children that will be enrolled in this school come from a wide variety of cultural backgrounds and reflect a rich diversity of race, ethnicity, and religious practices. The school will also have at least forty students enrolled whose families have recently immigrated from other countries from around the world.

The school was founded because parents in the community wanted an educational environment that would train their children in important virtues. The only problem is that, because the children come from such a wide variety of backgrounds, it has been difficult to reach a consensus on what these virtues should be.

To solve this problem a committee made up of parents, administrators, teachers, and community and religious leaders has been formed to devise a list of twenty virtues that everyone agrees are essential for all the children in this school to practice on a consistent basis.

You have agreed to serve on this committee. List at least five virtues that you believe are essential to include on this list. Be sure to give an explanation as to why you think each virtue deserves to be included on the master list.

Sources and Further Reading

Adams, Robert Merrihew. *A Theory of Virtue.* New York: Oxford University Press, 2006.

Aristotle. *Nicomachean Ethics.* Trans. Martin Ostwald. Englewood Cliffs, NJ: Prentice Hall, 1962.

Baron, Marcia. "Varities of Ethics of Virtue." *American Philosophical Quarterly* 22 (1985): 47-53.

Crisp, Roger and Slote, Michael, eds. *Virtue Ethics.* New York: Oxford University Press, 1997.

Darwell, Stephen, ed. *Virtue Ethics.* Malden, MA: Blackwell, 2003.

Foot, Phillipa. *Natural Goodness.* Oxford: Oxford University Press, 2001.

Franklin, Benjamin. *Autobiography.* New York: Houghton Mifflin, 1923.

Hardie, W.F.R. *Aristotle's Ethical Theory.* Oxford: Clarendon, 1968.

Hunt, Lester H. *Character and Culture.* Lanham, MD: Rowman and Littlefield, 1997.

Hursthouse, Rosalind. *On Virtue Ethics.* Oxford: Oxford University Press, 1999.

—. *Virtues and Vices.* Berkeley, CA: University of California, 1978.

Keenan, James F. "Proposing Cardinal Virtues." *Theological Studies* 56 (1995).

MacIntyre, Alasdair. *After Virtue.* Notre Dame, IN: University of Notre Dame Press, 1984.

Nussbaum, Martha. "Non-Relative Virtues: An Aristotelian Approach." *Midwest Studies in Philosophy* 13 (1988).

Porter, Jean. "Perennial and Timely Virtues: Practical Wisdom, Courage and Temperance." *Changing Values and Virtues.* Ed. Dietmar Mieth and Jacques Pohier. Edinburgh: T. and T. Clark, 1987.

Sherman, Nancy. *Aristotle's Ethics: Critical Essays.* New York: Rowman and Littlefield, 1999.

Slote, Michael. *From Morality to Virtue*. New York: Oxford University Press, 1992.

Taylor, Richard. *Pride: The Lost Virtue of Our Age*. Amherst, NY: Prometheus, 1995.

—. *Virtue Ethics: An Introduction*. Amherst, NY: Prometheus Books, 2001.

Wallace, James. *Virtue and Vice*. Ithaca, NY: Cornell University Press, 1978.

chapter 11

THE GREAT THEORIES: PUTTING IT ALL TOGETHER

Case Study: The Family Home

Mrs. Grace Hightower has inherited a house on a piece of waterfront property in the town of Crystal Cove, Florida, which has been in her family for several generations. She has lived in the house for over thirty years, has raised three children in it, and has had many wonderful memories associated with the house and property. A widow for over ten years with a very limited income, Mrs Hightower was planning to spend her remaining years living in the house and eventually, after she died, pass the property on to her children.

In recent years the town of Crystal Cove has grown significantly and has witnessed an influx of extremely wealthy retirees, seeking to live by the seashore. Unfortunately, there is a limit to the amount of seafront property available in the town because most of it is either owned already by people like Mrs. Hightower or is sensitive wetlands that the town has been trying to preserve. A local developer has convinced the mayor of the town, Bill Shuntell, that if he was allowed to build high rise condominiums along the coast, the taxes generated from these properties could help lift the town out of its fiscal difficulties and pay for projects, like school construction, that would benefit all the citizens of the town. In addition, the presence of so many wealthy retirees living in the town would be a boon to local restaurants and businesses that have not been doing so well in recent years.

Convinced of the importance of the project to the town, Mayor Shuntell immediately went before the town board and got them to agree to use a legal proceeding known as eminent domain to condemn and take over about fifty acres of waterfront property with about forty houses on them. Eminent domain has been used for some time by towns around the country to take over private property that is considered blighted in order to allow for public projects that would benefit all citizens (e.g., the creation of roads, hospitals, schools); in more recent years the Supreme Court has ruled that eminent domain could be used to allow towns to take over property for commercial development like the project being considered by the town of Crystal Cove.

On July 14, 2006, Mrs. Hightower was informed by the sheriff of Crystal Cove that her property would be taken over by the town at the end of the year and her house demolished to make room for the new condominiums. She would be compensated for her loss in the amount of $240,000, which is what the town determined that her house and property were worth. Upon hearing this news, Mrs. Hightower immediately went on the offensive, speaking out publicly against the mayor and the town board members and beginning legal proceedings against the town.

Although Mayor Shuntell knew that the law was on his side, he also knew that Mrs. Hightower was becoming a lightening rod for opposition to his plan and that her court case could potentially hold up his building project for several years. He decided that the smartest thing to do would be to neutralize Mrs. Hightower's opposition to the plan as quickly as possible.

One day in September, Mayor Shuntell goes to Mrs. Hightower's house to make her an offer she can't refuse. Mayor Shuntell says that he has a plan to spare Mrs. Hightower's house and those of some of her immediate neighbors. His plan is to move the development project further south along the coast. This would mean that other people's property would be taken by the town, but, because of their limited incomes, the people in this area have less political clout than Mrs. Hightower and her neighbors, and, therefore, would be less successful in raising opposition to the project. Moving the project south also means that the town's beautiful wetlands, which house numerous species of wildlife, would have to be destroyed to allow for building. Mayor Shuntell goes on to say that, if Mrs. Hightower promises to publicly support the new development plans, she can keep her home; if not he would keep the project location as is and her home would be condemned by the town.

Mrs. Hightower is torn by this proposition. On the one hand, she loves her home and wants to be able to spend the rest of her life living in it. On the other hand, she is philosophically opposed to the way that the Mayor is using eminent domain and has a great deal of pity for the new families that would now be affected by the move of the project location, many of whom she knows personally. She is also horrified that the town's wetlands would now have to be sacrificed so that she could remain in her home.

FOR DISCUSSION

What would an ethical egoist, utilitarian, deontologist, rights

theorist, and virtue ethicist say is the right thing for Mrs. Hightower to do in this situation? Be sure to explain why each moral theorist would argue the way they do using the specifics of the case.

Although there are many more moral theories than those presented in this text, we have focused on five of most significant theories in the field of ethics. Let's sum these five up one last time for comparison sake:

Ethical Egoism: "An act is morally right if, more than any other alternative available at the time, it brings about the greatest amount of good, or happiness, for oneself."

Utilitarianism: "An act is morally right if, more than any other alternative available at the time, it brings about the greatest amount of good, or happiness, for all those who are affected by the act."

Deontology: "An act is morally right if, and only if, it accords with a universal rule that all can follow."

Rights Ethics: "An act is morally right if, and only if, in performing it, one does not violate the basic rights of others."

Virtue Ethics: "An act is morally right if, and only if, it is performed by a person of virtuous moral character."

After examining these theories in some detail, and going through case studies and exercises to illuminate them further, you should have formed some intelligent opinions about these theories. One or two of these theories in particular may have struck you more forcefully than the others. It's now time for you to take a stand and specify which of these theories you think has the greatest degree of validity and would provide the best possible guidance for your own moral decision making.

Of course, it may be the case that none of the theories presented in this book resonates very much with you. As I have already mentioned, however, there are many more moral theories in the field of ethics than the few that we have focused upon in this text. If you haven't been able to commit yourself to any moral theory by this point, you will have to keep exploring the field of ethics in order to find a more satisfactory theory.

It might also be the case that you feel it necessary to combine different theories—for example, virtue ethics and deontology or utilitarianism and rights theory—in order to create an ethical system that makes the most sense to you. Or you may want to pick and choose different aspects of the theories that we have examined in an attempt to hobble together a more satisfactory theory. Feel free to try this as well.

The point is that ethics is a creative science, one that demands both critical reflection as well as imaginative insight. If you keep thinking about moral issues in a creative way, you may even come up with your own original moral theory, one that is as innovative and original as anything the great moral theorists profiled in this text were able to devise. If nothing else, your reflections on moral theory will probably serve to make you just a bit more ethical in your daily life...and that can't be such a bad thing now, can it?

PART THREE

READING THE SOURCES

The works included in this section of the text are for those who would like to delve further into the history and development of the various ethical theories we've been exploring by reading the original source materials for those theories. As I mentioned in the Introduction to this text, reading the works of great ethical thinkers can be challenging, but it can often be extremely rewarding as well. There's no better way to understand the great ideas that have influenced the course of Western ethics than to examine those ideas in their original context—in the very words of those intellectual luminaries whose vision helped shape those theories in the first place. If you've done a good job reading through Parts 1 and 2 of this text, you basically have enough background to handle these original sources. Ideally, you should read the primary sources right after you've gone through my explanation of the specific ethical system to which they belong in Part 2 of this text, so that the ideas presented in the earlier chapters will still be fresh in your mind when you are reading the primary sources.

Egoism

The first selection included in this section comes from Book 2 of Plato's *Republic* (360 B.C.) and focuses on the famous Ring of Gyges argument of Thrasymachus, one of the main characters in this work. The argument is considered one of the oldest and most important expositions of the theory of psychological egoism. Using the metaphor of a ring that renders its wearer invisible, Thrasymachus makes the case that human beings are selfish by nature and that it is only the fear of punishment that prevents us at times from acting on our natural—and often unjust—inclinations.

The theory of psychological egoism was challenged in the 18th century by the Scottish philosopher, David Hume. In his major work on ethics, *A Treatise of Human Nature* (1739), Hume is highly critical of the idea that acts of altruism and benevolence are impossible. He contends that the temptation to reduce the motivations for all of our actions to self-interest is overly simplistic and ignores the reality of human experience.

The human propensity towards selfishness is also addressed by the 17th century English philosopher Thomas Hobbes in political treatises such as *De Cive* (1651). Hobbes was the originator of the idea of the "state of nature"—the natural condition of human beings prior to the establishment of political communities. In such a state, he argue,s daily existence becomes a state of war of all against all, and human life "solitary, poor, nasty, brutish and short." To preserve their lives in the state of nature, human beings have absolute freedom to do whatever they think necessary. But the state of nature is one of continuous insecurity: in it human beings can follow their selfish inclinations, but no individual is powerful enough to prevent harm at the hands of other individuals and groups. For this very reason, Hobbes thought it was perfectly rational for human beings to sacrifice their egoistic inclinations and form political communities in which one's absolute freedom is given over to the state in return for the kind of peace and security that only an organized political community can provide.

A very different moral and political vision is found in the writings of Ayn Rand, who is the founder of an ethical and political movement called "Objectivism"—a contemporary reformulation of ethical egoism. Rand's promotion of the virtue of self-interest and her outright rejection of altruism as dangerous and immoral, provided the intellectual foundations of the libertarian movement in the late 20th and early 21st centuries.

Utilitarianism

In Chapter 7 we saw that Utilitarianism has had a very long and interesting history. The classic Utilitarians, Jeremy Bentham and John Stuart Mill, attemped to answer the question, "What makes ad act morally right" by referring to the principle of utility. An act becomes right, they thought, because it produces the greatest amount of happiness or pleasure possible for all those who are affected by the act. In *An Introduction to the Principles of Morals and Legislation* (1789), Bentham devised a fairly elaborate scheme—his hedonistic calculus—for determining which actions are likely to produce the greatest amount of pleasure over pain.

John Stuart Mill, as we've seen, rejects Bentham's focus on the quantity of pleasure that an act produces and argues that we also need to take into consideration the quality of pleasure involved. In the selection from *Utilitarianism* (1859), Mill goes on to defend utilitarian theory from objections raised by critics of the system that it amounts to little more than expediency and selfishness.

A response of sorts to the kinds of criticisms of utilitarian theory that Mill experienced can be found in William Godwin's *An Enquiry Concerning Political Justice* (1793), where Godwin takes utilitarianism to its logical conclusion by arguing that certain lives are indeed more valuable than others. In his example of the Archbishop of Cambria and his chambermaid, Godwin is forced to concede that if it came to a decision to save one or the other, the chambermaid, according to the principle of utility, ought to be sacrificed. This would be true, Godwin argues, even if the chambermaid was one's own wife or mother.

The 19th century British utilitarian, Henry Sidgwick, while a less innovative thinker than John Stuart Mill, was able to anticipate some of the problems inherent in utilitarian ethics and attempted to resolve them. In his work, *The Method of Ethics* (1874), he argued that the universal desire that human beings have to promote their own happiness (the basic tenant of psychological egoism) does not necessarily lead to a desire to promote the happiness of others. Sidgwick also raises the question of extent of our moral obligation to all those who are affected by our actions. Does this "all" include all sentient beings? All human beings? All future human beings? In any of these cases, a hedonistic calculus, such as the one devised by Bentham, will be extraordinarily difficult—if not impossible—to undertake.

Deontology

The history of ethics can often seem like an endless debate between utilitarians and deontologists over which moral system is most likely to aid human beings in living ethically. Immanuel Kant, the most prominent spokesperson for a deontological approach to ethics, makes it perfectly clear in his *Foundations of the Metaphysics of Morals* (1785) that the moral worth of an action is in no way to be measured by its consequences. For Kant, morality demands that we follow a law that can be universalized. This law becomes his famous categorical imperative. In his essay, "On the Supposed Right to Lie For Benevolent Motives" (1797) Kant draws out the implications of the categorical imperative when he argues that lying under any circumstances—even when doing so may protect human life—is always wrong.

Highly critical of Kant's approach to ethics, the 20th century English philosopher G.E. Moore challenged Kant's assumption that "this ought to be" is synonymous with "this is commanded." Moore questions the very possibility, therefore, of any kind of legitimate moral imperative.

Rights Theory

Although the source of rights theory can be found in Thomas Hobbes' *Leviathan* (1651), where Hobbes formulated his ideas on the social contract, it is John Locke who is considered the father of rights theory. In his *Second Treatise of Civil Government* (1689), Locke describes three basic rights that have formed the cornerstone of all democratic forms of government—the rights to life, liberty, and property. So influential was Locke's thought in the 18th century, that his views on natural human rights became incorporated into the "U.S. Declaration of Independence" (1776) and the "U.S. Constitution" (1787), most notably in its "Bill of Rights." In the 20th century human rights theory took an even more expansive turn after World War II when the United Nations adopted its "Universal Declaration of Human Rights" in 1948.

Although rights theory has become universally accepted in most democratic societies, there have always been those who considered the idea of natural human rights to be problematic for various reasons. Libertarians as we have seen, accept only the possibility of negative rights, and so many of the rights innumerated in the U.N.'s "Universal Declaration" are flatly rejected by them. Jeremy Bentham challenged the very idea of natural human rights, which he famously refers to in his "Anarchical Fallacies" (1843) as "nonsense on stilts." In his critique of the "French Declaration of the Rights of Man and Citizen" (1789) he argued that the idea of natural human rights was a fabrication and a fiction. As Bentham puts it, "a reason for wishing that a certain right were established, is not that right; want is not supply; hunger is not bread."

Virtue Ethics

Virtue ethics is probably the oldest of the ethical theories that we've examined in this text. As we've seen, this approach differs from other ethical theories because, instead of asking "how should I do?" a proponent of virtue ethics asks "what kind of person should I be?" The answer to this question becomes a list of virtues—qualities of character—that facilitate human flourishing.

Although Aristotle was by no means the first philosopher in antiquity to develop a theory of the virtues, his approach, particularly in the *Nicomachean Ethics* (350 B.C.), is certainly the best developed of any philosopher in the ancient world. In fact, although the text is well over two thousand years old, many still regard it as the most important work on virtue ethics ever written.

In the first two books of the *Nicomachean Ethics,* Aristotle begins by discussing the nature of human happiness. Ultimately he argues that it is impossible to become truly happy unless one is also morally virtuous. He then goes into a lengthy discussion of the nature of a moral virtue (a means between two extremes with respect to action and emotion) and how virtues are acquired (by habit rather than by learning). Beginning in Book III, Aristotle applies his ideas to such important virtues as courage, generosity, pride, and good temper.

Although there are some virtues that may be perennial—that is, they have been recognized as important qualities of character throughout human history—different societies will recognize different virtues as being uniquely important to them. In his *Autobiography* (1791), American founding father Benjamin Franklin describes his own program of moral self-improvement that includes the practice of developing what were to become decidedly American virtues, like frugality and industry.

A very different collection of virtues is developed by the 19th century existential philosopher, Friedrich Nietzsche, who is known for his rejection of traditional (i.e., Christian) values and ideals. In the selection provided from *Human, All-Too-Human* (1878), Nietzsche examines three qualities of character that traditionally were considered vices— malicious joy (*Schadenfreude*), envy, and the desire for revenge against one's enemies. He contends that all of these qualities are a natural part of what it means to be human.

For centuries, virtues and vices were explained to children through fairy tales. And no authors were better at drawing out the implications of the exercise of virtue and vice better than the German Brothers Grimm, who published their now-famous collection of fairy tales in 1812. These tales are still read to children by their parents, although usually in a modified, less violent, form. One of my favorite tales of the Brothers Grimm is "The Fisherman and His Wife." The story works on a number of different levels—as a critique of ethical egoism, as an allegory of consequentialist ethics, and as a simple tale reminding us of the penalty of vicious behavior—and, as such, is a perfect conclusion to our text.

The Ring Of Gyges
Plato

They say that to do injustice is, by nature, good; to suffer injustice, evil; but that the evil is greater than the good. And so when men have both done and suffered injustice and have had experience of both, not being able to avoid the one and obtain the other, they think that they had better agree among themselves to have neither; hence there arise laws and mutual covenants; and that which is ordained by law is termed by them lawful and just. This they affirm to be the origin and nature of justice; it is a mean or compromise, between the best of all, which is to do injustice and not be punished, and the worst of all, which is to suffer injustice without the power of retaliation; and justice, being at a middle point between the two, is tolerated not as a good, but as the lesser evil, and honored by reason of the inability of men to do injustice. For no man who is worthy to be called a man would ever submit to such an agreement if he were able to resist; he would be mad if he did. Such is the received account, Socrates, of the nature and origin of justice.

Now that those who practise justice do so involuntarily and because they have not the power to be unjust will best appear if we imagine something of this kind: having given both to the just and the unjust power to do what they will, let us watch and see whither desire will lead them; then we shall discover in the very act the just and unjust man to be proceeding along the same road, following their interest, which all natures deem to be their good, and are only diverted into the path of justice by the force of law. The liberty which we are supposing may be most completely given to them in the form of such a power as is said to have been possessed by Gyges, the ancestor of Croesus the Lydian. According to the tradition, Gyges was a shepherd in the service of the King of Lydia; there was a great storm, and an earthquake made an opening in the earth at the place where he was feeding his flock. Amazed at the sight, he descended into the opening, where, among other marvels,

---

Plato. "Republic." *The Dialogues of Plato*. Vol. 2. Translated by Benjamin Jowett. Oxford: Oxford University Press, 1892.

he beheld a hollow brazen horse, having doors, at which he, stooping and looking in, saw a dead body of stature, as appeared to him, more than human and having nothing on but a gold ring; this he took from the finger of the dead and reascended. Now the shepherds met together, according to custom, that they might send their monthly report about the flocks to the King; into their assembly he came having the ring on his finger, and as he was sitting among them he chanced to turn the collet of the ring inside his hand, when instantly he became invisible to the rest of the company and they began to speak of him as if he were no longer present. He was astonished at this, and again touching the ring he turned the collet outward and reappeared; he made several trials of the ring, and always with the same result—when he turned the collet inward he became invisible, when outward he reappeared. Whereupon he contrived to be chosen one of the messengers who were sent to the court; where as soon as he arrived he seduced the Queen, and with her help conspired against the King and slew him and took the kingdom.

Suppose now that there were two such magic rings, and the just put on one of them and the unjust the other; no man can be imagined to be of such an iron nature that he would stand fast in justice. No man would keep his hands off what was not his own when he could safely take what he liked out of the market, or go into houses and lie with anyone at his pleasure, or kill or release from prison whom he would, and in all respects be like a god among men. Then the actions of the just would be as the actions of the unjust; they would both come at last to the same point. And this we may truly affirm to be a great proof that a man is just, not willingly or because he thinks that justice is any good to him individually, but of necessity, for wherever anyone thinks that he can safely be unjust, there he is unjust. For all men believe in their hearts that injustice is far more profitable to the individual than justice, and he who argues as I have been supposing, will say that they are right. If you could imagine anyone obtaining this power of becoming invisible, and never doing any wrong or touching what was another's, he would be thought by the lookerson to be a most wretched idiot, although they would praise him to one another's faces, and keep up appearances with one another from a fear that they too might suffer injustice. Enough of this.

Now, if we are to form a real judgment of the life of the just and unjust, we must isolate them; there is no other way; and how is the isolation to be effected? I answer: Let the unjust man be entirely unjust, and the just man entirely just; nothing is to be taken away from either of them, and both are to be perfectly furnished for the work of their respective lives. First, let the unjust be like other distinguished masters of craft; like the skilful pilot or physician, who knows intuitively his own powers and keeps within their limits, and who, if he fails at any point, is able to recover himself. So let the unjust make his unjust attempts in the right way, and lie hidden if he means to be great in his injustice (he who is found out is nobody): for the highest reach of injustice is, to be deemed just when you are not. Therefore I say that in the perfectly unjust man we must assume the most perfect injustice; there is to be no deduction, but we must allow him, while doing the most unjust acts, to have acquired the greatest reputation for justice. If he have taken a false step he must be able to recover himself; he must be one who can speak with effect, if any of his deeds come to light, and who can force his way where force is required by his courage and strength, and command of money and friends. And at his side let us place the just man in his nobleness and simplicity, wishing, as Aeschylus says, to be and not to seem good. There must be no seeming, for if he seem to be just he will be honored and rewarded, and then we shall not know whether he is just for the sake of justice or for the sake of honor and rewards; therefore, let him be clothed in justice only, and have no other covering; and he must be imagined in a state of life the opposite of the former. Let him be the best of men, and let him be thought the worst; then he will have been put to the proof; and we shall see whether he will be affected by the fear of infamy and its consequences. And let him continue thus to the hour of death; being just and seeming to be unjust. When both have reached the uttermost extreme, the one of justice and the other of injustice, let judgment be given which of them is the happier of the two.

Heavens! my dear Glaucon, I said, how energetically you polish them up for the decision, first one and then the other, as if they were two statues.

I do my best, he said. And now that we know what they are like there is no difficulty in tracing out the sort of life which awaits either of them. This I will proceed to describe; but as you may think the description a little too coarse, I ask you to suppose, Socrates, that the words which follow are not mine. Let me put them into the mouths of the eulogists of injustice: They will tell you that the just man who is thought unjust will be scourged, racked, bound—will have his eyes burnt out; and, at last, after suffering every kind of evil, he will be impaled. Then he will understand that he ought to seem only, and not to be, just; the words of Aeschylus may be more truly spoken of the unjust than of the just. For the unjust is pursuing a reality; he does not live with a view to appearances—he wants to be really unjust and not to seem only—"His mind has a soil deep and fertile, Out of which spring his prudent counsels."

In the first place, he is thought just, and therefore bears rule in the city; he can marry whom he will, and give in marriage to whom he will; also he can trade and deal where he likes, and always to his own advantage, because he has no misgivings about injustice; and at every contest, whether in public or private, he gets the better of his antagonists, and gains at their expense, and is rich, and out of his gains he can benefit his friends, and harm his enemies; moreover, he can offer sacrifices, and dedicate gifts to the gods abundantly and magnificently, and can honor the gods or any man whom he wants to honor in a far better style than the just, and therefore he is likely to be dearer than they are to the gods. And thus, Socrates, gods and men are said to unite in making the life of the unjust better than the life of the just.

Of Self-Love
David Hume

There is a principle, supposed to prevail among many, which is utterly incompatible with all virtue or moral sentiment; and as it can proceed from nothing but the most depraved disposition, so in its turn it tends still further to encourage that depravity. This principle is, that all benevolence is mere hypocrisy, friendship a cheat, public spirit a farce, fidelity a snare to procure trust and confidence; and that while all of us, at bottom, pursue only our private interest, we wear these fair disguises, in order to put others off their guard, and expose them the more to our wiles and machinations. What heart one must be possessed of who possesses such principles, and who feels no internal sentiment that belies so pernicious a theory, it is easy to imagine: and also what degree of affection and benevolence he can bear to a species whom he represents under such odious colours, and supposes so little susceptible of gratitude or any return of affection. Or if we should not ascribe these principles wholly to a corrupted heart, we must at least account for them from the most careless and precipitate examination. Superficial reasoners, indeed, observing many false pretences among mankind, and feeling, perhaps, no very strong restraint in their own disposition, might draw a general and a hasty conclusion that all is equally corrupted, and that men, different from all other animals, and indeed from all other species of existence, admit of no degrees of good or bad, but are, in every instance, the same creatures under different disguises and appearances.

There is another principle, somewhat resembling the former; which has been much insisted on by philosophers, and has been the foundation of many a system; that, whatever affection one may feel, or imagine he feels for others, no passion is, or can be disinterested; that the most generous friendship, however sincere, is a modification of self-love; and that, even unknown to ourselves, we seek only our own

---

David Hume. "Of Self-Love." A Treatise of Human Nature. Oxford: Clarendon Press, 1888.

gratification, while we appear the most deeply engaged in schemes for the liberty and happiness of mankind. By a turn of imagination, by a refinement of reflection, by an enthusiasm of passion, we seem to take part in the interests of others, and imagine ourselves divested of all selfish considerations: but, at bottom, the most generous patriot and most niggardly miser, the bravest hero and most abject coward, have, in every action, an equal regard to their own happiness and welfare.

Whoever concludes from the seeming tendency of this opinion, that those, who make profession of it, cannot possibly feel the true sentiments of benevolence, or have any regard for genuine virtue, will often find himself, in practice, very much mistaken. Probity and honour were no strangers to Epicurus and his sect. Atticus and Horace seem to have enjoyed from nature, and cultivated by reflection, as generous and friendly dispositions as any disciple of the austerer schools. And among the modern, Hobbes and Locke, who maintained the selfish system of morals, lived irreproachable lives; though the former lay not under any restraint of religion which might supply the defects of his philosophy.

An epicurean or a Hobbist readily allows, that there is such a thing as a friendship in the world, without hypocrisy or disguise; though he may attempt, by a philosophical chymistry, to resolve the elements of this passion, if I may so speak, into those of another, and explain every affection to be self-love, twisted and moulded, by a particular turn of imagination, into a variety of appearances. But as the same turn of imagination prevails not in every man, nor gives the same direction to the original passion; this is sufficient even according to the selfish system to make the widest difference in human characters, and denominate one man virtuous and humane, another vicious and meanly interested. I esteem the man whose self-love, by whatever means, is so directed as to give him a concern for others, and render him serviceable to society; as I hate or despise him, who has no regard to any thing beyond his own gratifications and enjoyments. In vain would you suggest that these characters, though seemingly opposite, are at bottom the same, and that a very inconsiderable turn of thought forms the whole difference between them. Each character, notwithstanding these inconsiderable differences, appears to me, in practice, pretty durable and untransmutable. And I find not in this more than in other subjects, that the natural sentiments arising from the general appearances of things are easily destroyed by subtile reflections concerning the minute origin of these appearances. Does not the lively, cheerful colour of a countenance inspire me with complacency and pleasure; even though I learn from philosophy that all difference of complexion arises from the most minute differences of thickness, in the most minute parts of the skin; by means of which a superficies is qualified to reflect one of the original colours of light, and absorb the others?

But though the question concerning the universal or partial selfishness of man be not so material as is usually imagined to morality and practice, it is certainly of consequence in the speculative science of human nature, and is a proper object of curiosity and enquiry. It may not, therefore, be unsuitable, in this place, to bestow a few reflections upon it.

The most obvious objection to the selfish hypothesis is, that, as it is contrary to common feeling and our most unprejudiced notions, there is required the highest stretch of philosophy to establish so extraordinary a paradox. To the most careless observer there appear to be such dispositions as benevolence and generosity; such affections as love, friendship, compassion, gratitude. These sentiments have their causes, effects, objects, and operations, marked by common language and observation, and plainly distinguished from those of the selfish passions. And as this is the obvious appearance of things, it must be admitted, till some hypothesis be discovered, which by penetrating deeper into human nature, may prove the former affections to be nothing but modifications of the latter. All attempts of this kind have hitherto proved fruitless, and seem to have proceeded entirely from that love of simplicity which has been the source of much false reasoning in philosophy. I shall not here enter into any detail on the present subject. Many able philosophers have shown the insufficiency of these systems. And I shall take for granted what, I believe, the smallest reflection will make evident to every impartial enquirer.

But the nature of the subject furnishes the strongest presumption, that no better system will ever, for the future, be invented, in order to account for the origin of the benevolent from the selfish affections, and reduce all the various emotions of the human mind to a perfect simplicity. The case is not the same in this species of philosophy as in physics. Many an hypothesis in nature, contrary to first appearances, has been found, on more accurate scrutiny, solid and satisfactory. Instances of this kind are so frequent that a judicious, as well as witty philosopher , has ventured to affirm, if there be more than one way in which any phenomenon may be produced, that there is general presumption for its arising from the causes which are the least obvious and familiar. But the presumption always lies on the other side, in all enquiries concerning the origin of our passions, and of the internal operations of the human mind. The simplest and most obvious cause which can there be assigned for any phenomenon, is probably the true one. When a philosopher, in the explication of his system, is obliged to have recourse to some very intricate and refined reflections, and to suppose them essential to the production of any passion or emotion, we have reason to be extremely on our guard against so fallacious an hypothesis. The affections are not susceptible of any impression from the refinements of reason or imagination; and it is always found that a vigorous exertion of the latter faculties, necessarily, from the narrow capacity of the human mind, destroys all activity in the former. Our predominant motive or intention is, indeed, frequently concealed from ourselves when it is mingled and confounded with other motives which the mind, from vanity or self-conceit, is desirous of supposing more prevalent: but there is no instance that a concealment of this nature has ever arisen from the abstruseness and intricacy of the motive. A man that has lost a friend and patron may flatter himself that all his grief arises from generous sentiments, without any mixture of narrow or interested considerations: but a man that grieves for a valuable friend, who needed his patronage and protection; how can we suppose, that his passionate tenderness arises from some metaphysical regards to a self-interest, which has no foundation or reality? We may as well imagine that minute wheels and springs, like those of a watch, give motion to a loaded wagon, as account for the origin of passion from such abstruse reflections.

Animals are found susceptible of kindness, both to their own species and to ours; nor is there, in this case, the least suspicion of disguise or artifice. Shall we account for all their sentiments, too, from refined deductions of self-interest? Or if we admit a disinterested benevolence in the inferior species, by what rule of analogy can we refuse it in the superior?

Love between the sexes begets a complacency and good-will, very distinct from the gratification of an appetite. Tenderness to their offspring, in all sensible beings, is commonly able alone to counter-balance the strongest motives of self-love, and has no manner of dependance on that affection. What interest can a fond mother have in view, who loses her health by assiduous attendance on her sick child, and afterwards languishes and dies of grief, when freed, by its death, from the slavery of that attendance?

Is gratitude no affection of the human breast, or is that a word merely, without any meaning or reality? Have we no satisfaction in one man's company above another's, and no desire of the welfare of our friend, even though absence or death should prevent us from all participation in it? Or what is it commonly, that gives us any participation in it, even while alive and present, but our affection and regard to him?

These and a thousand other instances are marks of a general benevolence in human nature, where no real interest binds us to the object. And how an imaginary interest known and avowed for such, can be the origin of any passion or emotion, seems difficult to explain. No satisfactory hypothesis of this kind has yet been discovered; nor is there the smallest probability that the future industry of men will ever be attended with more favourable success.

But farther, if we consider rightly of the matter, we shall find that the hypothesis which allows of a disinterested benevolence, distinct from self-love, has really more simplicity in it, and is more conformable to the analogy of nature than that which pretends to resolve all friendship and humanity into this latter principle. There are bodily wants or appetites acknowledged by every one, which necessarily precede all sensual enjoyment, and carry us directly to seek possession of the object. Thus, hunger and thirst have eating and drinking for their end; and from the gratification of these primary appetites arises a pleasure, which may become the object of another species of desire or inclination that is secondary and interested. In the same manner there are mental passions by which we are impelled immediately to seek particular objects, such as fame or power, or vengeance without any regard to interest; and when these objects are attained a pleasing enjoyment ensues, as the consequence of our indulged affections. Nature must, by the internal frame and constitution of the mind, give an original propensity to fame, ere we can reap any pleasure from that acquisition, or pursue it from motives of self-love, and desire of happiness. If I have no vanity, I take no delight in praise: if I be void of ambition, power gives me no enjoyment: if I be not angry, the punishment of an adversary is totally indifferent to me. In all these cases there is a passion which points immediately to the object, and constitutes it our good or happiness; as there are other secondary passions which afterwards arise and pursue it as a part of our happiness, when once it is constituted such by our original affections. Were there no appetite of any kind antecedent to self-love, that propensity could scarcely ever exert itself; because we should, in that case, have felt few and slender pains or pleasures, and have little misery or happiness to avoid or to pursue.

Now where is the difficulty in conceiving, that this may likewise be the case with benevolence and friendship, and that, from the original frame of our temper, we may feel a desire of another's happiness or good, which, by means of that affection, becomes our own good, and is afterwards pursued, from the combined motives of benevolence and self-enjoyments? Who sees not that vengeance, from the force alone of passion, may be so eagerly pursued, as to make us knowingly neglect every consideration of ease, interest, or safety; and, like some vindictive animals, infuse our very souls into the wounds we give an enemy ; and what a malignant philosophy must it be, that will not allow to humanity and friendship the same privileges which are undisputably granted to the darker passions of enmity and resentment; such a philosophy is more like a satyr than a true delineation or description of human nature; and may be a good foundation for paradoxical wit and raillery, but is a very bad one for any serious argument or reasoning.

Of the State of Men Civil Society

Thomas Hobbes

The faculties of human nature may be reduced unto four kinds: bodily strength, experience, reason, passion. Taking the beginning of this following doctrine from these, we will declare in the first place what manner of inclinations men who are endued with these faculties bear towards each other and whether and by what faculty they are born apt for society and so preserve themselves against mutual violence; then proceeding, we will show what advice was necessary to be taken for this business and what are the conditions of society or of human peace—that is to say (changing the words only), what are the fundamental laws of nature.

The greatest part of those men who have written aught concerning commonwealths either suppose or require us or beg of us to believe that man is a creature born fit for society. The Greeks call him *zoon politikon*; and on this foundation, they so build up the doctrine of civil society, as if for the preservation of peace and the government of mankind there were nothing else necessary than that men should agree to make certain covenants and conditions together, which themselves should then call laws. Which axiom, though received by most, is yet certainly false and an error proceeding from our too slight contemplation of human nature. For they who shall more narrowly look into the causes for which men come together and delight in each other's company, shall easily find that this happens not because naturally it could not happen otherwise, but by accident. For, if by nature one man should move another (that is) as man, there could no reason be returned why every man should not equally love every man, as being equally man, or why he should rather frequent those whose society affords him honor or profit. We do not therefore by nature seek society for its own sake, but that we may receive some honor or profit from it; these we desire primarily, that secondarily. How by what

---

Thomas Hobbes. *De Cive*. Chapter 1. London, 1651. Text language updated.

advice men do meet, will be best known by observing those things which they do when they are met. For if they meet for traffic, it's plain every man regards not his fellow, but his business; if to discharge some office, a certain market friendship is begotten, which has more of jealousy in it than true love and whence factions sometimes may arise, but good will never; if for pleasure and recreation of mind, every man is wont to please himself most with those things which stir up laughter; whence he may (according to the nature of that which is ridiculous) by comparison of another man's defects and infirmities, pass the more current in his own opinion. And although this be sometimes innocent and without offence, yet it is manifest they are not so much delighted with the society as their own vain glory. But for the most part, in these kinds of meetings, we wound the absent; their whole life, sayings, actions are examined, judged, condemned. Nay, it is very rare, but some present receive a fling before they part; so as his reason was not ill, who was wont always at parting to go out last. And these are indeed the true delights of society unto which we are carried by nature, i.e. by those passions which are incident to all creatures, until, either by sad experience or good precepts, it so fall out (which in many never happens) that the appetite of present matters be dulled with the memory of things past, without which the discourse of most quick and nimble men on this subject is but cold and hungry.

But if it so happen that being met, they pass their time in relating some stories and one of them begins to tell one which concerns himself; instantly every one of the rest most greedily desires to speak of himself too. If one relate some wonder, the rest will tell you miracles, if they have them; if not, they'll feign them. Lastly, that I may say somewhat of them who pretend to be wiser then others, if they meet to talk of Philosophy, look how many men, so many would be esteemed masters, or else they not only love not their fellows, but even persecute them with hatred. So clear is it by experience to all men who a little more narrowly consider human affairs, that all free congress arises either from mutual poverty or from vain glory; whence the parties met, endeavor to carry with them either some benefit or to leave behind them that same some esteem and honor with those with whom they have been conversant: The same is also collected by reason out of the definitions themselves of will, good, honor, profitable. For when we voluntarily contract society, in all manner of society we look after the object of the will, i.e. that which every one of those who gather together propounds to himself for good, now whatsoever seems good, is pleasant and relates either to the senses or the mind; but all the mind's pleasure is either glory (or to have a good opinion of one's self) or refers to glory in the end; the rest are sensual or conducing to sensuality, which may be all comprehended under the word conveniences. All society therefore is either for gain or for glory; i.e., not so much for love of our fellows, as for love of ourselves. But no society can be great or lasting, which begins from vain glory, because that glory is like honor: If all, men have it, no man has it; for they consist in comparison and precellence. Neither does the society of others advance any whit the cause of my glorying in my self; for every man must account himself such as he can make himself without the help of others. But though the benefits of this life may be much furthered by mutual help, since yet those may be better attained to by dominion than by the society of others, I hope nobody will doubt but that men would much more greedily be carried by nature, if all fear were removed, to obtain dominion, than to gain society. We must therefore resolve that the original of all great and lasting societies consisted not in the mutual good will men had towards each other, but in the mutual fear they had of each other.

The cause of mutual fear consists partly in the natural equality of men, partly in their mutual will of hurting; whence it comes to pass that we can neither expect from others nor promise to ourselves the least security. For if we look on men full grown and consider how brittle the frame of our human body is (which perishing, all its strength, vigor, and wisdom itself perishes with it) and how easy a matter it is even for the weakest man to kill the strongest, there is no reason why any man trusting to his own strength should conceive himself made by nature above others. They are equals who can do equal things one against the other; but they who can do the greatest things (namely kill) can do equal things. All men therefore among themselves are by nature equal. The inequality we now discern, has its spring from the civil law.

All men in the state of nature have a desire and will to hurt, but not proceeding from the same cause, neither equally to be condemned. For one man, according to that natural equality which is among us, permits as much to others as he assumes to himself (which is an argument of a temperate man, and one that rightly values his power); another, supposing himself above others, will have a license to do what he lists and challenges respect and honor as due to him before others (which is an argument of a fiery spirit). This man's will to hurt arises from vain glory, and the false esteem he has of his own strength; the other's from the necessity of defending himself, his liberty, and his goods against this man's violence.

Furthermore, since the combat of wits is the fiercest, the greatest discords which are, must necessarily arise from this contention. For in this case it is not only odious to contend against, but also not to consent; for not to approve of what a man says is no less then tacitly to accuse him of an error in that thing which he speaks; as in very many things, to dissent is as much as if you accounted him a fool whom you dissent from; which may appear hence, that there are no wars so sharply waged as between sects of the same religion and factions of the same commonweal, where the contestation is either concerning doctrines or politic prudence. And since all the pleasure and jollity of the mind consists in this, even to get some, with whom comparing, it may find somewhat wherein to triumph, and vaunt itself; it's impossible but men must declare sometimes some mutual scorn and contempt either by laughter or by words or by gesture or some sign or other, than which there is no greater vexation of mind and than from which there cannot possibly arise a greater desire to do hurt.

But the most frequent reason why men desire to hurt each other, arises hence that many men at the same time have an appetite to the same thing, which yet very often they can neither enjoy in common, nor yet divide it. Whence it follows that the strongest must have it, and who is strongest must be decided by the sword.

Among so many dangers therefore, as the natural lusts of men do daily threaten each other withal, to have a care of one's self is not a matter so scornfully to be looked upon, as if so be there had not been a power and will left in one to have done otherwise. For every man is desirous of what is good for him and shuns what is evil, but chiefly the chiefest of natural evils, which is death; and this he does, by a certain impulsion of nature, no less then that whereby a stone moves downward: It is therefore neither absurd nor reprehensible, neither against the dictates of true reason, for a man to use all his endeavors to preserve and defend his body, and the members thereof from death and sorrows; but that which is not contrary to right reason, that all men account to be done justly and with right; neither by the word right is any thing else signified than that liberty which every man has to make use of his natural faculties according to right reason. Therefore the first foundation of natural right is this, that every man as much as in him lies endeavor to protect his life and members.

But because it is in vain for a man to have a right to the end, if the right to the necessary means be denied him; it follows, that since every man has a right to preserve himself, he must also be allowed a right to use all the means and do all the actions, without which he cannot preserve himself.

Now whether the means which he is about to use and the action he is performing be necessary to the preservation of his life and members or not, he himself, by the right of nature, must be judge. For, say another man judge that it is contrary to right reason that I should judge of mine own peril, why now, because he judges of what concerns me, by the same reason, because we are equal by nature, will I judge also of things which do belong to him; therefore it agrees with right reason—that is, it is the right of nature that I judge of his opinion, i.e. whether it conduce to my preservation or not.

Nature has given to every one a right to all. That is, it was lawful for every man in the bare state of nature, or before such time as men had engaged themselves by any covenants or bonds, to do what he would and against whom he thought fit and to possess, use, and enjoy all what he would or could get. Now because whatsoever a man would, it therefore seems good to him because he wills it, and either it really does, or at least seems to him to contribute toward his preservation, (but we have already allowed him to be judge in the foregoing article whether it does or not, in so much as we are to hold all for necessary whatsoever he shall esteem so) and by the 7. article it appears that by the right of nature those things may be done and must be had, which necessarily conduce to the protection of life and members, it follows that in the state of nature to have all and do all is lawful for all. And this is that which is meant by that common saying, nature has given all to all; from whence we understand likewise, that in the state of nature, profit is the measure of right. In the mere state of nature, this is thus to be understood: What any man does in the bare state of nature is injurious to no man; not that in such a state he cannot offend God, or break the laws of nature; for injustice against men presupposes human laws, such as in the state of nature there are none. Now the truth of this proposition thus conceived is sufficiently demonstrated to the mindful reader in the articles immediately foregoing; but because in certain cases the difficulty of the conclusion makes us forget the premises, I will contract this argument, and make it most evident to a single view. Every man has right to protect himself, as appears by the seventh article. The same man therefore has a right to use all the means which necessarily conduce to this end by the eight article. But those are the necessary means which he shall judge to be such by the ninth article. He therefore has a right to make use of and to do all whatsoever he shall judge requisite for his preservation; wherefore by the judgment of him that does it, the thing done is either right or wrong and therefore right. True it is therefore in the bare state of nature, but if any man pretend somewhat to tend necessarily to his preservation, which yet he himself does not confidently believe so, he may offend against the laws of nature, as in the third chapter of this book is more at large declared. It has been objected by some: If a son kill his father, does he him no injury? I have answered, That a son cannot be understood to be at any time in the state of nature, as being under the power and command of them to whom he owns his protection as soon as ever he is born, namely either his fathers, or his mothers, or his that nourished him, as is demonstrated in the ninth chapter.

But it was the least benefit for men thus to have a common right to all things; for the effects of this right are the same, almost, as if there had been no right at all; for although any man might say of everything, this is mine, yet could he not enjoy it, by reason of his neighbor who, having equal right and equal power, would pretend the same thing to be his.

If now to this natural proclivity of men to hurt each other, which they derive from their passions, but chiefly from a vain esteem of themselves, you add the right of all to all, wherewith one by right invades, the other by right resists, and whence arise perpetual jealousies and suspicions on all hands, and how hard a thing it is to provide against an enemy invading us, with an intention to oppress and ruin, though he come with a small number, and no great provision. It cannot be denied but that the natural state of men, before they entered into society, was a mere war, and that not simply, but a war of all men against all men; for what is war, but that same time in which the will of contesting by force is fully declared either by words or deeds? The time remaining is termed peace.

But it is easily judged how disagreeable a thing to the preservation either of mankind or of each single man, a perpetual war is: But it is perpetual in its own nature, because in regard of the equality of those that strive, it cannot be ended by victory; for in this state the conqueror is subject to so much danger, as it were to be accounted a miracle, if any, even the most strong should close up his life with many years, and old age. They of America are examples hereof, even in this present age. Other nations have been in former ages, which now indeed are become civil, and flourishing, but were then few, fierce, short-lived, poor, nasty, and destroyed of all that pleasure, and beauty of life, which peace and society are wont to bring with them. Whosoever therefore holds, that it had been best to have continued in that state in which all things were lawful for all men, he contradicts himself; for every man, by natural necessity desires that which is good for him: nor is there any that esteems a war of all against all, which necessarily adheres to such a state, to be good for him. And so it happens that through fear of each other we think it fit to rid ourselves of this condition, and to get some fellows; that if there needs must be war, it may not yet be against all men, nor without some helps.

Fellows are gotten either by constraint or by consent: By constraint, when after fight the conqueror makes the conquered serve him either through fear of death or by laying fetters on him. By consent, when men enter into society to help each other, both parties consenting without any constraint. But the conqueror may by right compel the conquered, or the strongest the weaker (as a man in health may one that is sick, or he that is of riper years a child), unless he will choose to die, to give caution of his future obedience. For since the right of protecting ourselves according to our own wills proceeded from our danger, and our danger from our equality, it's more consonant to reason and more certain for our conservation, using the present advantage to secure ourselves by taking caution, than when they shall be full grown and strong and got out of our power, to endeavor to recover that power again by doubtful fight. And on the other side, nothing can be thought more absurd, then by discharging whom you already have weak in your power, to make him at once both an enemy and a strong one. From whence we may understand likewise as a corollary in the natural state of men, that a sure and irresistible power confers the right of dominion; and ruling over those who cannot resist; insomuch, as the right of all things, that can be done, adheres essentially and immediately unto this omnipotence hence arising.

Yet men cannot expect any lasting preservation continuing thus in the state of nature, i.e. of war, by reason of that equality of power and other human faculties they are endued withal. Wherefore to seek peace, where there is any hope of obtaining it, and where there is none, to enquire out for auxiliaries of war, is the dictate of right reason; that is, the law of nature, as shall be shown in the next chapter.

The Virtue of Selfishness
Ayn Rand

The title of this book may evoke the kind of question that I hear once in a while: "Why do you use the word 'selfishness' to denote virtuous qualities of character, when that word antagonizes so many people to whom it does not mean the things you mean?"

To those who ask it, my answer is: "For the reason that makes you afraid of it."

But there are others, who would not ask that question, sensing the moral cowardice it implies, yet who are unable to formulate my actual reason or to identify the profound moral issue involved. It is to them that I will give a more explicit answer.

It is not a mere semantic issue nor a matter of arbitrary choice. The meaning ascribed in popular usage to the word "selfishness" is not merely wrong: it represents a devastating intellectual "package-deal," which is responsible, more than any other single factor, for the arrested moral development of mankind.

In popular usage, the word "selfishness" is a synonym of evil; the image it conjures is of a murderous brute who tramples over piles of corpses to achieve his own ends, who cares for no living being and pursues nothing but the gratification of the mindless whims of any immediate moment.

Yet the exact meaning and dictionary definition of the word "selfishness" is: *concern with one's own interests.*

This concept does *not* include a moral evaluation; it does not tell us whether concern with one's own interests is good or evil; nor does it tell us what constitutes man's actual interests. It is the task of ethics to answer such questions.

The ethics of altruism has created the image of the brute, as its answer, in order to make men accept two inhuman tenets: (a) that any concern with one's own interests is evil, regardless of what these interests might

---

Ayn Rand. *The Virtue of Selfishness.* Introduction. New York: Pengiun Books, 1964. Reprinted by permission of the Ayn Rand Foundation.

be, and (b) that the brute's activities are *in fact* to one's own interest (which altruism enjoins man to renounce for the sake of his neighbors).

For a view of the nature of altruism, its consequences and the enormity of the moral corruption it perpetrates, I shall refer you to *Atlas Shrugged*—or to any of today's newspaper headlines. What concerns us here is altruism's *default* in the field of ethical theory.

There are two moral questions which altruism lumps together into one "package-deal": (1) What are values? (2) Who should be the beneficiary of values? Altruism substitutes the second for the first; it evades the task of defining a code of moral values, thus leaving man, in fact, without moral guidance.

Altruism declares that any action taken for the benefit of others is good, and any action taken for one's own benefit is evil. Thus the *beneficiary* of an action is the only criterion of moral value—and so long as that beneficiary is anybody other than oneself, anything goes.

Hence the appalling immorality, the chronic injustice, the grotesque double standards, the insoluble conflicts and contradictions that have characterized human relationships and human societies throughout history, under all the variants of the altruist ethics.

Observe the indecency of what passes for moral judgments today. An industrialist who produces a fortune, and a gangster who robs a bank are regarded as equally immoral, since they both sought wealth for their own "selfish" benefit. A young man who gives up his career in order to support his parents and never rises beyond the rank of grocery clerk is regarded as morally superior to the young man who endures an excruciating struggle and achieves his personal ambition. A dictator is regarded as moral, since the unspeakable atrocities he committed were intended to benefit "the people," not himself.

Observe what this beneficiary-criterion of morality does to a man's life. The first thing he learns is that morality is his enemy: he has nothing to gain from it, he can only lose; self-inflicted loss, self-inflicted pain and the gray, debilitating pall of an incomprehensible duty is all that he can expect. He may hope that others might occasionally sacrifice themselves for his benefit, as he grudgingly sacrifices himself for theirs, but he knows that the relationship will bring mutual resentment, not pleasure—and that, morally, their pursuit of values will be like an exchange of unwanted, unchosen Christmas presents, which neither is morally permitted to buy for himself. Apart from such times as he manages to perform some act of self-sacrifice, he possesses no moral significance: morality takes no cognizance of him and has nothing to say to him for guidance in the crucial issues of his life; it is only his own personal, private, "selfish" life and, as such, it is regarded either as evil or, at best, *amoral*.

Since nature does not provide man with an automatic form of survival, since he has to support his life by his own effort, the doctrine that concern with one's own interests is evil means that man's desire to live is evil—that man's life, as such, is evil. No doctrine could be more evil than that.

Yet that is the meaning of altruism, implicit in such examples as the equation of an industrialist with a robber. There is a fundamental moral difference between a man who sees his self-interest in production and a man who sees it in robbery. The evil of a robber does not lie in the fact that he pursues his own interests, but in *what* he regards as to his own interest; *not* in the fact that he pursues his values, but in what he chose to value; not in the fact that he wants to live, but in the fact that he wants to live on a subhuman level....

If it is true that what I mean by "selfishness" is not what is meant conventionally, then *this* is one of the worst indictments of altruism: it means that altruism *permits no concept* of a self-respecting, self-supporting man—a man who supports his life by his own effort and neither sacrifices himself nor others. It means that altruism permits no view of men except as sacrificial animals and profiteers-on-sacrifice, as victims and parasites—that it permits no concept of a benevolent co-existence among me—that it permits no concept of *justice*.

If you wonder about the reasons behind the ugly mixture of cynicism and guilt in which most men spend their lives, these are the reasons: cynicism, because they neither practice nor accept the altruist morality—guilt, because they dare not reject it.

To rebel against so devastating an evil, one has to rebel against its basic premise. To redeem both man and morality, it is the concept of *"selfishness"* that one has to redeem. The first step is to assert man's right to a moral existence—that is: to recognize his need of a moral code to guide the course and the fulfillment of his own life.

Utility and Pleasure
Jeremy Bentham

Nature has placed mankind under the governance of two sovereign masters, *pain* and *pleasure*. It is for them alone to point out what we ought to do, as well as to determine what we shall do. On the one hand the standard of right and wrong, on the other the chain of causes and effects, are fastened to their throne. They govern us in all we do, in all we say, in all we think: every effort we can make to throw off our subjection, will serve but to demonstrate and confirm it. In words a man may pretend to abjure their empire: but in reality he will remain. subject to it all the while. The *principle of utility* recognizes this subjection, and assumes it for the foundation of that system, the object of which is to rear the fabric of felicity by the hands of reason and of law. Systems which attempt to question it, deal in sounds instead of sense, in caprice instead of reason, in darkness instead of light.

But enough of metaphor and declamation: it is not by such means that moral science is to be improved.

The principle of utility is the foundation of the present work: it will be proper therefore at the outset to give an explicit and determinate account of what is meant by it. By the principle of utility is meant that principle which approves or disapproves of every action whatsoever. according to the tendency it appears to have to augment or diminish the happiness of the party whose interest is in question: or, what is the same thing in other words to promote or to oppose that happiness. I say of every action whatsoever, and therefore not only of every action of a private individual, but of every measure of government.

By utility is meant that property in any object, whereby it tends to produce benefit, advantage, pleasure, good, or happiness, (all this in the present case comes to the same thing) or (what comes again to the same thing) to prevent the happening of mischief, pain, evil, or unhappiness to the party whose interest is considered: if that party be the community in

Jeremy Bentham. *An Introduction to the Principles of Morals and Legislation.* 1789.

general, then the happiness of the community: if a particular individual, then the happiness of that individual.

IV. The interest of the community is one of the most general expressions that can occur in the phraseology of morals: no wonder that the meaning of it is often lost. When it has a meaning, it is this. The community is a fictitious *body*, composed of the individual persons who are considered as constituting as it were its *members*. The interest of the community then is, what is it? — the sum of the interests of the several members who compose it.

It is in vain to talk of the interest of the community, without understanding what is the interest of the individual. A thing is said to promote the interest, or to be *for* the interest, of an individual, when it tends to add to the sum total of his pleasures: or, what comes to the same thing, to diminish the sum total of his pains.

An action then may be said to be conformable to then principle of utility, or, for shortness sake, to utility, (meaning with respect to the community at large) when the tendency it has to augment the happiness of the community is greater than any it has to diminish it.

A measure of government (which is but a particular kind of action, performed by a particular person or persons) may be said to be conformable to or dictated by the principle of utility, when in like manner the tendency which it has to augment the happiness of the community is greater than any which it has to diminish it....

When an action, or in particular a measure of government, is supposed by a man to be conformable to the principle of utility, it may be convenient, for the purposes of discourse, to imagine a kind of law or dictate, called a law or dictate of utility: and to speak of the action in question, as being conformable to such law or dictate.

A man may be said to be a partizan of the principle of utility, when the approbation or disapprobation he annexes to any action, or to any measure, is determined by and proportioned to the tendency which he conceives it to have to augment or to diminish the happiness of the community: or in other words, to its conformity or unconformity to the laws or dictates of utility.

Of an action that is conformable to the principle of utility one may always say either that it is one that ought to be done, or at least that it is not one that ought not to be done. One may say also, that it is right it should be done; at least that it is not wrong it should be done: that it is a right action; at least that it is not a wrong action. When thus interpreted, the words *ought*, and *right* and *wrong* and others of that stamp, have a meaning: when otherwise, they have none....

Measuring Pleasure and Pain

Pleasures then, and the avoidance of pains, are the *ends* that the legislator has in view; it behoves him therefore to understand their *value*. Pleasures and pains are the instruments he has to work with: it behoves him therefore to understand their force, which is again, in other words, their value.

To a person considered by *himself*, the value of a pleasure or pain considered *by itself*, will be greater or less, according to the four following *circumstances*:

1. Its *intensity*.
2. Its *duration*.
3. Its *certainty* or *uncertainty*.
4. Its *propinquity* or *remoteness*.

These are the circumstances which are to be considered in estimating a pleasure or a pain considered each of them by itself. But when the value of any pleasure or pain is considered for the purpose of estimating the tendency of any *act* by which it is produced, there are two other circumstances to be taken into the account; these are,

5. Its *fecundity*, or the chance it has of being followed by sensations of the *same* kind: that is, pleasures, if it be a pleasure: pains, if it be a pain.
6. Its *purity*, or the chance it has of not being followed by sensations of the *opposite* kind: that is, pains, if it be a pleasure: pleasures, if it be a pain.

These two last, however, are in strictness scarcely to be deemed properties of the pleasure or the pain itself; they are not, therefore, in strictness to be taken into the account of the value of that pleasure or that pain. They are in strictness to be deemed properties only of the act, or other event, by which such pleasure or pain has been produced; and accordingly are only to be taken into the account of the tendency of such act or such event.

To a *number* of persons, with reference to each of whom to the value of a pleasure or a pain is considered, it will be greater or less, according to seven circumstances: to wit, the six preceding ones; viz.

1. Its *intensity*.

2. Its *duration*.
3. Its *certainty* or *uncertainty*.
4. Its *propinquity* or *remoteness*.
5. Its *fecundity*.
6. Its *purity*.
And one other; to wit:
7. Its *extent*; that is, the number of persons to whom it *extends*; or (in other words) who are affected by it.

To take an exact account then of the general tendency of any act, by which the interests of a community are affected, proceed as follows. Begin with any one person of those whose interests seem most immediately to be affected by it: and take an account,

1. Of the value of each distinguishable *pleasure* which appears to be produced by it in the *first* instance.
2. Of the value of each *pain* which appears to be produced by it in the *first* instance.
3. Of the value of each pleasure which appears to be produced by it *after* the first. This constitutes the *fecundity* of the first *pleasure* and the *impurity* of the first *pain*.
4. Of the value of each *pain* which appears to be produced by it after the first. This constitutes the *fecundity* of the first *pain*, and the *impurity* of the first pleasure.
5. Sum up all the values of all the *pleasures* on the one side, and those of all the pains on the other. The balance, if it be on the side of pleasure, will give the *good* tendency of the act upon the whole, with respect to the interests of that *individual* person; if on the side of pain, the *bad* tendency of it upon the whole.
6. Take an account of the *number* of persons whose interests appear to be concerned; and repeat the above process with respect to each. *Sum up* the numbers expressive of the degrees of *good* tendency, which the act has, with respect to each individual, in regard to whom the tendency of it is *good* upon the whole: do this again with respect to each individual, in regard to whom the tendency of it is *good* upon the whole: do this again with respect to each individual, in regard to whom the tendency of it is *bad* upon the whole. Take the *balance* which if on the side of *pleasure*, will give the general *good tendency* of the act, with respect to the total number or community of individuals concerned; if on the side of pain, the general *evil tendency*, with respect to the same

community.

It is not to be expected that this process should be strictly pursued previously to every moral judgment, or to every legislative or judicial operation. It may, however, be always kept in view: and as near as the process actually pursued on these occasions approaches to it, so near will such process approach to the character of an exact one....

2.2

Utilitarianism
John Stuart Mill

The creed which accepts as the foundation of morals, Utility, or the Greatest Happiness Principle, holds that actions are right in proportion as they tend to promote happiness, wrong as they tend to produce the reverse of happiness. By happiness is intended pleasure, and the absence of pain; by unhappiness, pain, and the privation of pleasure. To give a clear view of the moral standard set up by the theory, much more requires to be said; in particular, what things it includes in the ideas of pain and pleasure; and to what extent this is left an open question. But these supplementary explanations do not affect the theory of life on which this theory of morality is grounded—namely, that pleasure, and freedom from pain, are the only things desirable as ends; and that all desirable things (which are as numerous in the utilitarian as in any other scheme) are desirable either for the pleasure inherent in themselves, or as means to the promotion of pleasure and the prevention of pain.

Now, such a theory of life excites in many minds, and among them in some of the most estimable in feeling and purpose, inveterate dislike. To suppose that life has (as they express it) no higher end than pleasure—no better and nobler object of desire and pursuit—they designate as utterly mean and grovelling; as a doctrine worthy only of swine....

Higher and Lower Pleasures

It is quite compatible with the principle of utility to recognise the fact, that some kinds of pleasure are more desirable and more valuable than others. It would be absurd that while, in estimating all other things, quality is considered as well as quantity, the estimation of pleasures should be supposed to depend on quantity alone.

If I am asked, what I mean by difference of quality in pleasures, or what makes one pleasure more valuable than another, merely as a

John Stuart Mill. *Utilitarianism.* Chapter 2. London: Longmans, Green, Reader and Dyer, 1871.

pleasure, except its being greater in amount, there is but one possible answer. Of two pleasures, if there be one to which all or almost all who have experience of both give a decided preference, irrespective of any feeling of moral obligation to prefer it, that is the more desirable pleasure. If one of the two is, by those who are competently acquainted with both, placed so far above the other that they prefer it, even though knowing it to be attended with a greater amount of discontent, and would not resign it for any quantity of the other pleasure which their nature is capable of, we are justified in ascribing to the preferred enjoyment a superiority in quality, so far outweighing quantity as to render it, in comparison, of small account.

Now it is an unquestionable fact that those who are equally acquainted with, and equally capable of appreciating and enjoying, both, do give a most marked preference to the manner of existence which employs their higher faculties. Few human creatures would consent to be changed into any of the lower animals, for a promise of the fullest allowance of a beast's pleasures; no intelligent human being would consent to be a fool, no instructed person would be an ignoramus, no person of feeling and conscience would be selfish and base, even though they should be persuaded that the fool, the dunce, or the rascal is better satisfied with his lot than they are with theirs. They would not resign what they possess more than he for the most complete satisfaction of all the desires which they have in common with him. If they ever fancy they would, it is only in cases of unhappiness so extreme, that to escape from it they would exchange their lot for almost any other, however undesirable in their own eyes. A being of higher faculties requires more to make him happy, is capable probably of more acute suffering, and certainly accessible to it at more points, than one of an inferior type; but in spite of these liabilities, he can never really wish to sink into what he feels to be a lower grade of existence. We may give what explanation we please of this unwillingness; we may attribute it to pride, a name which is given indiscriminately to some of the most and to some of the least estimable feelings of which mankind are capable: we may refer it to the love of liberty and personal independence, an appeal to which was with the Stoics one of the most effective means for the inculcation of it; to the love of power, or to the love of excitement, both of which do really enter into and contribute to it: but its most appropriate appellation is a sense of dignity, which all human beings possess in one form or other, and in some, though by no means in exact, proportion to their higher faculties, and which is so essential a part of the happiness of those in whom it is strong, that nothing which conflicts with it could be, otherwise than momentarily, an object of desire to them.

Whoever supposes that this preference takes place at a sacrifice of happiness—that the superior being, in anything like equal circumstances, is not happier than the inferior— confounds the two very different ideas, of *happiness*, and *content*. It is indisputable that the being whose capacities of enjoyment are low, has the greatest chance of having them fully satisfied; and a highly endowed being will always feel that any happiness which he can look for, as the world is constituted, is imperfect. But he can learn to bear its imperfections, if they are at all bearable; and they will not make him envy the being who is indeed unconscious of the imperfections, but only because he feels not at all the good which those imperfections qualify. It is better to be a human being dissatisfied than a pig satisfied; better to be Socrates dissatisfied than a fool satisfied. And if the fool, or the pig, are a different opinion, it is because they only know their own side of the question. The other party to the comparison knows both sides....

Further Considerations on Happiness

According to the Greatest Happiness Principle...the ultimate end, with reference to and for the sake of which all other things are desirable (whether we are considering our own good or that of other people), is an existence exempt as far as possible from pain, and as rich as possible in enjoyments, both in point of quantity and quality; the test of quality, and the rule for measuring it against quantity, being the preference felt by those who in their opportunities of experience, to which must be added their habits of self-consciousness and self-observation, are best furnished with the means of comparison. This, being, according to the utilitarian opinion, the end of human action, is necessarily also the standard of morality; which may accordingly be defined, the rules and precepts for human conduct, by the observance of which an existence such as has been described might be, to the greatest extent possible, secured to all mankind; and not to them only, but, so far as the nature of things admits, to the whole sentient creation....

...If by happiness be meant a continuity of highly pleasurable excitement, it is evident enough that this is impossible. A state of exalted pleasure lasts only moments, or in some cases, and with some intermissions, hours or days, and is the occasional brilliant flash of enjoyment, not its permanent and steady flame. Of this the philosophers who have taught that happiness is the end of life were as fully aware as those who taunt them. The happiness which they meant was not a life of rapture; but moments of such, in an existence made up of few and transitory pains, many and various pleasures, with a decided predominance of the active over the passive, and having as the foundation of the whole, not to expect more from life than it is capable of bestowing. A life thus composed, to those who have been fortunate enough to obtain it, has always appeared worthy of the name of happiness. And such an existence is even now the lot of many, during some considerable portion of their lives. The present wretched education, and wretched social arrangements, are the only real hindrance to its being attainable by almost all.

The objectors perhaps may doubt whether human beings, if taught to consider happiness as the end of life, would be satisfied with such a moderate share of it. But great numbers of mankind have been satisfied with much less. The main constituents of a satisfied life appear to be two, either of which by itself is often found sufficient for the purpose: tranquillity, and excitement. With much tranquillity, many find that they can be content with very little pleasure: with much excitement, many can reconcile themselves to a considerable quantity of pain. There is assuredly no inherent impossibility in enabling even the mass of mankind to unite both; since the two are so far from being incompatible that they are in natural alliance, the prolongation of either being a preparation for, and exciting a wish for, the other. It is only those in whom indolence amounts to a vice, that do not desire excitement after an interval of repose: it is only those in whom the need of excitement is a disease, that feel the tranquillity which follows excitement dull and insipid, instead of pleasurable in direct proportion to the excitement which preceded it. When people who are tolerably fortunate in their outward lot do not find in life sufficient enjoyment to make it valuable to them, the cause generally is, caring for nobody but themselves. To those who have neither public nor private affections, the excitements of life are much curtailed, and in any case dwindle in value as the time approaches when all selfish interests must be terminated by death: while those who leave after them objects of personal affection, and especially those who have also cultivated a fellow-feeling with the collective interests of mankind, retain as lively an interest in life on the eve of death as in the vigour of youth and health. Next to selfishness, the principal cause which makes life unsatisfactory is want of mental cultivation. A cultivated mind - I do not mean that of a philosopher, but any mind to which the fountains of knowledge have been opened, and which has been taught, in any tolerable degree, to exercise its faculties- finds sources of inexhaustible interest in all that surrounds it; in the objects of nature, the achievements of art, the imaginations of poetry, the incidents of history, the ways of mankind, past and present, and their prospects in the future. It is possible, indeed, to become indifferent to all this, and that too without having exhausted a thousandth part of it; but only when one has had from the beginning no moral or human interest in these things, and has sought in them only the gratification of curiosity.

Now there is absolutely no reason in the nature of things why an amount of mental culture sufficient to give an intelligent interest in these objects of contemplation, should not be the inheritance of every one born in a civilised country. As little is there an inherent necessity that any human being should be a selfish egotist, devoid of every feeling or care but those which centre in his own miserable individuality. Something far superior to this is sufficiently common even now, to give ample earnest of what the human species may be made. Genuine private affections and a sincere interest in the public good, are possible, though in unequal degrees, to every rightly brought up human being. In a world in which there is so much to interest, so much to enjoy, and so much also to correct and improve, every one who has this moderate amount of moral and intellectual requisites is capable of an existence which may be called enviable; and unless such a person, through bad laws, or subjection to the will of others, is denied the liberty to use the sources of happiness within his reach, he will not fail to find this enviable existence, if he escape the positive evils of life, the great sources of physical and mental suffering- such as indigence, disease, and the unkindness, worthlessness, or premature loss of objects of affection. The main stress of the problem lies, therefore, in the contest with these calamities, from which it is a rare good fortune entirely to escape; which, as things now are, cannot be obviated, and often cannot be in any material degree mitigated. Yet no one whose opinion deserves a moment's consideration can doubt that most of the great positive evils of the world are in themselves removable, and will, if human affairs continue to improve, be in the end reduced within narrow limits. Poverty, in any sense implying suffering, may be completely extinguished by the wisdom of society, combined with the good sense and providence of individuals. Even that most intractable of enemies, disease, may be indefinitely reduced in dimensions by good physical and moral education, and proper control of noxious influences; while the progress of science holds out a promise for the future of still more direct conquests over this detestable foe. And every advance in that direction relieves us from some, not only of the chances which cut short our own lives, but, what concerns us still more, which deprive us of those in whom our happiness is wrapt up. As for vicissitudes of fortune, and other disappointments connected with worldly circumstances, these are principally the effect either of gross imprudence, of ill-regulated desires, or of bad or imperfect social institutions.

All the grand sources, in short, of human suffering are in a great degree, many of them almost entirely, conquerable by human care and effort; and though their removal is grievously slow—though a long succession of generations will perish in the breach before the conquest is completed, and this world becomes all that, if will and knowledge were not wanting, it might easily be made—yet every mind sufficiently intelligent and generous to bear a part, however small and unconspicuous, in the endeavour, will draw a noble enjoyment from the contest itself, which he would not for any bribe in the form of selfish indulgence consent to be without.

And this leads to the true estimation of what is said by the objectors concerning the possibility, and the obligation, of learning to do without happiness. Unquestionably it is possible to do without happiness; it is done involuntarily by nineteen-twentieths of mankind, even in those parts of our present world which are least deep in barbarism; and it often has to be done voluntarily by the hero or the martyr, for the sake of something which he prizes more than his individual happiness. But this something, what is it, unless the happiness of others or some of the requisites of happiness? It is noble to be capable of resigning entirely one's own portion of happiness, or chances of it: but, after all, this self-sacrifice must be for some end; it is not its own end; and if we are told that its end is not happiness, but virtue, which is better than happiness, I ask, would the sacrifice be made if the hero or martyr did not believe that it would earn for others immunity from similar sacrifices? Would it be made if he thought that his renunciation of happiness for himself would produce no fruit for any of his fellow creatures, but to make their lot like his, and place them also in the condition of persons who have renounced happiness? All honour to those who can abnegate for themselves the personal enjoyment of life, when by such renunciation they contribute worthily to increase the amount of happiness in the world; but he who does it, or professes to do it, for any other purpose, is no more deserving of admiration than the ascetic mounted on his pillar. He may be an inspiriting proof of what men can do, but assuredly not an example of what they *should*.

Though it is only in a very imperfect state of the world's arrangements that any one can best serve the happiness of others by the absolute sacrifice of his own, yet so long as the world is in that imperfect state, I fully acknowledge that the readiness to make such a sacrifice is the highest virtue which can be found in man. I will add, that in this condition the world, paradoxical as the assertion may be, the conscious ability to do without happiness gives the best prospect of realising, such happiness as is attainable. For nothing except that consciousness can raise a person above the chances of life, by making him feel that, let fate and fortune do their worst, they have not power to subdue him: which, once felt, frees him from excess of anxiety concerning the evils of life, and enables him, like many a Stoic in the worst times of the Roman Empire, to cultivate in tranquillity the sources of satisfaction accessible to him, without concerning himself about the uncertainty of their duration, any more than about their inevitable end.

Meanwhile, let utilitarians never cease to claim the morality of self devotion as a possession which belongs by as good a right to them, as either to the Stoic or to the Transcendentalist. The utilitarian morality does recognise in human beings the power of sacrificing their own greatest good for the good of others. It only refuses to admit that the sacrifice is itself a good. A sacrifice which does not increase, or tend to increase, the sum total of happiness, it considers as wasted. The only self-renunciation which it applauds, is devotion to the happiness, or to some of the means of happiness, of others; either of mankind collectively, or of individuals within the limits imposed by the collective interests of mankind.

Defending Utilitarianism

I must again repeat, what the assailants of utilitarianism seldom have the justice to acknowledge, that the happiness which forms the utilitarian standard of what is right in conduct, is not the agent's own happiness, but that of all concerned. As between his own happiness and that of others, utilitarianism requires him to be as strictly impartial as a disinterested and benevolent spectator. In the golden rule of Jesus of Nazareth, we read the complete spirit of the ethics of utility. To do as you would be done by, and to love your neighbour as yourself, constitute the ideal perfection of utilitarian morality. As the means of making the nearest approach to this ideal, utility would enjoin, first, that laws and social arrangements should place the happiness, or (as speaking practically it may be called) the interest, of every individual, as nearly as possible in harmony with the interest of the whole; and secondly, that education and opinion, which have so vast a power over human character, should so use that power as to establish in the mind of every individual an indissoluble association between his own happiness and the good of the whole; especially between his own happiness and the practice of such modes of conduct, negative and positive, as regard for the universal happiness prescribes; so that not only he may be unable to conceive the possibility of happiness to himself, consistently with conduct opposed to the general good, but also that a direct impulse to promote the general good may be in every individual one of the habitual motives of action, and the sentiments connected therewith may fill a large and prominent place in every human being's sentient existence. If the, impugners of the utilitarian morality represented it to their own minds in this its, true character, I know not what recommendation possessed by any other morality they could possibly affirm to be wanting to it; what more beautiful or more exalted developments of human nature any other ethical system can be supposed to foster, or what springs of action, not accessible to the utilitarian, such systems rely on for giving effect to their mandates.

The objectors to utilitarianism cannot always be charged with representing it in a discreditable light. On the contrary, those among them who entertain anything like a just idea of its disinterested character, sometimes find fault with its standard as being too high for humanity. They say it is exacting too much to require that people shall always act from the inducement of promoting the general interests of society. But this is to mistake the very meaning of a standard of morals, and confound the rule of action with the motive of it. It is the business of ethics to tell us what are our duties, or by what test we may know them; but no system of ethics requires that the sole motive of all we do shall be a feeling of duty; on the contrary, ninety-nine hundredths of all our actions are done from other motives, and rightly so done, if the rule of duty does not condemn them. It is the more unjust to utilitarianism that this particular misapprehension should be made a ground of objection to it, inasmuch as utilitarian moralists have gone beyond almost all others in affirming that the motive has nothing to do with the morality of the action, though much with the worth of the agent. He who saves a fellow creature from drowning does what is morally right, whether his motive be duty, or the hope of being paid for his trouble; he who betrays the friend that trusts him, is guilty of a crime, even if his object be to serve another friend to whom he is under greater obligations.

But to speak only of actions done from the motive of duty, and in direct obedience to principle: it is a misapprehension of the utilitarian mode of thought, to conceive it as implying that people should fix their minds upon so wide a generality as the world, or society at large. The great majority of good actions are intended not for the benefit of the world, but for that of individuals, of which the good of the world is made up; and the thoughts of the most virtuous man need not on these occasions travel beyond the particular persons concerned, except so far as is necessary to assure himself that in benefiting them he is not violating the rights, that is, the legitimate and authorised expectations, of any one else. The multiplication of happiness is, according to the utilitarian ethics, the object of virtue: the occasions on which any person (except one in a thousand) has it in his power to do this on an extended scale, in other words to be a public benefactor, are but exceptional; and on these occasions alone is he called on to consider public utility; in every other case, private utility, the interest or happiness of some few persons, is all he has to attend to. Those alone the influence of whose actions extends to society in general, need concern themselves habitually about large an object. In the case of abstinences indeed—of things which people forbear to do from moral considerations, though the consequences in the particular case might be beneficial—it would be unworthy of an intelligent agent not to be consciously aware that the action is of a class which, if practised generally, would be generally injurious, and that this is the ground of the obligation to abstain from it. The amount of regard for the public interest implied in this recognition, is no greater than is demanded by every system of morals, for they all enjoin to abstain from whatever is manifestly pernicious to society....

Again, Utility is often summarily stigmatised as an immoral doctrine by giving it the name of Expediency, and taking advantage of the popular use of that term to contrast it with Principle. But the Expedient, in the sense in which it is opposed to the Right, generally means that which is expedient for the particular interest of the agent himself; as when a minister sacrifices the interests of his country to keep himself in place. When it means anything better than this, it means that which is expedient for some immediate object, some temporary purpose, but which violates a rule whose observance is expedient in a much higher degree. The Expedient, in this sense, instead of being the same thing with the useful, is a branch of the hurtful.

Thus, it would often be expedient, for the purpose of getting over some momentary embarrassment, or attaining some object immediately useful to ourselves or others, to tell a lie. But inasmuch as the cultivation in ourselves of a sensitive feeling on the subject of veracity, is one of the most useful, and the enfeeblement of that feeling one of the most hurtful, things to which our conduct can be instrumental; and inasmuch as any, even unintentional, deviation from truth, does that much towards weakening the trustworthiness of human assertion, which is not only the principal support of all present social well-being, but the insufficiency of which does more than any one thing that can be named to keep back civilisation, virtue, everything on which human happiness on the largest scale depends; we feel that the violation, for a present advantage, of a rule of such transcendant expediency, is not expedient, and that he who, for the sake of a convenience to himself or to some other individual, does what depends on him to deprive mankind of the good, and inflict upon them the evil, involved in the greater or less reliance which they can place in each other's word, acts the part of one of their worst enemies.

Yet that even this rule, sacred as it is, admits of possible exceptions, is acknowledged by all moralists; the chief of which is when the withholding of some fact (as of information from a malefactor, or of bad news from a person dangerously ill) would save an individual (especially an individual other than oneself) from great and unmerited evil, and when the withholding can only be effected by denial. But in order that the exception may not extend itself beyond the need, and may have the least possible effect in weakening reliance on veracity, it ought to be recognised, and, if possible, its limits defined; and if the principle of utility is good for anything, it must be good for weighing these conflicting utilities against one another, and marking out the region within which one or the other preponderates.

Again, defenders of utility often find themselves called upon to reply to such objections as this—that there is not time, previous to action, for calculating and weighing the effects of any line of conduct on the general happiness. This is exactly as if any one were to say that it is impossible to guide our conduct by Christianity, because there is not time, on every occasion on which anything has to be done, to read through the Old and New Testaments. The answer to the objection is, that there has been ample time, namely, the whole past duration of the human species. During all that time, mankind have been learning by experience the tendencies of actions; on which experience all the prudence, as well as all the morality of life, are dependent. People talk as if the commencement of this course of experience had hitherto been put off, and as if, at the moment when some man feels tempted to meddle with the property or life of another, he had to begin considering for the first time whether murder and theft are injurious to human happiness. Even then I do not think that he would find the question very puzzling; but, at all events, the matter is now done to his hand. It is truly a whimsical supposition that, if mankind were agreed in considering utility to be the test of morality, they would remain without any agreement as to what is useful, and would take no measures for having their notions on the subject taught to the young, and enforced by law and opinion. There is no difficulty in proving any ethical standard whatever to work ill, if we suppose universal idiocy to be conjoined with it; but on any hypothesis short of that, mankind must by this time have acquired positive beliefs as to the effects of some actions on their happiness; and the beliefs which have thus come down are the rules of morality for the multitude, and for the philosopher until he has succeeded in finding better.

That philosophers might easily do this, even now, on many subjects; that the received code of ethics is by no means of divine right; and that mankind have still much to learn as to the effects of actions on the general happiness, I admit, or rather, earnestly maintain. The corollaries from the principle of utility, like the precepts of every practical art, admit of indefinite improvement, and, in a progressive state of the human mind, their improvement is perpetually going on.

But to consider the rules of morality as improvable, is one thing; to pass over the intermediate generalisations entirely, and endeavour to test each individual action directly by the first principle, is another. It is a strange notion that the acknowledgment of a first principle is inconsistent with the admission of secondary ones. To inform a traveller respecting the place of his. ultimate destination, is not to forbid the use of landmarks and direction-posts on the way. The proposition that happiness is the end and aim of morality, does not mean that no road ought to be laid down to that goal, or that persons going thither should not be advised to take one direction rather than another. Men really ought to leave off talking a kind of nonsense on this subject, which they would neither talk nor listen to on other matters of practical concernment. Nobody argues that the art of navigation is not founded on astronomy, because sailors cannot wait to calculate the Nautical Almanack. Being rational creatures, they go to sea with it ready calculated; and all rational creatures go out upon the sea of life with their minds made up on the common questions of right and wrong, as well as on many of the far more difficult questions of wise and foolish. And this, as long as foresight is a human quality, it is to be presumed they will continue to do. Whatever we adopt as the fundamental principle of morality, we require subordinate principles to apply it by; the impossibility of doing without them, being common to all systems, can afford no argument against any one in particular; but gravely to argue as if no such secondary principles could be had, and as if mankind had remained till now, and always must remain, without drawing any general conclusions from the experience of human life, is as high a pitch, I think, as absurdity has ever reached in philosophical controversy.

The remainder of the stock arguments against utilitarianism mostly consist in laying to its charge the common infirmities of human nature, and the general difficulties which embarrass conscientious persons in shaping their course through life. We are told that a utilitarian will be apt to make his own particular case an exception to moral rules, and, when under temptation, will see a utility in the breach of a rule, greater than he will see in its observance. But is utility the only creed which is able to furnish us with excuses for evil doing, and means of cheating our own conscience? They are afforded in abundance by all doctrines which recognise as a fact in morals the existence of conflicting considerations; which all doctrines do, that have been believed by sane persons. It is not the fault of any creed, but of the complicated nature of human affairs, that rules of conduct cannot be so framed as to require no exceptions, and that hardly any kind of action can safely be laid down as either always obligatory or always condemnable. There is no ethical creed which does not temper the rigidity of its laws, by giving a certain latitude, under the moral responsibility of the agent, for accommodation to peculiarities of circumstances; and under every creed, at the opening thus made, self-deception and dishonest casuistry get in. There exists no moral system under which there do not arise unequivocal cases of conflicting obligation. These are the real difficulties, the knotty points both in the theory of ethics, and in the conscientious guidance of personal conduct. They are overcome practically, with greater or with less success, according to the intellect and virtue of the individual; but it can hardly be pretended that any one will be the less qualified for dealing with them, from possessing an ultimate standard to which conflicting rights and duties can be referred. If utility is the ultimate source of moral obligations, utility may be invoked to decide between them when their demands are incompatible. Though the application of the standard may be difficult, it is better than none at all: while in other systems, the moral laws all claiming independent authority, there is no common umpire entitled to interfere between them; their claims to precedence one over another rest on little better than sophistry, and unless determined, as they generally are, by the unacknowledged influence of considerations of utility, afford a free scope for the action of personal desires and partialities. We must remember that only in these cases of conflict between secondary principles is it requisite that first principles should be appealed to. There is no case of moral obligation in which some secondary principle is not involved; and if only one, there can seldom be any real doubt which one it is, in the mind of any person by whom the principle itself is recognised.

2.3

The Archbishop and the Chambermaid
William Godwin

Justice is a rule of conduct originating in the connection of one percipient being with another. A comprehensive maxim which has been laid down upon the subject is, 'that we should love our neighbour as ourselves.' But this maxim, though possessing considerable merit as a popular principle, is not modelled with the strictness of philosophical accuracy.

In a loose and general view I and my neighbour are both of us men; and of consequence entitled to equal attention. But in reality it is probable that one of us is a being of more worth and importance than the other. A man is of more worth than a beast; because, being possessed of higher faculties, he is capable of a more refined and genuine happiness. In the same manner the illustrious archbishop of Cambray was of more worth than his chambermaid, and there are few of us that would hesitate to pronounce, if his palace were in flames, and the life of only one of them could be preserved, which of the two ought to be preferred.

But there is another ground of preference, beside the private consideration of one of them being farther removed from the state of a mere animal. We are not connected with one or two percipient beings, but with a society, a nation, and in some sense with the whole family of mankind. Of consequence that life ought to be preferred which will be most conducive to the general good. In saving the life of Fenelon, suppose at the moment when he was conceiving the project of his immortal Telemachus, I should be promoting the benefit of thousands, who have been cured by the perusal of it of some error, vice and consequent unhappiness. Nay, my benefit would extend farther than this, for every individual thus cured has become a better member of society, and has contributed in his turn to the happiness, the information and

William Godwin. *An Enquiry Concerning Political Justice*. Chapter 2. 1793.

improvement of others.

Supposing I had been myself the chambermaid, I ought to have chosen to die, rather than that Fenelon should have died. The life of Fenelon was really preferable to that of the chambermaid. But understanding is the faculty that perceives the truth of this and similar propositions; and justice is the principle that regulates my conduct accordingly. It would have been just in the chambermaid to have preferred the archbishop to herself. To have done otherwise would have been a breach of justice.

Supposing the chambermaid had been my wife, my mother or my benefactor. This would not alter the truth of the proposition. The life of Fenelon would still be more valuable that that of the chambermaid; and justice, pure, unadulterated justice, would still have preferred that which was most valuable. Justice would have taught me to save the life of Fenelon at the expence of the other. What magic is there in the pronoun 'my,' to overturn the decisions of everlasting truth? My wife or my mother may be a fool or a prostitute, malicious, lying or dishonest. If they be, of what consequence is it that they are mine?

'But my mother endured for me the pains of child bearing, and nourished me in the helplessness of infancy.' When she first subjected herself to the necessity of these cares, she was probably influenced by no particular motives of benevolence to her future offspring. Every voluntary benefit however entitles the bestower to some kindness and retribution. But why so? Because a voluntary benefit is an evidence of benevolent intention, that is, of virtue. It is the disposition of the mind, not the external action, that entitles to respect. But the merit of this disposition is equal, whether the benefit was conferred upon me or upon another. I and another man cannot both be right in preferring {84} our own individual benefactor, for no man can be at the same time both better and worse than his neighbour. My benefactor ought to be esteemed, not because he bestowed a benefit upon me, but because he bestowed it upon a human being. His desert will be in exact proportion to the degree, in which that human being was worthy of the distinction conferred. Thus every view of the subject brings us back to the consideration of my neighbour's moral worth and his importance to the general weal, as the only standard to determine the treatment to which he is entitled. Gratitude therefore, a principle which has so often been the theme of the moralist and the poet, is no part either of justice or virtue.

2.4

The Problems of Utilitarianism
Henry Sidgwick

The term Utilitarianism is, at the present day, in common use, and is supposed to designate a doctrine or method with which we are all familiar. But on closer examination, it appears to be applied to several distinct theories, having no necessary connexion with one another, and not even referring to the same subject-matter. It will be well, therefore, to define, as carefully as possible, the doctrine that is to be denoted by the term in the present Book: at the same time distinguishing this from other doctrines to which usage would allow the name to be applied, and indicating, so far as seems necessary, its relation to these.

By Utilitarianism is here meant the ethical theory, that the conduct which, under any given circumstances, is objectively right, is that which will produce the greatest amount of happiness on the whole; that is, taking into account all whose happiness is affected by the conduct. It would tend to clearness if we might call this principle, and the method based upon it, by some such name as ``Universalistic Hedonism''; and I have therefore sometimes ventured to use this term, in spite of its cumbrousness.

The first doctrine from which it seems necessary to distinguish this, is the Egoistic Hedonism....The difference, however, between the propositions (1) that each ought to seek his own happiness, and (2) that each ought to seek the happiness of all, is so obvious and glaring, that instead of dwelling upon it we seem rather called upon to explain how the two ever came to be confounded, or in any way included under one notion. This question and the general relation between the two doctrines were briefly discussed in a former chapter. Among other points it was there noticed that the confusion between these two ethical theories was partly assisted by the confusion with both of the psychological theory that in voluntary actions every agent does, universally or normally, seek his own

Henry Sidgwick. *The Method of Ethics*. Book 4, Chapter 1. London: Macmillan, 1907.

individual happiness or pleasure. Now there seems to be no *necessary* connection between this latter proposition and any ethical theory: but in so far as there is a natural tendency to pass from psychological to ethical Hedonism, the transition must be—at least primarily—to the Egoistic phase of the latter. For clearly, from the fact that every one actually does seek his own happiness we cannot conclude, as an immediate and obvious inference, that he ought to seek the happiness of other people.

Nor, again, is Utilitarianism, as an ethical doctrine, necessarily connected with the psychological theory that the moral sentiments are derived, by ``association of ideas'' or otherwise, from experiences of the non-moral pleasures and pains resulting to the agent or to others from different kinds of conduct. An Intuitionist might accept this theory, so far as it is capable of scientific proof, and still hold that these moral sentiments, being found in our present consciousness as independent impulses, ought to possess the authority that they seem to claim over the more primary desires and aversions from which they have sprung: and an Egoist on the other hand might fully admit the altruistic element of the derivation, and still hold that these and all other impulses (including even Universal Benevolence) are properly under the rule of Rational Self-love: and that it is really only reasonable to gratify them in so far as we may expect to find our private happiness in such gratification. In short, what is often called the "utilitarian" theory of the origin of the moral sentiments cannot by itself provide a proof of the ethical doctrine to which I in this treatise restrict the term Utilitarianism....

Finally, the doctrine that Universal Happiness is the ultimate *standard* must not be understood to imply that Universal Benevolence is the only right or always best *motive* of action. For, as we have before observed, it is not necessary that the end which gives the criterion of rightness should always be the end at which we consciously aim: and if experience shows that the general happiness will be more satisfactorily attained if men frequently act from other motives than pure universal philanthropy, it is obvious that these other motives are reasonably to be preferred on Utilitarian principles.

Let us now examine the principle itself somewhat closer....We shall understand, then, that by Greatest Happiness is meant the greatest possible surplus of pleasure over pain, the pain being conceived as balanced against an equal amount of pleasure, so that the two contrasted amounts annihilate each other for purposes of ethical calculation. And of course, here as before, the assumption is involved that all pleasures included in our calculation are capable of being compared quantitatively with one another and with all pains; that every such feeling has a certain intensive quantity, positive or negative (or, perhaps, zero), in respect of its desirableness, and that this quantity may be to some extent known: so that each may be at least roughly weighed in ideal scales against any other. This assumption is involved in the very notion of Maximum Happiness; as the attempt to make `as great as possible' a sum of elements not quantitatively commensurable would be a mathematical absurdity. Therefore whatever weight is to be attached to the objections brought against this assumption (which was discussed in chap. iii. of Book ii.) must of course tell against the present method.

We have next to consider who the ``all'' are, whose happiness is to be taken into account. Are we to extend our concern to all the beings capable of pleasure and pain whose feelings are affected by our conduct? or are we to confine our view to human happiness? The former view is the one adopted by Bentham and Mill, and (I believe) by the Utilitarian school generally: and is obviously most in accordance with the universality that is characteristic of their principle. It is the Good *Universal*, interpreted and defined as `happiness' or `pleasure,' at which a Utilitarian considers it his duty to aim: and it seems arbitrary and unreasonable to exclude from the end, as so conceived, any pleasure of any sentient being.

It may be said that by giving this extension to the notion, we considerably increase the scientific difficulties of the hedonistic comparison...: for if it be difficult to compare the pleasures and pains of other men accurately with our own, a comparison of either with the pleasures and pains of brutes is obviously still more obscure. Still, the difficulty is at least not greater for Utilitarians than it is for any other moralists who recoil from the paradox of disregarding altogether the pleasures and pains of brutes. But even if we limit our attention to human beings, the extent of the subjects of happiness is not yet quite determinate. In the first place, it may be asked, How far we are to consider the interests of posterity when they seem to conflict with those of existing human beings? It seems, however, clear that the time at which a man exists cannot affect the value of his happiness from a universal point of view; and that the interests of posterity must concern a Utilitarian as much as those of his contemporaries, except in so far as the effect of his actions on posterity—and even the existence of human beings to be affected— must necessarily be more uncertain. But a further question arises when we consider that we can to some extent influence the number of future human (or sentient) beings. We have to ask how, on Utilitarian principles, this influence is to be exercised. Here I shall assume that, for human beings generally, life on the average yields a positive balance of pleasure over pain. This has been denied by thoughtful persons: but the denial seems to me clearly opposed to the common experience of mankind, as expressed in their commonly accepted principles of action. The great majority of men, in the great majority of conditions under which human life is lived, certainly act as if death were one of the worst of evils, for themselves and for those whom they love: and the administration of criminal justice proceeds on a similar assumption.

Assuming, then, that the average happiness of human beings is a positive quantity, it seems clear that, supposing the average happiness enjoyed remains undiminished, Utilitarianism directs us to make the number enjoying it as great as possible. But if we foresee as possible that an increase in numbers will be accompanied by a decrease in average happiness or *vice versa*, a point arises which has not only never been formally noticed, but which seems to have been substantially overlooked by many Utilitarians. For if we take Utilitarianism to prescribe, as the ultimate end of action, happiness on the whole, and not any individual's happiness, unless considered as an element of the whole, it would follow that, if the additional population enjoy on the whole positive happiness, we ought to weigh the amount of happiness gained by the extra number against the amount lost by the remainder. So that, strictly conceived, the point up to which, on Utilitarian principles, population ought to be encouraged to increase, is not that at which average happiness is the greatest possible, as appears to be often assumed by political economists of the school of Malthus—but that at which the product formed by multiplying the number of persons living into the amount of average happiness reaches its maximum.

It may be well here to make a remark which has a wide application in Utilitarian discussion. The conclusion just given wears a certain air of absurdity to the view of Common Sense; because its show of exactness is grotesquely incongruous with our consciousness of the inevitable inexactness of all such calculations in actual practice. But, that our practical Utilitarian reasonings must necessarily be rough, is no reason for not making them as accurate as the case admits; and we shall be more likely to succeed in this if we keep before our mind as distinctly as possible the strict type of the calculation that we should have to make, if all the relevant considerations could be estimated with mathematical precision.

There is one more point that remains to be noticed. It is evident that there may be many different ways of distributing the same quantum of happiness among the same number of persons; in order, therefore, that the Utilitarian criterion of right conduct may be as complete as possible, we ought to know which of these ways is to be preferred. This question is often ignored in expositions of Utilitarianism. It has perhaps seemed somewhat idle as suggesting a purely abstract and theoretical perplexity, that could have no practical exemplification; and no doubt, if all the consequences of actions were capable of being estimated and summed up with mathematical precision, we should probably never find the excess of pleasure over pain exactly equal in the case of two competing alternatives of conduct. But the very indefiniteness of all hedonistic calculations, which was sufficiently shown in Book ii., renders it by no means unlikely that there may be no cognisable difference between the quantities of happiness involved in two sets of consequences respectively; the more rough our estimates necessarily are, the less likely we shall be to come to any clear decision between two apparently balanced alternatives. In all such cases, therefore, it becomes practically important to ask whether any mode of distributing a given quantum of happiness is better than any other. Now the Utilitarian formula seems to supply no answer to this question: at least we have to supplement the principle of seeking the greatest happiness on the whole by some principle of Just or Right distribution of this happiness. The principle which most Utilitarians have either tacitly or expressly adopted is that of pure equality—as given in Bentham's formula, "everybody to count for one, and nobody for more than one." And this principle seems the only one which does not need a special justification; for, as we saw, it must be reasonable to treat any one man in the same way as any other, if there be no reason apparent for treating him differently.

Foundations of the Metaphysics of Morals

Immanuel Kant

The Good Will

Nothing can possibly be conceived in the world, or even out of it, which can be called good without qualification, except a Good Will. Intelligence, wit, judgment, and the other *talents* of the mind, however they may be named, or courage, resolution, perseverance, as qualities of temperament, are undoubtedly good and desirable in many respects; but these gifts of nature may also become extremely bad and mischievous if the will which is to make use of them, and which, therefore, constitutes what is called *character,* is not good. It is the same with the *gifts of fortune.* Power, riches, honour, even health, and the general well-being and contentment with one's condition which is called *happiness,* inspire pride, and often presumption, if there is not a good will to correct the influence of these on the mind, and with this also to rectify the whole principle of acting, and adapt it to its end. The sight of a being who is not adorned with a single feature of a pure and good will, enjoying unbroken prosperity, can never give pleasure to an impartial rational spectator. Thus a good will appears to constitute the indispensable condition even of being worthy of happiness.

There are even some qualities which are of service to this good will itself, and may facilitate its action, yet which have no intrinsic unconditional value, but always presuppose a good will, and this qualifies the esteem that we justly have for them, and does not permit us to regard them as absolutely good. Moderation in the affections and passions, self-control and calm deliberation are not only good in many respects, but even seem to constitute part of the intrinsic worth of the person; but they are far from deserving to be called good without qualification, although they have been so unconditionally praised by the ancients. For without

Kant's Critique of Practical Reason and Other Works on the Theory of Ethics. Trans. Thomas Kingsmill Abbott. 4th ed. London: Longman, Green, and Co., 1889.

the principles of a good will, they may become extremely bad, and the coolness of a villain not only makes him far more dangerous, but also directly makes him more abominable in our eyes than he would have been without it.

A good will is good not because of what it performs or effects, not by its aptness for the attainment of some proposed end, but simply by virtue of the volition, that is, it is good in itself, and considered by itself is to be esteemed much higher than all that can be brought about by it in favour of any inclination, nay, even of the sum total of all inclinations. Even if it should happen that, owing to special disfavour of fortune, or the nig-gardly provision of a step-motherly nature, this will should wholly lack power to accomplish its purpose, if with its greatest efforts it should yet achieve nothing, and there should remain only the good will (not, to be sure, a mere wish, but the summoning of all means in our power), then, like a jewel, it would still shine by its own light, as a thing which has its whole value in itself....

Duty Vs. Inclination

We have then to develop the notion of a will which deserves to be highly esteemed for itself, and is good without a view to anything further, a no-tion which exists already in the sound natural understanding, requiring rather to be cleared up than to be taught, and which in estimating the value of our actions always takes the first place, and constitutes the con-dition of all the rest. In order to do this we will take the notion of duty, which includes that of a good will, although implying certain subjective restrictions and hindrances. These, however, far from concealing it, or rendering it unrecognisable, rather bring it out by contrast, and make it shine forth so much the brighter.

I omit here all actions which are already recognised as inconsistent with duty, although they may be useful for this or that purpose, for with these the question whether they are done *from duty* cannot arise at all, since they even conflict with it. I also set aside those actions which really conform to duty, but to which men have *no* direct *inclination,* performing them because they are impelled thereto by some other inclination. For in this case we can readily distinguish whether the action which agrees with duty is done *from duty,* or from a selfish view. It is much harder to make this distinction when the action accords with duty, and the subject has besides a *direct* inclination to it. For example, it is always a matter of duty that a dealer should not overcharge an inexperienced purchaser, and wherever there is much commerce the prudent tradesman does not over-charge, but keeps a fixed price for everyone, so that a child buys of him as well as any other. Men are thus *honestly* served; but this is not enough to make us believe that the tradesman has so acted from duty and from principles of honesty: his own advantage required it; it is out of the question in this case to suppose that he might besides have a direct inclination in favour of the buyers, so that, as it were, from love he should give no advantage to one over another. Accordingly the action was done neither from duty nor from direct inclination, but merely with a selfish view.

On the other hand, it is a duty to maintain one's life; and, in addition, every one has also a direct inclination to do so. But on this account the often anxious care which most men take for it has no intrinsic worth, and their maxim has no moral import. They preserve their life *as duty requires,* no doubt, but not *because duty requires.* On the other hand, if adversity and hopeless sorrow have completely taken away the relish for life; if the unfortunate one, strong in mind, indignant at his fate rather than desponding or dejected, wishes for death, and yet preserves his life without loving it—not from inclination or fear, but from duty—then his maxim has a moral worth.

To be beneficent when we can is a duty; and besides this, there are many minds so sympathetically constituted that, without any other motive of vanity or self-interest, they find a pleasure in spreading joy around them, and can take delight in the satisfaction of others so far as it is their own work. But I maintain that in such a case an action of this kind, however proper, however amiable it may be, has nevertheless no true moral worth, but is on a level with other inclinations, *e. g.* the inclination to honour, which, if it is happily directed to that which is in fact of public utility and accordant with duty, and consequently honourable, deserves praise and encouragement, but not esteem. For the maxim lacks the moral import, namely, that such actions be done *from duty,* not from inclination. Put the case that the mind of that philanthropist were clouded by sorrow of his own, extinguishing all sympathy with the lot of others, and that while he still has the power to benefit others in distress, he is not touched by their trouble because he is absorbed with his own; and now suppose that he tears himself out of this dead insensibility, and performs the action without any inclination to it, but simply from duty, then first has his action its genuine moral worth. Further still; if nature has put little sympathy in the heart of this or that man; if he, supposed to be an upright man, is by temperament cold and indifferent to the sufferings of others, perhaps because in respect of his own he is provided with the special gift of patience and fortitude, and supposes, or even requires, that others should have the same—and such a man would certainly not be the meanest product of nature—but if nature had not specially framed him for a philanthropist, would he not still find in himself a source from whence to give himself a far higher worth than that of a good-natured temperament could be? Unquestionably. It is just in this that the moral worth of the character is brought out which is incomparably the highest of all, namely, that he is beneficent, not from inclination, but from duty.

To secure one's own happiness is a duty, at least indirectly; for discontent with one's condition, under a pressure of many anxieties and amidst unsatisfied wants, might easily become a great *temptation to transgression of duty....*

It is in this manner, undoubtedly, that we are to understand those passages of Scripture also in which we are commanded to love our neighbour, even our enemy. For love, as an affection, cannot be commanded, but beneficence for duty's sake may; even though we are not impelled to it by any inclination—nay, are even repelled by a natural and unconquerable aversion. This is *practical* love, and not *pathological*—a love which is seated in the will, and not in the propensions of sense—in principles of action and not of tender sympathy; and it is this love alone which can be commanded.

The second proposition is: That an action done from duty derives its moral worth, *not from the purpose* which is to be attained by it, but from the maxim by which it is determined, and therefore does not depend on the realization of the object of the action, but merely on the *principle of volition* by which the action has taken place, without regard to any object of desire. It is clear from what precedes that the purposes which we may have in view in our actions, or their effects regarded as ends and springs of the will, cannot give to actions any unconditional or moral worth. In what, then, can their worth lie, if it is not to consist in the will and in reference to its expected effect? It cannot lie anywhere but in the *principle of the will* without regard to the ends which can be attained by the action. For the will stands between its *à priori* principle, which is formal, and its *à posteriori* spring, which is material, as between two roads, and as it must be determined by something, it follows that it must be determined by the formal principle of volition when an action is done from duty, in which case every material principle has been withdrawn from it.

Respect for the Moral Law

The third proposition, which is a consequence of the two preceding, I would express thus: *Duty is the necessity of acting from respect for the law.* I may have *inclination* for an object as the effect of my proposed action, but I cannot have *respect* for it, just for this reason, that it is an effect and not an energy of will. Similarly, I cannot have respect for inclination, whether my own or another's; I can at most, if my own, approve it; if another's, sometimes even love it; *i. e.* look on it as favourable to my own interest. It is only what is connected with my will as a principle, by no means as an effect—what does not subserve my inclination, but overpowers it, or at least in case of choice excludes it from its calculation—in other words, simply the law of itself, which can be an object of respect, and hence a command. Now an action done from duty must wholly exclude the influence of inclination, and with it every object of the will, so that nothing remains which can determine the will except objectively the *law,* and subjectively *pure respect* for this practical law, and consequently the maxim that I should follow this law even to the thwarting of all my inclinations.

Thus the moral worth of an action does not lie in the effect expected from it, nor in any principle of action which requires to borrow its motive from this expected effect. For all these effects—agreeableness of one's condition, and even the promotion of the happiness of others—could have been also brought about by other causes, so that for this there would have been no need of the will of a rational being; whereas it is in this alone that the supreme and unconditional good can be found. The preeminent good which we call moral can therefore consist in nothing else than *the conception of law* in itself, *which certainly is only possible in a rational being,* in so far as this conception, and not the expected effect, determines the will. This is a good which is already present in the person who acts accordingly, and we have not to wait for it to appear first in the result.

The Categorical Imperative

But what sort of law can that be, the conception of which must determine the will, even without paying any regard to the effect expected from it, in order that this will may be called good absolutely and without qualification? As I have deprived the will of every impulse which could arise to it from obedience to any law, there remains nothing but the universal conformity of its actions to law in general, which alone is to serve the will as a principle, *i. e.* I am never to act otherwise than so *that I could also will that my maxim should become a universal law.* Here now, it is the simple conformity to law in general, without assuming any particular law applicable to certain actions, that serves the will as its principle, and must so serve it, if duty is not to be a vain delusion and a chimerical notion. The common reason of men in its practical judgments perfectly coincides with this, and always has in view the principle here suggested. Let the question be, for example: May I when in distress make a promise with the intention not to keep it? I readily distinguish here between the two significations which the question may have: Whether it is prudent, or whether it is right, to make a false promise. The former may undoubtedly often be the case. I see clearly indeed that it is not enough to extricate myself from a present difficulty by means of this subterfuge, but it must be well considered whether there may not hereafter spring from this lie much greater inconvenience than that from which I now free myself, and as, with all my supposed *cunning,* the consequences cannot be so easily foreseen but that credit once lost may be much more injurious to me than any mischief which I seek to avoid at present, it should be considered whether it would not be more *prudent* to act herein according to a universal maxim, and to make it a habit to promise nothing except with the intention of keeping it. But it is soon clear to me that such a maxim will still only be based on the fear of consequences. Now it is a wholly different thing to be truthful from duty, and to be so from apprehension of injurious consequences. In the first case, the very notion of the action already implies a law for me; in the second case, I must first look about elsewhere to see what results may be combined with it which would affect myself. For to deviate from the principle of duty is beyond all doubt wicked; but to be unfaithful to my maxim of prudence may often be very advantageous to me, although to abide by it is certainly safer. The shortest way, however, and an unerring one, to discover the answer to this question whether a lying promise is consistent with duty, is to ask myself, Should I be content that my maxim (to extricate myself from difficulty by a false promise) should hold good as a universal law, for myself as well as for others? and should I be able to say to myself, "Every one may make a deceitful promise when he finds himself in a difficulty from which he cannot otherwise extricate himself"? Then I presently become aware that while I can will the lie, I can by no means will that lying should be a universal law. For with such a law there would be no promises at all, since it would be in vain to allege my intention in regard to my future actions to those who would not believe this allegation, or if they over-hastily did so would pay me back in my own coin. Hence my maxim, as soon as it should be made a universal law, would necessarily destory itself.

I do not, therefore, need any far-reaching penetration to discern what I have to do in order that my will may be morally good. Inexperienced in the course of the world, incapable of being prepared for all its contingencies, I only ask myself: Canst thou also will that thy maxim should be a universal law? If not, then it must be rejected, and that not because of a disadvantage accruing from it to myself or even to others, but because it cannot enter as a principle into a possible universal legislation, and reason extorts from me immediate respect for such legislation. I do not indeed as yet *discern* on what this respect is based (this the philosopher may inquire), but at least I understand this, that it is an estimation of the worth which far outweighs all worth of what is recommended by inclination, and that the necessity of acting from *pure* respect for the practical law is what constitutes duty, to which every other motive must give place, because it is the condition of a will being good *in itself,* and the worth of such a will is above everything.

Thus then, without quitting the moral knowledge of common human reason, we have arrived at its principle. And although no doubt common men do not conceive it in such an abstract and universal form, yet they always have it really before their eyes, and use it as the standard of their decision....

Hypothetical and Categorical Imperatives

Everything in nature works according to laws. Rational beings alone have the faculty of acting according *to the conception* of laws, that is according to principles, *i. e.* have a *will.* Since the deduction of actions from principles requires *reason,* the will is nothing but practical reason. If reason infallibly determines the will, then the actions of such a being which are recognised as objectively necessary are subjectively necessary also, *i. e.* the will is a faculty to choose *that only* which reason independent on inclination recognises as practically necessary, *i. e.* as good. But if reason of itself does not sufficiently determine the will, if the latter is subject also to subjective conditions (particular impulses) which do not always coincide with the objective conditions; in a word, if the will does not *in itself* completely accord with reason (which is actually the case with men), then the actions which objectively are recognised as necessary are subjectively contingent, and the determination of such a will according to objective laws is *obligation,* that is to say, the relation of the objective laws to a will that is not thoroughly good is conceived as the determination of the will of a rational being by principles of reason, but which the will from its nature does not of necessity follow.

The conception of an objective principle, in so far as it is obligatory for a will, is called a command (of reason), and the formula of the command is called an Imperative.

All imperatives are expressed by the word *ought* [or *shall*], and thereby indicate the relation of an objective law of reason to a will, which from its subjective constitution is not necessarily determined by it (an obligation). They say that something would be good to do or to forbear, but they say it to a will which does not always do a thing because it is conceived to be good to do it. That is practically *good,* however, which determines the will by means of the conceptions of reason, and consequently not from subjective causes, but objectively, that is on principles which are valid for every rational being as such. It is distinguished from the *pleasant,* as that which influences the will only by means of sensation from merely subjective causes, valid only for the sense of this or that one, and not as a principle of reason, which holds for every one.

A perfectly good will would therefore be equally subject to objective laws (viz. laws of good), but could not be conceived as *obliged* thereby to act lawfully, because of itself from its subjective constitution it can only be determined by the conception of good. Therefore no imperatives hold for the Divine will, or in general for a *holy* will; *ought* is here out of place, because the volition is already of itself necessarily in unison with the law. Therefore imperatives are only formulæ to express the relation of objective laws of all volition to the subjective imperfection of the will of this or that rational being, *e.g.* the human will.

Now all *imperatives* command either *hypothetically* or *categorically.* The former represent the practical necessity of a possible action as means to something else that is willed (or at least which one might possibly will). The categorical imperative would be that which represented an action as necessary of itself without reference to another end, *i.e.* as objectively necessary.

Since every practical law represents a possible action as good, and on this account, for a subject who is practically determinable by reason, necessary, all imperatives are formulæ determining an action which is necessary according to the principle of a will good in some respects. If now the action is good only as a means *to something else,* then the imperative is *hypothetical;* if it is conceived as good *in itself* and consequently as being necessarily the principle of a will which of itself conforms to reason, then it is *categorical.*

Thus the imperative declares what action possible by me would be good, and presents the practical rule in relation to a will which does not forthwith perform an action simply because it is good, whether because the subject does not always know that it is good, or because, even if it know this, yet its maxims might be opposed to the objective principles of practical reason.

Accordingly the hypothetical imperative only says that the action is good for some purpose, *possible* or *actual.* In the first case it is a Problematical, in the second an Assertorial practical principle. The categorical imperative which declares an action to be objectively necessary in itself without reference to any purpose, *i.e.* without any other end, is valid as an Apodictic (practical) principle.

Whatever is possible only by the power of some rational being may also be conceived as a possible purpose of some will; and therefore the principles of action as regards the means necessary to attain some possible purpose are in fact infinitely numerous. All sciences have a practical part, consisting of problems expressing that some end is possible for us, and of imperatives directing how it may be attained. These may, therefore, be called in general imperatives of Skill. Here there is no question whether the end is rational and good, but only what one must do in order to attain it. The precepts for the physician to make his patient thoroughly healthy, and for a poisoner to ensure certain death, are of equal value in this respect, that each serves to effect its purpose perfectly. Since in early youth it cannot be known what ends are likely to occur to us in the course of life, parents seek to have their children taught a *great many things,* and provide for their *skill* in the use of means for all sorts of arbitrary ends, of none of which can they determine whether it may not perhaps hereafter be an object to their pupil, but which it is at all events *possible* that he might aim at; and this anxiety is so great that they commonly neglect to form and correct their judgment on the value of the things which may be chosen as ends.

There is *one* end, however, which may be assumed to be actually such to all rational beings (so far as imperatives apply to them, viz. as dependent beings), and therefore, one purpose which they not merely *may* have, but which we may with certainty assume that they all actually *have* by a natural necessity, and this is *happiness.* The hypothetical imperative which expresses the practical necessity of an action as means to the advancement of happiness is Assertorial. We are not to present it as necessary for an uncertain and merely possible purpose, but for a purpose which we may presuppose with certainty and *à priori* in every man, because it belongs to his being. Now skill in the choice of means to his own greatest well-being may be called *prudence,* in the narrowest sense. And thus the imperative which refers to the choice of means to one's own happiness, *i. e.* the precept of prudence, is still always *hypothetical;* the action is not commanded absolutely, but only as means to another purpose.

Finally, there is an imperative which commands a certain conduct immediately, without having as its condition any other purpose to be attained by it. This imperative is Categorical. It concerns not the matter of the action, or its intended result, but its form and the principle of which it is itself a result; and what is essentially good in it consists in the mental disposition, let the consequence be what it may. This imperative may be called that of Morality.

There is a marked distinction also between the volitions on these three sorts of principles in the *dissimilarity* of the obligation of the will.

In order to mark this difference more clearly, I think they would be most suitably named in their order if we said they are either *rules* of skill, or *counsels* of prudence, or *commands* (*laws*) of morality. For it is *law* only that involves the conception of an *unconditional* and objective necessity, which is consequently universally valid; and commands are laws which must be obeyed, that is, must be followed, even in opposition to inclination. *Counsels,* indeed, involve necessity, but one which can only hold under a contingent subjective condition, viz. they depend on whether this or that man reckons this or that as part of his happiness; the categorical imperative, on the contrary, is not limited by any condition, and as being absolutely, although practically, necessary, may be quite properly called a command. We might also call the first kind of imperatives *technical* (belonging to art), the second *pragmatic* (to welfare), the third *moral* (belonging to free conduct generally, that is, to morals).

Now arises the question, how are all these imperatives possible? This question does not seek to know how we can conceive the accomplishment of the action which the imperative ordains, but merely how we can conceive the obligation of the will which the imperative expresses. No special explanation is needed to show how an imperative of skill is possible. Whoever wills the end, wills also (so far as reason decides his conduct) the means in his power which are indispensably necessary thereto....

We shall therefore have to investigate *à priori* the possibility of a categorical imperative, as we have not in this case the advantage of its reality being given in experience, so that [the elucidation of] its possibility should be requisite only for its explanation, not for its establishment. In the meantime it may be discerned beforehand that the categorical imperative alone has the purport of a practical law: all the rest may indeed be called *principles* of the will but not laws, since whatever is only necessary for the attainment of some arbitrary purpose may be considered as in itself contingent, and we can at any time be free from the precept if we give up the purpose: on the contrary, the unconditional command leaves the will no liberty to choose the opposite; consequently it alone carries with it that necessity which we require in a law.

Secondly, in the case of this categorical imperative or law of morality, the difficulty (of discerning its possibility) is a very profound one. It is an *à priori* synthetical practical proposition; and as there is so much difficulty in discerning the possibility of speculative propositions of this kind, it may readily be supposed that the difficulty will be no less with the practical.

In this problem we will first inquire whether the mere conception of a categorical imperative may not perhaps supply us also with the formula

of it, containing the proposition which alone can be a categorical imperative; for even if we know the tenor of such an absolute command, yet
how it is possible will require further special and laborious study, which
we postpone to the last section.

When I conceive a hypothetical imperative in general I do not know
beforehand what it will contain until I am given the condition. But when
I conceive a categorical imperative I know at once what it contains. For
as the imperative contains besides the law only the necessity that the
maxims shall conform to this law, while the law contains no conditions
restricting it, there remains nothing but the general statement that the
maxim of the action should conform to a universal law, and it is this
conformity alone that the imperative properly represents as necessary.

First Formulation of the Categorical Imperative

There is therefore but one categorical imperative, namely this: *Act only
on that maxim whereby thou canst at the same time will that it should
become a universal law.*

Now if all imperatives of duty can be deduced from this one imperative as from their principle, then, although it should remain undecided
whether what is called duty is not merely a vain notion, yet at least we
shall be able to show what we understand by it and what this notion
means.

Since the universality of the law according to which effects are produced constitutes what is properly called *nature* in the most general
sense (as to form), that is the existence of things so far as it is determined
by general laws, the imperative of duty may be expressed thus: *Act as if
the maxim of thy action were to become by thy will a Universal Law of
Nature.*

We will now enumerate a few duties, adopting the usual division of
them into duties to ourselves and to others, and into perfect and imperfect duties.

1. A man reduced to despair by a series of misfortunes feels wearied of life, but is still so far in possession of his reason that he can ask
himself whether it would not be contrary to his duty to himself to take
his own life. Now he inquires whether the maxim of his action could
become a universal law of nature. His maxim is: From self-love I adopt it
as a principle to shorten my life when its longer duration is likely to bring
more evil than satisfaction. It is asked then simply whether this principle
founded on self-love can become a universal law of nature. Now we see
at once that a system of nature of which it should be a law to destroy
life by means of the very feeling whose special nature it is to impel to

the improvement of life would contradict itself, and therefore could not exist as a system of nature; hence that maxim cannot possibly exist as a universal law of nature, and consequently would be wholly inconsistent with the supreme principle of all duty.

2. Another finds himself forced by necessity to borrow money. He knows that he will not be able to repay it, but sees also that nothing will be lent to him, unless he promises stoutly to repay it in a definite time. He desires to make this promise, but he has still so much conscience as to ask himself: Is it not unlawful and inconsistent with duty to get out of a difficulty in this way? Suppose however that he resolves to do so, then the maxim of his action would be expressed thus: When I think myself in want of money, I will borrow money and promise to repay it, although I know that I never can do so. Now this principle of self-love or of one's own advantage may perhaps be consistent with my whole future welfare; but the question now is, Is it right? I change then the suggestion of self-love into a universal law, and state the question thus: How would it be if my maxim were a universal law? Then I see at once that it could never hold as a universal law of nature, but would necessarily contradict itself. For supposing it to be a universal law that everyone when he thinks himself in a difficulty should be able to promise whatever he pleases, with the purpose of not keeping his promise, the promise itself would become impossible, as well as the end that one might have in view in it, since no one would consider that anything was promised to him, but would ridicule all such statements as vain pretences.

3. A third finds in himself a talent which with the help of some culture might make him a useful man in many respects. But he finds himself in comfortable circumstances, and prefers to indulge in pleasure rather than to take pains in enlarging and improving his happy natural capacities. He asks, however, whether his maxim of neglect of his natural gifts, besides agreeing with his inclination to indulgence, agrees also with what is called duty. He sees then that a system of nature could indeed subsist with such a universal law although men (like the South Sea islanders) should let their talents rust, and resolve to devote their lives merely to idleness, amusement, and propagation of their species—in a word, to enjoyment; but he cannot possibly *will* that this should be a universal law of nature, or be implanted in us as such by a natural instinct. For, as a rational being, he necessarily wills that his faculties be developed, since they serve him, and have been given him, for all sorts of possible purposes.

4. A fourth, who is in prosperity, while he sees that others have to contend with great wretchedness and that he could help them, thinks: What concern is it of mine? Let everyone be as happy as heaven pleases,

or as he can make himself; I will take nothing from him nor even envy him, only I do not wish to contribute anything to his welfare or to his assistance in distress! Now no doubt if such a mode of thinking were a universal law, the human race might very well subsist, and doubtless even better than in a state in which everyone talks of sympathy and good-will, or even takes care occasionally to put it into practice, but on the other side, also cheats when he can, betrays the rights of men, or otherwise violates them. But although it is possible that a universal law of nature might exist in accordance with that maxim, it is impossible to *will* that such a principle should have the universal validity of a law of nature. For a will which resolved this would contradict itself, inasmuch as many cases might occur in which one would have need of the love and sympathy of others, and in which, by such a law of nature, sprung from his own will, he would deprive himself of all hope of the aid he desires.

These are a few of the many actual duties, or at least what we regard as such, which obviously fall into two classes on the one principle that we have laid down. We must be *able to will* that a maxim of our action should be a universal law. This is the canon of the moral appreciation of the action generally. Some actions are of such a character that their maxim cannot without contradiction be even *conceived* as a universal law of nature, far from it being possible that we should *will* that it *should* be so. In others this intrinsic impossibility is not found, but still it is impossible to *will* that their maxim should be raised to the universality of a law of nature, since such a will would contradict itself. It is easily seen that the former violate strict or rigorous (inflexible) duty; the latter only laxer (meritorious) duty. Thus it has been completely shown by these examples how all duties depend as regards the nature of the obligation (not the object of the action) on the same principle....

Second Formulation of the Categorical Imperative

The will is conceived as a faculty of determining oneself to action *in accordance with the conception of certain laws.* And such a faculty can be found only in rational beings. Now that which serves the will as the objective ground of its self-determination is the *end,* and if this is assigned by reason alone, it must hold for all rational beings. On the other hand, that which merely contains the ground of possibility of the action of which the effect is the end, this is called the *means....*

The ends which a rational being proposes to himself at pleasure as *effects* of his actions (material ends) are all only relative, for it is only their relation to the particular desires of the subject that gives them their worth, which therefore cannot furnish principles universal and necessary for all rational beings and for every volition, that is to say practical laws. Hence all these relative ends can give rise only to hypothetical imperatives.

Supposing, however, that there were something *whose existence* has *in itself* an absolute worth, something which, being *an end in itself,* could be a source of definite laws, then in this and this alone would lie the source of a possible categorical imperative, *i.e.* a practical law.

Now I say: man and generally any rational being *exists* as an end in himself, *not merely as a means* to be arbitrarily used by this or that will, but in all his actions, whether they concern himself or other rational beings, must be always regarded at the same time as an end. All objects of the inclinations have only a conditional worth, for if the inclinations and the wants founded on them did not exist, then their object would be without value. But the inclinations themselves being sources of want, are so far from having an absolute worth for which they should be desired, that on the contrary it must be the universal wish of every rational being to be wholly free from them. Thus the worth of any object which is *to be acquired* by our action is always conditional. Beings whose existence depends not on our will but on nature's, have nevertheless, if they are irrational beings, only a relative value as means, and are therefore called *things;* rational beings, on the contrary, are called *persons,* because their very nature points them out as ends in themselves, that is as something which must not be used merely as means, and so far therefore restricts freedom of action (and is an object of respect). These, therefore, are not merely subjective ends whose existence has a worth *for us* as an effect of our action, but *objective ends,* that is things whose existence is an end in itself: an end moreover for which no other can be substituted, which they should subserve *merely* as means, for otherwise nothing whatever would possess *absolute worth;* but if all worth were conditioned and therefore contingent, then there would be no supreme practical principle of reason whatever.

If then there is a supreme practical principle or, in respect of the human will, a categorical imperative, it must be one which (57), being drawn from the conception of that which is necessarily an end for every one because it is *an end in itself,* constitutes an *objective* principle of will, and can therefore serve as a universal practical law. The foundation of this principle is: *rational nature exists as an end in itself.* Man necessarily conceives his own existence as being so: so far then this is a *subjective* principle of human actions. But every other rational being regards its existence similarly, just on the same rational principle that holds for me: so that it is at the same time an objective principle, from which as a supreme practical law all laws of the will must be capable of being deduced. Accordingly the practical imperative will be as follows: *So act as to treat humanity, whether in thine own person or in that of any other, in every case as an end withal, never as means only.* We will now inquire whether this can be practically carried out.

To abide by the previous examples:

Firstly, under the head of necessary duty to oneself: He who contemplates suicide should ask himself whether his action can be consistent with the idea of humanity *as an end in itself.* If he destroys himself in order to escape from painful circumstances, he uses a person merely as *a mean* to maintain a tolerable condition up to the end of life. But a man is not a thing, that is to say, something which can be used merely as means, but must in all his actions be always considered as an end in himself. I cannot, therefore, dispose in any way of a man in my own person so as to mutilate him, to damage or kill him. (It belongs to ethics proper to define this principle more precisely so as to avoid all misunderstanding, *e.g.* as to the amputation of the limbs in order to preserve myself; as to exposing my life to danger with a view to preserve it, &c. This question is therefore omitted here.)

Secondly, as regards necessary duties, or those of strict obligation, towards others; he who is thinking of making a lying promise to others will see at once that he would be using another man *merely as a mean,* without the latter containing at the same time the end in himself. For he whom I propose by such a promise to use for my own purposes cannot possibly assent to my mode of acting towards him, and therefore cannot himself contain the end of this action. This violation of the principle of humanity in other men is more obvious if we take in examples of attacks on the freedom and property of others. For then it is clear that he who transgresses the rights of men, intends to use the person of others merely as means, without considering that as rational beings they ought always to be esteemed also as ends, that is, as beings who must be capable of containing in themselves the end of the very same action.

Thirdly, as regards contingent (meritorious) duties to oneself; is not enough that the action does not violate humanity in our own person as an end in itself, it must also *harmonise with* it. Now there are in humanity capacities of greater perfection, which belong to the end that nature has in view in regard to humanity in ourselves as the subject: to neglect these might perhaps be consistent with the *maintenance* of humanity as an end in itself, but not with the *advancement* of this end.

Fourthly, as regards meritorious duties towards others: the natural end which all men have is their own happiness. Now humanity might indeed subsist, although no one should contribute anything to the happiness of others, provided he did not intentionally withdraw anything from it; but after all this would only harmonise negatively not positively with *humanity as an end in itself,* if every one does not also endeavour, as far as in him lies, to forward the ends of others. For the ends of any subject which is an end in himself, ought as far as possible to be *my* ends also, if that conception is to have its *full* effect with me.

On the Supposed Right to Lie
From Benevolent Motives
Immanuel Kant

In the work called *France,* for the year 1797, Part VI. No. 1, on Political Reactions, by *Benjamin Constant,* the following passage occurs, p. 123:—

"The moral principle that it is one's duty to speak the truth, if it were taken singly and unconditionally, would make all society impossible. We have the proof of this in the very direct consequences which have been drawn from this principle by a German philosopher, who goes so far as to affirm that to tell a falsehood to a murderer who asked us whether our friend, of whom he was in pursuit, had not taken refuge in our house, would be a crime."

The French philosopher opposes this principle in the following manner—

"It is a duty to tell the truth. The notion of duty is inseparable from the notion of right. A duty is what in one being corresponds to the right of another. Where there are no rights there are no duties. To tell the truth then is a duty, but only towards him who has a right to the truth. But no man has a right to a truth that injures others." The πρω˜τον ψευˆδος here lies in the statement that *"To tell the truth is a duty, but only towards him who has a right to the truth."*

It is to be remarked, first, that the expression "to have a right to the truth" is unmeaning. We should rather say, a man has a right to his own *truthfulness* (*veracitas*), that is, to subjective truth in his own person. For

Immauel Kant. *Critique of Practical Reason and Other Works on the Theory of Ethics,* 4th ed. Trans. Thomas Kingsmill Abbott. London: Kongmans, Green and Co., 1889.

to have a right objectively to truth would mean that, as in *meum* and *tuum* generally, it depends on his *will* whether a given statement shall be true or false, which would produce a singular logic.

Now, the *first* question is whether a man—in cases where he cannot avoid answering Yes or No—has the *right* to be untruthful. The *second* question is whether, in order to prevent a misdeed that threatens him or some one else, he is not actually bound to be untruthful in a certain statement to which an unjust compulsion forces him.

Truth in utterances that cannot be avoided is the formal duty of a man to everyone, however great the disadvantage that may arise from it to him or any other; and although by making a false statement I do no wrong to him who unjustly compels me to speak, yet I do wrong to men in general in the most essential point of duty, so that it may be called a lie (though not in the jurist's sense), that is, so far as in me lies I cause that declarations in general find no credit, and hence that all rights founded on contract should lose their force; and this is a wrong which is done to mankind.

If, then, we define a lie merely as an intentionally false declaration towards another man, we need not add that it must injure another; as the jurists think proper to put in their definition (*mendacium est falsiloquium in præjudicium alterius*). For it always injures another; if not another individual, yet mankind generally, since it vitiates the source of justice. This benevolent lie *may*, however, by *accident* (*casus*) become punishable even by civil laws; and that which escapes liability to punishment only by accident may be condemned as a wrong even by external laws. For instance, if you have *by a lie* hindered a man who is even now planning a murder, you are legally responsible for all the consequences. But if you have strictly adhered to the truth, public justice can find no fault with you, be the unforeseen consequence what it may. It is possible that whilst you have honestly answered Yes to the murderer's question, whether his intended victim is in the house, the latter may have gone out unobserved, and so not have come in the way of the murderer, and the deed therefore have not been done; whereas, if you lied and said he was not in the house, and he had really gone out (though unknown to you) so that the murderer met him as he went, and executed his purpose on him, then you might with justice be accused as the cause of his death. For, if you had spoken the truth as well as you knew it, perhaps the murderer while seeking for his enemy in the house might have been caught by neighbours coming up and the deed been prevented. Whoever then *tells a lie,* however good his intentions may be, must answer for the consequences of it, even before the civil tribunal, and must pay the penalty for them, however unforeseen they may have been; because truthfulness is a duty that must be regarded as the basis of all duties founded on contract, the laws of which would be rendered uncertain and useless if even the least exception to them were admitted.

To be *truthful* (honest) in all declarations is therefore a sacred unconditional command of reason, and not to be limited by any expediency.

Critique of Kantian Ethics
G. E. Moore

T he fallacy of supposing moral law to be analogous to natural law in respect of asserting that some action is one which is always necessarily done is contained in one of the most famous doctrines of Kant. Kant identifies what ought to be with the law according to which a Free or Pure Will *must* act—with the only kind of action which is possible for it. And by this identification he does not mean merely to assert that Free Will is *also* under the necessity of doing what it ought; he means that what it ought to do *means* nothing but its own law—the law according to which it must act. It differs from the human will just in that, what *we* ought to do, is what *it* necessarily does. It is "autonomous"; and by this is meant (among other things) that there is no separate standard by which it can be judged: that the question "Is the law by which this Will acts a good one?" is, in its case, meaningless. It follows that what is necessarily willed by this Pure Will is good, not *because* that Will is good, nor for any other reason; but merely because it is what is necessarily willed by a Pure Will.

Kant's assertion of the "Autonomy of the Practical Reason" thus has the very opposite effect to that which he desired; it makes his Ethics ultimately and hopelessly "heteronomous." His Moral Law is "independent" of Metaphysics only in the sense that according to him we can *know* it independently; he holds that we can only infer that there is Freedom, from the fact that the Moral Law is true. And so far as he keeps strictly to this view, he does avoid the error, into which most metaphysical writers fall, of allowing his opinions as to what is real to influence his judgments of what is good. But he fails to see that on his view the Moral Law is dependent upon Freedom in a far more important sense than that in which Freedom depends on the Moral Law. He admits that Freedom is the *ratio essendi* of the Moral Law, whereas the latter is only the *ratio cognoscendi* of Freedom. And this means that, unless

G.E. Moore. *Principia Ethica.* Chapter 4. Cambridge: Cambridge University Press, 1903.

Reality be such as he says, no assertion that "This is good" can possibly be true: it can indeed have no meaning. He has, therefore, furnished his opponents with a conclusive method of attacking the validity of the Moral Law. If they can only show by some other means (which he denies to be possible but leaves theoretically open) that the nature of Reality is not such as he says, he cannot deny that they will have proved his ethical principle to be false. If what "This ought be done" *means* "This is willed by a Free Will," then, if it can be shewn that there is no Free Will which wills anything, it will follow that nothing ought to be done.

76. And Kant also commits the fallacy of supposing that "This ought to be" means "This is commanded." He conceives the Moral Law to be an Imperative. And this is a very common mistake. "This ought to be," it is assumed, must mean "This is commanded"; nothing, therefore, would be good unless it were commanded; and since commands in this world are liable to be erroneous, what ought to be in its ultimate sense means "what is commanded by some real supersensible authority." With regard to this authority it is, then, no longer possible to ask "Is it righteous?" Its commands cannot fail to be right, because to be right means to be what it commands. Here, therefore, law, in the moral sense, is supposed to be analogous to law, in the legal sense, rather than, as in the last instance, to law in the natural sense. It is supposed that moral obligation is analogous to legal obligation, with this difference only that whereas the source of legal obligation is earthly, that of moral obligation is heavenly. Yet it is obvious that if by a source of obligation is meant only a power which binds you or compels you to do a thing, it is not because it does do this that you ought to obey it. It is only if it be itself so good, that it commands and enforces only what is good, that it can be a source of moral obligation. And in that case what it commands and enforces would be good, whether commanded and enforced or not. Just that which makes an obligation legal, namely the fact that it is commanded by a certain kind of authority, is entirely irrelevant to moral obligation. However an authority be defined, its commands will be *morally* binding only if they are—morally binding; only if they tell us what ought to be or what is a means to that which ought to be.

77. In this last error, in the supposition that when I say "You ought to do this" I must mean "You are commanded to do this," we have one of the reasons which has led to the supposition that the particular supersensible property by reference to which good must be defined is Will. And that ethical conclusion may be obtained by enquiring into the nature of a fundamentally real Will seems to be by far the commonest assumption of Metaphysical Ethics at the present day. But this assumption seems to owe its plausibility, not so much to the supposition that "ought" expresses a

"command," as to a far more fundamental error. This error consists in supposing that to ascribe certain predicates to a thing is the same thing as to say that that thing is the object of a certain kind of psychical state. It is supposed that to say that a thing is real or true is the same thing as to say that it is known in a certain way; and that the difference between the assertion that it is good and the assertion that it is real—between an ethical, therefore, and a metaphysical proposition—*consists* in the fact that whereas the latter asserts its relation to Cognition the former asserts its relation to Will.

Now that this is an error has been already shown….That the assertion "This is good" is *not* identical with the assertion "This is willed," either by a supersensible will, or otherwise, nor with any other proposition, has been proved; nor can I add anything to that proof. But in face of this proof it may be anticipated that two lines of defence may be taken up. (1) It may be maintained that, nevertheless, they really are identical, and facts may be pointed out which seem to prove that identity. Or else (2) it may be said that an *absolute* identity is not maintained: that it is only meant to assert that there is some special connection between will and goodness, such as makes an enquiry into the real nature of the former an essential step in the proof of ethical conclusions. In order to meet these two possible objections, I propose first to shew what possible connections there are or may be between goodness and will; and that none of these can justify us in asserting that "This is good" is identical with "This is willed." On the other hand it will appear that some of them may be easily confused with this assertion of identity; and that therefore the confusion is likely to have been made. This part of my argument will, therefore, already go some way towards meeting the second objection. But what must be conclusive against this is to shew that any possible connection between will and goodness *except* the *absolute* identity in question, would not be sufficient to give an enquiry into Will the smallest relevance to the proof of any ethical conclusion.

Second Treatise of Civil Government
John Locke

Chapter 2
Of the State of Nature

4. To understand political power right, and derive it from its original, we must consider, what state all men are naturally in, and that is, a state of perfect freedom to order their actions, and dispose of their possessions and persons, as they think fit, within the bounds of the law of nature, without asking leave, or depending upon the will of any other man.

A state also of equality wherin all the power and jurisdiction is reciprocal, no one having more than another; there being nothing more evident, than that the creatures of the same species and rank, promiscuously born to all the same advantages of nature, and the use of the same faculties, should also be equal one amongst another without subordination or subjection, unless the lord and master of them all should, by any manifest declaration of his will, set one above another, and confer on him, by an evident and clear appointment, an undoubted right to dominion and sovereignty....

6. But though this be a state of liberty, yet it is not a state of licence: though man in that state have an uncontrollable liberty to dispose of his person or possessions, yet he has not liberty to destroy himself, or so much as any creature in his possession, but where some nobler use than its bare preservation calls for it. The state of nature has a law of nature to govern it, which obliges every one: and reason, which is that law, teaches all mankind, who will but consult it, that being all equal and independent, no one ought to harm another in his life, health, liberty, or possessions: for men being all the workmanship of one omnipotent, and infinitely wise maker; all the servants of one sovereign master, sent

---

John Locke. Second Treatise on Civil Government. London: Routledge and Sons, 1887.

into the world by his order, and about his business; they are his property, whose workmanship they are, made to last during his, not one another's pleasure: and being furnished with like faculties, sharing all in one community of nature, there cannot be supposed any such subordination among us, that may authorize us to destroy one another, as if we were made for one another's uses, as the inferior ranks of creatures are for our's. Every one, as he is bound to preserve himself, and not to quit his station willfully, so by the like reason, when his own preservation comes not in competition, ought he, as much as he can, to preserve the rest of mankind, and may not, unless it be to do justice on an offender, take away, or impair the life, or what tends to the preservation of the life, the liberty, health, limb, or goods of another.

7. And that all men may be restrained from invading others rights, and from doing hurt to one another, and the law of nature be observed, which wills the peace and preservation of all mankind, the execution of the law of nature is, in that state, put into every man's hands, whereby everyone has a right to punish the transgressors of that law to such a degree, as may hinder its violation: for the law of nature would, as all other laws that concern men in this world 'be in vain, if there were no body that in the state of nature had a power to execute that law, and thereby preserve the innocent and restrain offenders. And if anyone in the state of nature may punish another for any evil he has done, every one may do so: for in that state of perfect equality, where naturally there is no superiority or jurisdiction of one over another, what any may do in prosecution of that law, everyone must needs have a right to do.

8. And thus, in the state of nature, one man comes by a power over another; but yet no absolute or arbitrary power, to use a criminal, when he has got him in his hands, according to the passionate heats, or boundless extravagancy of his own will; but only to retribute to him, so far as calm reason and conscience dictate, what is proportionate to his transgression, which is so much as may serve for reparation and restraint: for these two are the only reasons, why one man may lawfully do harm to another, which is that we call punishment. In transgressing the law of nature, the offender declares himself to live by another rule than that of reason and common equity, which is that measure God has set to the actions of men, for their mutual security; and so he becomes dangerous to mankind, the tie, which is to secure them from injury and violence, being slighted and broken by him. Which being a trespass against the whole species, and the peace and safety of it, provided for by the law of nature, every man upon this score, by the right he hath to preserve mankind in general, may restrain, or where it is necessary, destroy things noxious to them, and so may bring such evil on any one, who hath transgressed that

law, as may make him repent the doing of it, and thereby deter him, and by his example others, from doing the like mischief. And in the case, and upon this ground, every man hath a right to punish the offender, and be executioner of the law of nature....

10. Besides the crime which consists in violating the law, and varying from the right rule of reason, whereby a man so far becomes degenerate, and declares himself to quit the principles of human nature, and to be a noxious creature, there is commonly injury done to some person or other, and some other man receives damage by his transgression: in which case he who hath received any damage, has, besides the right of punishment common to him with other men, a particular right to seek reparation from him that has done it: and any other person, who finds it just, may also join with him that is injured, and assist him in recovering from the offender so much as may make satisfaction for the harm he has suffered.

11. From these two distinct rights, the one of punishing the crime for restraint, and preventing the like offence, which right of punishing is in everybody; the other of taking reparation, which belongs only to the injured party, comes it to pass that the magistrate, who by being magistrate hath the common right of punishing put into his hands, can often, where the public good demands not the execution of the law, remit the punishment of criminal offences by his own authority, but yet cannot remit the satisfaction due to any private man for the damage he has received. That, he who has suffered the damage has a right to demand in his own name, and he alone can remit: the damnified person has this power of appropriating to himself the goods or service of the offender, by right of self-preservation, as every man has a power to punish the crime, to prevent its being committed again, by the right he has of preserving all mankind, and doing all reasonable things he can in order to that end: and thus it is, that every man, in the state of nature, has a power to kill a murderer, both to deter others from doing the like injury, which no reparation can compensate, by the example of the punishment that attends it from everybody, and also to secure men from the attempts of a criminal, who having renounced reason, the common rule and measure God hath given to mankind, hath, by the unjust violence and slaughter he hath committed upon one, declared war against all mankind, and therefore may be destroyed as a lion or a tiger, one of those wild savage beasts, with whom men can have no society nor security: and upon this is grounded that great law of nature, Whoso sheds man's blood, by man shall his blood be shed. And Cain was so fully convinced, that every one had a right to destroy such a criminal, that after the murder of his brother, he cries out, Everyone that finds me, shall slay me; so plain was it writ in the hearts of all mankind.

12. By the same reason may a man in the state of nature punish the lesser breaches of that law. It will perhaps be demanded, with death? I answer, each transgression may be punished to that degree, and with so much severity, as will suffice to make it an ill bargain to the offender, give him cause to repent, and terrify others from doing the like. Every offence, that can be committed in the state of nature, may in the state of nature be also punished equally, and as far forth as it may, in a common-wealth: for though it would be besides my present purpose, to enter here into the particulars of the law of nature, or its measures of punishment; yet, it is certain there is such a law, and that too, as intelligible and plain to a rational creature, and a studier of that law, as the positive laws of commonwealths; nay, possibly plainer; as much as reason is easier to be understood, than the fancies and intricate contrivances of men, following contrary and hidden interests put into words; for so truly are a great part of the municipal laws of countries, which are only so far right, as they are founded on the law of nature, by which they are to be regulated and interpreted.

13. To this strange doctrine, viz. That in the state of nature everyone has the executive power of the law of nature, I doubt not but it will be objected, that it is unreasonable for men to be judges in their own cases, that self-love will make men partial to themselves and their friends: and on the other side, that ill nature, passion and revenge will carry them too far in punishing others; and hence nothing but confusion and disorder will follow, and that therefore God hath certainly appointed government to restrain the partiality and violence of men. I easily grant, that civil government is the proper remedy for the inconveniencies of the state of nature, which must certainly be great, where men may be judges in their own case, since it is easy to be imagined, that he who was so unjust as to do his brother an injury, will scarce be so just as to condemn himself for it: but I shall desire those who make this objection, to remember, that absolute monarchs are but men; and if government is to be the remedy of those evils, which necessarily follow from men's being judges in their own cases, and the state of nature is therefore not to how much better it is than the state of nature, where one man, commanding a multitude, has the liberty to be judge in his own case, and may do to all his sub-jects whatever he pleases, without the least liberty to anyone to question or control those who execute his pleasure? And in whatsoever he doth, whether led by reason, mistake or passion, must be submitted to? much better it is in the state of nature, wherein men are not bound to submit to the unjust will of another: and if he that judges, judges amiss in his own, or any other case, he is answerable for it to the rest of mankind.

14. It is often asked as a mighty objection, where are, or ever were

there any men in such a state of nature? To which it may suffice as an answer at present, that since all princes and rulers of independent governments all through the world, are in a state of nature, it is plain the world never was, nor ever will be, without numbers of men in that state. I have named all governors of independent communities, whether they are, or are not, in league with others: for it is not every compact that puts an end to the state of nature between men, but only this one of agreeing together mutually to enter into one community, and make one body politic; other promises, and compacts, men may make one with another, and yet still be in the state of nature. The promises and bargains for truck, &c.; between the two men in the desert island, mentioned by Garcilasso de la Vega, in his history of Peru; or between a Swiss and an Indian, in the woods of America, are binding to them, though they are perfectly in a state of nature, in reference to one another: for truth and keeping of faith belongs to men, as men, and not as members of society.

15. To those that say, there were never any men in the state of nature...I...affirm, that all men are naturally in that state, and remain so, till by their own consents they make themselves members of some politic society; and I doubt not in the sequel of this discourse, to make it very clear....

Chapter 3
Of the State of War

16. THE state of war is a state of enmity and destruction: and therefore declaring by word or action, not a passionate and hasty, but a sedate settled design upon another man's life, puts him in a state of war with him against whom he has declared such an intention, and so has exposed his life to the other's power to be taken away by him, or any one that joins with him in his defense, and espouses his quarrel; it being reasonable and just, I should have a right to destroy that which threatens me with destruction: for, by the fundamental law of nature, man being to be preserved as much as possible, when all cannot be preserved, the safety of the innocent is to be preferred: and one may destroy a man who makes war upon him, or has discovered an enmity to his being, for the same reason that he may kill a wolf or a lion; because such men are not under the ties of the common law of reason, have no other rule, but that of force and violence, and so may be treated as beasts of prey, those dangerous and noxious creatures, that will be sure to destroy him whenever he falls into their power.

17. And hence it is, that he who attempts to get another man into his absolute power, does thereby put himself into a state of war with him;

it being to be understood as a declaration of a design upon his life: for I have reason to conclude, that he who would get me into his power without my consent, would use me as he pleased when he had got me there, and destroy me too when he had a fancy to it; for nobody can desire to have me in his absolute power, unless it be to compel me by force to that which is against the right of my freedom, i.e. make me a slave. To be free from such force is the only security of my preservation; and reason bids me look on him, as an enemy to my preservation, who would take away that freedom which is the fence to it; so that he who makes an attempt to enslave me, thereby puts himself into a state of war with me. He that, in the state of nature, would take away the freedom that belongs to any one in that state, must necessarily be supposed to have a design to take away everything else, that freedom being the foundation of all the rest; as he that, in the state of society, would take away the freedom belonging to those of that society or commonwealth, must be supposed to design to take away from them everything else, and so be looked on as in a state of war.

18. This makes it lawful for a man to kill a thief, who has not in the least hurt him, nor declared any design upon his life, any farther than, by the use of force, so to get him in his power, as to take away his money, or what he pleases, from him; because using force, where he has no right, to get me into his power, let his pretence be what it will, I have no reason to suppose, that he, who would take away my liberty, would not, when he had me in his power, take away every thing else. And therefore it is lawful for me to treat him as one who has put himself into a state of war with me, i.e. kill him if I can; for to that hazard does he justly expose himself, whoever introduces a state of war, and is aggressor in it.

19. And here we have the plain difference between the state of nature and the state of war, which however some men have confounded, are as far distant, as a state of peace, good will, mutual assistance and preservation, and a state of enmity, malice, violence and mutual destruction, are one from another. Men living together according to reason, without a common superior on earth, with authority to judge between them, is properly the state of nature. But force, or a declared design of force, upon the person of another, where there is no common superior on earth to appeal to for relief, is the state of war: and it is the want of such an appeal gives a man the right of war even against an aggressor, though he be in society and a fellow subject. Thus a thief, whom I cannot harm, but by appeal to the law, for having stolen all that I am worth, I may kill, when he sets on me to rob me but of my horse or coat; because the law, which was made for my preservation, where it cannot interpose to secure my life from present force, which, if lost, is capable of no reparation, permits

me my own defense, and the right of war, a liberty to kill the aggressor, because the aggressor allows not time to appeal to our common judge, nor the decision of the law, for remedy in a case where the mischief may be irreparable. Want of a common judge with authority, puts all men in a state of nature: force without right, upon a man's person, makes a state of war, both where there is, and is not, a common judge.

20. But when the actual force is over, the state of war ceases between those that are in society, and are equally on both sides subjected to the fair determination of the law; because then there lies open the remedy of appeal for the past injury, and to prevent future harm: but where no such appeal is, as in the state of nature, for want of positive laws, and judges with authority to appeal to, the state of war once begun, continues, with a right to the innocent party to destroy the other whenever he can, until the aggressor offers peace, and desires reconciliation on such terms as may repair any wrongs he has already done, and secure the innocent for the future; nay, where an appeal to the law, and constituted judges, lies open, but the remedy is denied by a manifest perverting of justice, and a barefaced wresting of the laws to protect or indemnify the violence or in-juries of some men, or party of men, there it is hard to imagine anything but a state of war: for wherever violence is used, and injury done, though by hands appointed to administer justice, it is still violence and injury, however coloured with the name, pretences, or forms of law, the end whereof being to protect and redress the innocent, by an unbiassed ap-plication of it, to all who are under it; wherever that is not bona fide done, war is made upon the sufferers, who having no appeal on earth to right them, they are left to the only remedy in such cases, an appeal to heaven.

21. To avoid this state of war (wherein there is no appeal but to heav-en, and wherein every the least difference is apt to end, where there is no authority to decide between the contenders) is one great reason of men's putting themselves into society, and quitting the state of nature: for where there is an authority, a power on earth, from which relief can be had by appeal, there the continuance of the state of war is excluded, and the controversy is decided by that power....

Chapter 5
Of Property

25. Whether we consider natural reason, which tells us, that men, being once born, have a right to their preservation, and consequently to meat and drink, and such other things as nature affords for their subsistence: or revelation, which gives us an account of those grants God made of the world to Adam, and to Noah, and his sons, it is very clear, that God, as

king David says, has given the earth to the children of men; given it to mankind in common....

26. God, who hath given the world to men in common, hath also given them reason to make use of it to the best advantage of life, and convenience. The earth, and all that is therein, is given to men for the support and comfort of their being. And though all the fruits it naturally produces, and beasts it feeds, belong to mankind in common, as they are produced by the spontaneous hand of nature; and no body has originally a private dominion, exclusive of the rest of mankind, in any of them, as they are thus in their natural state: yet being given for the use of men, there must of necessity be a means to appropriate them some way or other, before they can be of any use, or at all beneficial to any particular man. The fruit, or venison, which nourishes the wild Indian, who knows no enclosure, and is still a tenant in common, must be his, and so his, i.e. a part of him, that another can no longer have any right to it, before it can do him any good for the support of his life.

Though the earth, and all inferior creatures, be common to all men, yet every man has a property in his own person: this nobody has any right to but himself. The labour of his body, and the work of his hands, we may say, are properly his. Whatsoever then he removes out of the state that nature hath provided, and left it in, he hath mixed his labour with, and joined to it something that is his own, and thereby makes it his property. It being by him removed from the common state nature hath placed it in, it hath by this labour something annexed to it, that excludes the common right of other men: for this labour being the unquestionable property of the labourer, no man but he can have a right to what that is once joined to, at least where there is enough, and as good, left in common for others.

He that is nourished by the acorns he picked up under an oak, or the apples he gathered from the trees in the wood, has certainly appropriated them to himself. Nobody can deny but the nourishment is his. I ask then, when did they begin to be his? When he digested? Or when he eat? Or when he boiled? Or when he brought them home? or when he picked them up? And it is plain, if the first gathering made them not his, nothing else could. That labour put a distinction between them and common: that added something to them more than nature, the common mother of all, had done; and so they became his private right. And will anyone say, he had no right to those acorns or apples, he thus appropriated, because he had not the consent of all mankind to make them his? Was it a robbery thus to assume to himself what belonged to all in common? If such a consent as that was necessary, man had starved, notwithstanding the plenty

God had given him. We see in commons, which remain so by compact, that it is the taking any part of what is common, and removing it out of the state nature leaves it in, which begins the property; without which the common is of no use. And the taking of this or that part, does not depend on the express consent of all the commoners. Thus the grass my horse has bit; the turfs my servant has cut; and the ore I have digged in any place, where I have a right to them in common with others, become my property, without the assignation or consent of any body. The labour that was mine, removing them out of that common state they were in, hath fixed my property in them....

Chapter 7
Of Political or Civil Society

...87. Man being born, as has been proved, with a title to perfect freedom, and an uncontrolled enjoyment of all the rights and privileges of the law of nature, equally with any other man, or number of men in the world, hath by nature a power, not only to preserve his property, that is, his life, liberty and estate, against the injuries and attempts of other men; but to judge of, and punish the breaches of that law in others, as he is persuaded the offence deserves, even with death itself, in crimes where the heinousness of the fact, in his opinion, requires it. But because no political society can be, nor subsist, without having in itself the power to preserve the property, and in order thereunto, punish the offences of all those of that society; there, and there only is political society, where every one of the members hath quitted this natural power, resigned it up into the hands of the community in all cases that exclude him not from appealing for protection to the law established by it. And thus all private judgment of every particular member being excluded, the community comes to be umpire, by settled standing rules, indifferent, and the same to all parties; and by men having authority from the community, for the execution of those rules, decides all the differences that may happen between any members of that society concerning any matter of right; and punishes those offences which any member hath committed against the society, with such penalties as the law has established: whereby it is easy to discern, who are, and who are not, in political society together. Those who are united into one body, and have a common established law and judicature to appeal to, with authority to decide controversies between them, and punish offenders, are in civil society one with another: but those who have no such common appeal, I mean on earth, are still in the state of nature, each being, where there is no other, judge for himself, and executioner; which is, as I have before showed it, the perfect state of nature.

88. And thus the commonwealth comes by a power to set down what punishment shall belong to the several transgressions which they think worthy of it, committed amongst the members of that society, (which is the power of making laws) as well as it has the power to punish any injury done unto any of its members, by any one that is not of it, (which is the power of war and peace;) and all this for the preservation of the property of all the members of that society, as far as is possible. But though every man who has entered into civil society, and is become a member of any commonwealth, has thereby quitted his power to punish offences, against the law of nature, in prosecution of his own private judgment, yet with the judgment of offences, which he has given up to the legislative in all cases, where he can appeal to the magistrate, he has given a right to the common-wealth to employ his force, for the execution of the judgments of the common-wealth, whenever he shall be called to it; which indeed are his own judgments, they being made by himself, or his representative. And herein we have the original of the legislative and executive power of civil society, which is to judge by standing laws, how far offences are to be punished, when committed within the common-wealth; and also to determine, by occasional judgments founded on the present circumstances of the fact, how far injuries from without are to be vindicated; and in both these to employ all the force of all the members, when there shall be need.

89. Whereever therefore any number of men are so united into one society, as to quit everyone his executive power of the law of nature, and to resign it to the public, there and there only is a political, or civil society. And this is done, where-ever any number of men, in the state of nature, enter into society to make one people, one body politic, under one supreme government; or else when any one joins himself to, and incorporates with any government already made: for hereby he authorizes the society, or which is all one, the legislative thereof, to make laws for him, as the public good of the society shall require; to the execution whereof, his own assistance (as to his own decrees) is due. And this puts men out of a state of nature into that of a common-wealth, by setting up a judge on earth, with authority to determine all the controversies, and redress the injuries that may happen to any member of the commonwealth; which judge is the legislative, or magistrates appointed by it. And where-ever there are any number of men, however associated, that have no such decisive power to appeal to, there they are still in the state of nature.

90. Hence it is evident, that absolute monarchy, which by some men

is counted the only government in the world, is indeed inconsistent with civil society, and so can be no form of civil government at all: for the end of civil society, being to avoid, and remedy those inconveniencies of the state of nature, which necessarily follow from every man's being judge in his own case, by setting up a known authority, to which every one of that society may appeal upon any injury received, or controversy that may arise, and which every one of the* society ought to obey; wherever any persons are, who have not such an authority to appeal to, for the decision of any difference between them, there those persons are still in the state of nature; and so is every absolute prince, in respect of those who are under his dominion.

91. For he being supposed to have all, both legislative and executive power in himself alone, there is no judge to be found, no appeal lies open to anyone, who may fairly, and indifferently, and with authority decide, and from whose decision relief and redress may be expected of any injury or inconvenience, that may be suffered from the prince, or by his order: so that such a man, however entitled, Czar, or Grand Seignior, or how you please, is as much in the state of nature, with all under his dominion, as he is with the rest of mankind: for where-ever any two men are, who have no standing rule, and common judge to appeal to on earth, for the determination of controversies of right betwixt them, there they are still in the state of nature, and under all the inconveniencies of it, with only this woful difference to the subject, or rather slave of an absolute prince: that whereas, in the ordinary state of nature, he has a liberty to judge of his right, and according to the best of his power, to maintain it; now, whenever his property is invaded by the will and order of his monarch, he has not only no appeal, as those in society ought to have, but as if he were degraded from the common state of rational creatures, is denied a liberty to judge of, or to defend his right; and so is exposed to all the misery and inconveniencies, that a man can fear from one, who being in the unrestrained state of nature, is yet corrupted with flattery, and armed with power....

Chapter 8
Of the Beginning of Political Societies

95. MEN being, as has been said, by nature, all free, equal, and independent, no one can be put out of this estate, and subjected to the political power of another, without his own consent. The only way whereby any one divests himself of his natural liberty, and puts on the bonds of civil society, is by agreeing with other men to join and unite into a community

for their comfortable, safe, and peaceable living one amongst another, in a secure enjoyment of their properties, and a greater security against any, that are not of it. This any number of men may do, because it injures not the freedom of the rest; they are left as they were in the liberty of the state of nature. When any number of men have so consented to make one community or government, they are thereby presently incorporated, and make one body politic, wherein the majority have a right to act and conclude the rest.

96. For when any number of men have, by the consent of every individual, made a community, they have thereby made that community one body, with a power to act as one body, which is only by the will and determination of the majority: for that which acts any community, being only the consent of the individuals of it, and it being necessary to that which is one body to move one way; it is necessary the body should move that way whither the greater force carries it, which is the consent of the majority: or else it is impossible it should act or continue one body, one community, which the consent of every individual that united into it, agreed that it should; and so everyone is bound by that consent to be concluded by the majority. And therefore we see, that in assemblies, empowered to act by positive laws, where no number is set by that positive law which impowers them, the act of the majority passes for the act of the whole, and of course determines, as having, by the law of nature and reason, the power of the whole.

97. And thus every man, by consenting with others to make one body politic under one government, puts himself under an obligation, to every one of that society, to submit to the determination of the majority, and to be concluded by it; or else this original compact, whereby he with others incorporates into one society, would signify nothing, and be no compact, if he be left free, and under no other ties than he was in before in the state of nature. For what appearance would there be of any compact? what new engagement if he were no farther tied by any decrees of the society, than he himself thought fit, and did actually consent to? This would be still as great a liberty, as he himself had before his compact, or any one else in the state of nature hath, who may submit himself, and consent to any acts of it if he thinks fit.

98. For if the consent of the majority shall not, in reason, be received as the act of the whole, and conclude every individual; nothing but the consent of every individual can make anything to be the act of the whole: but such a consent is next to impossible ever to be had, if we consider the infirmities of health, and avocations of business, which in a number, though much less than that of a common-wealth, will necessarily keep

many away from the public assembly. To which if we add the variety of opinions, and contrariety of interests, which unavoidably happen in all collections of men, the coming into society upon such terms would be only like Cato's coming into the theatre, only to go out again. Such a constitution as this would make the mighty Leviathan of a shorter duration, than the feeblest creatures, and not let it outlast the day it was born in: which cannot be supposed, till we can think, that rational creatures should desire and constitute societies only to be dissolved: for where the majority cannot conclude the rest, there they cannot act as one body, and consequently will be immediately dissolved again....

Chapter 9
Of the Ends of Political Society and Government

123. If man in the state of nature be so free, as has been said; if he be absolute lord of his own person and possessions, equal to the greatest, and subject to no body, why will he part with his freedom? why will he give up this empire, and subject himself to the dominion and control of any other power? To which it is obvious to answer, that though in the state of nature he hath such a right, yet the enjoyment of it is very uncertain, and constantly exposed to the invasion of others: for all being kings as much as he, every man his equal, and the greater part no strict observers of equity and justice, the enjoyment of the property he has in this state is very unsafe, very unsecure. This makes him willing to quit a condition, which, however free, is full of fears and continual dangers: and it is not without reason, that he seeks out, and is willing to join in society with others, who are already united, or have a mind to unite, for the mutual preservation of their lives, liberties and estates, which I call by the general name, property.

124. The great and chief end, therefore, of men's uniting into commonwealths, and putting themselves under government, is the preservation of their property. To which in the state of nature there are many things wanting.

First, There wants an established, settled, known law, received and allowed by common consent to be the standard of right and wrong, and the common measure to decide all controversies between them: for though the law of na ture be plain and intelligible to all rational creatures; yet men being biased by their interest, as well as ignorant for want of study of it, are not apt to allow of it as a law binding to them in the application of it to their particular cases.

125. Secondly, In the state of nature there wants a known and indif-

ferent judge, with authority to determine all differences according to the established law: for everyone in that state being both judge and executioner of the law of nature, men being partial to themselves, passion and revenge is very apt to carry them too far, and with too much heat, in their own cases; as well as negligence, and unconcernedness, to make them too remiss in other men's.

126. Thirdly, In the state of nature there often wants power to back and support the sentence when right, and to give it due execution. They who by any injustice offended, will seldom fail, where they are able, by force to make good their injustice; such resistance many times makes the punishment dangerous, and frequently destructive, to those who attempt it.

127. Thus mankind, notwithstanding all the privileges of the state of nature, being but in an ill condition, while they remain in it, are quickly driven into society. Hence it comes to pass, that we seldom find any number of men live any time together in this state. The inconveniencies that they are therein exposed to, by the irregular and uncertain exercise of the power every man has of punishing the transgressions of others, make them take sanctuary under the established laws of government, and therein seek the preservation of their property. It is this makes them so willingly give up every one his single power of punishing, to be exercised by such alone, as shall be appointed to it amongst them; and by such rules as the community, or those authorized by them to that purpose, shall agree on. And in this we have the original right and rise of both the legislative and executive power, as well as of the governments and societies themselves.

128. For in the state of nature, to omit the liberty he has of innocent delights, a man has two powers.

The first is to do whatsoever he thinks fit for the preservation of himself, and others within the permission of the law of nature: by which law, common to them all, he and all the rest of mankind are one community, make up one society, distinct from all other creatures. And were it not for the corruption and vitiousness of degenerate men, there would be no need of any other; no necessity that men should separate from this great and natural community, and by positive agreements combine into smaller and divided associations.

The other power a man has in the state of nature, is the power to punish the crimes committed against that law. Both these he gives up, when he joins in a private, if I may so call it, or particular politic society, and incorporates int o any common-wealth, separate from the rest of mankind.

129. The first power, viz. of doing whatsoever he thought for the preservation of himself, and the rest of mankind, he gives up to be regulated
by laws made by the society, so far forth as the preservation of himself,
and the rest of that society shall require; which laws of the society in
many things confine the liberty he had by the law of nature.

130. Secondly, The power of punishing he wholly gives up, and en-
gages his natural force, (which he might before employ in the execution
of the law of nature, by his own single authority, as he thought fit) to
assist the executive power of the society, as the law thereof shall require:
for being now in a new state, wherein he is to enjoy many conveniencies,
from the labour, assistance, and society of others in the same community,
as well as protection from its whole strength; he is to part also with as
much of his natural liberty, in providing for himself, as the good, prosperity, and safety of the society shall require; which is not only necessary, but just, since the other members of the society do the like.

131. But though men, when they enter into society, give up the equality, liberty, and executive power they had in the state of nature, into the
hands of the society, to be so far disposed of by the legislative, as the
good of the society shall require; yet it being only with an intention in
every one the better to preserve himself, his liberty and property; (for no
rational creature can be supposed to change his condition with an intention to be worse) the power of the society, or legislative constituted by
them, can never be supposed to extend farther, than the common good;
but is obliged to secure every one's property, by providing against those
three defects above mentioned, that made the state of nature so unsafe
and uneasy. And so whoever has the legislative or supreme power of
any common-wealth, is bound to govern by established standing laws,
promulgated and known to the people, and not by extemporary decrees;
by indifferent and upright judges, who are to decide controversies by
those laws; and to employ the force of the community at home, only in
the execution of such laws, or abroad to prevent or redress foreign injuries, and secure the community from inroads and invasion. And all this
to be directed to no other end, but the peace, safety, and public good of
the people.

4.2

The Bill of Rights
United States Government

Articles in addition to, and amendment of, the Constitution of the United States of America, proposed by Congress, and ratified by the legislatures of the several States pursuant to the fifth Article of the original Constitution.

ARTICLE I

Congress shall make no law respecting an establishment of religion, or prohibiting the free exercise thereof; or abridging the freedom of speech, or of the press; or the right of the people peaceably to assemble, and to petition the Government for a redress of grievances.

ARTICLE II

A well regulated Militia, being necessary to the security of a free State, the right of the people to keep and bear Arms, shall not be infringed.

ARTICLE III

No Soldier shall, in time of peace be quartered in any house, without the consent of the Owner, nor in time of war, but in a manner to be prescribed by law.

ARTICLE IV

The right of the people to be secure in their persons, houses, papers, and effects, against unreasonable searches and seizures, shall not be violated, and no Warrants shall issue, but upon probable cause, supported by Oath or affirmation, and particularly describing the place to be searched, and the persons or things to be seized.

ARTICLE V

No person shall be held to answer for a capital, or otherwise infamous crime, unless on a presentment or indictment of a Grand Jury, except in cases arising in the land or naval forces, or in the Militia, when in actual service in time of War or public danger; nor shall any person be subject for the same offence to be twice put in jeopardy of life or limb; nor shall be compelled in any criminal case to be a witness against himself, nor be deprived of life, liberty, or property, without due process of law; nor shall private property be taken for public use, without just compensation.

ARTICLE VI

In all criminal prosecutions, the accused shall enjoy the right to a speedy and public trial, by an impartial jury of the State and district wherein the crime shall have been committed, which district shall have been previously ascertained by law, and to be confronted with the witnesses against him; to have compulsory process for obtaining witnesses in his favor, and to have the Assistance of Counsel for his defence.

ARTICLE VII

In Suits at common law, where the value in controversy shall exceed twenty dollars, the right of trial by jury shall be preserved, and no fact tried by a jury, shall be otherwise re-examined in any Court of the United States, than according to the rules of the common law.

ARTICLE VIII

Excessive bail shall not be required, nor excessive fines imposed, nor cruel and unusual punishments inflicted.

ARTICLE IX

The enumeration in the Constitution, of certain rights, shall not be construed to deny or disparage others retained by the people.

ARTICLE X

The powers not delegated to the United States by the Constitution, nor prohibited by it to the States, are reserved to the States respectively, or to the people.

ARTICLE XI

The Judicial power of the United States shall not be construed to extend to any suit in law or equity, commenced or prosecuted against one of the United States by Citizens of another State, or by Citizens or Subjects of any Foreign State.

ARTICLE XII

The Electors shall meet in their respective states, and vote by ballot for President and Vice-President, one of whom, at least, shall not be an inhabitant of the same state with themselves; they shall name in their ballots the person voted for as President, and in distinct ballots the persons voted for as Vice-President, and of the number of votes for each, which lists they shall sign and certify, and transmit sealed to the seat of the government of the United States, directed to the President of the Senate; - The President of the Senate shall, in the presence of the Senate and House of Representatives, open all the certificates and the votes shall then be counted; - The person having the greatest number of votes for President, shall be President, if such number be a majority of the whole number of Electors appointed; and if no person have such majority, then from the persons having the highest numbers not exceeding three on the list of those voted for as President, the House of Representatives shall choose immediately, by ballot, the President. But in choosing the President, the votes shall be taken by states, the representation from each state having one vote; a quorum for this purpose shall consist of a member or members from two-thirds of the states, and a majority of all the states shall be necessary to a choice. And if the House of Representatives shall not choose a President whenever the right of choice shall devolve upon them, before the fourth day of March next following, then the Vice-President shall act as President, as in the case of the death or other constitutional disability of the President. The person having the greatest number of votes as Vice-President, shall be the Vice-President, if such number be a majority of the whole number of Electors appointed, and if no person have a majority, then from the two highest numbers on the list, the Senate shall choose the Vice-President; a quorum for the purpose shall consist of two-thirds of the whole number of Senators, and a majority of the whole number shall be necessary to a choice. But no person constitutionally ineligible to the office of President shall be eligible to that of Vice-President of the United States.

ARTICLE XIII

Sect. 1. Neither slavery nor involuntary servitude, except as a punishment for crime whereof the party shall have been duly convicted, shall exist within the United States, or any place subject to their jurisdiction.

Sect. 2. Congress shall have power to enforce this article by appropriate legislation.

ARTICLE XIV

Sect. 1. All persons born or naturalized in the United States, and subject to the jurisdictions thereof, are citizens of the United States and the State wherein they reside. No State shall make or enforce any law which shall abridge the privileges or immunities of citizens of the United States; nor shall any State deprive any person of life, liberty, or property, without due process of law; nor deny to any person within its jurisdiction the equal protection of the laws.

Sect. 2. Representatives shall be apportioned among the several States according to their respective numbers, counting the whole number of persons in each State, excluding Indians not taxed. But when the right to vote at any election for the choice of electors for President and Vice President of the United States, Representatives in Congress, the Executive and Judicial officers of a State, or the members of the Legislature thereof, is denied to any of the male inhabitants of such State, being twenty-one years of age, and citizens of the United States, or in any way abridged, except for participation in rebellion, or other crime, the basis of representation therein shall be reduced in the proportion which the number of such male citizens shall bear to the whole number of male citizens twenty-one years of age in such State.

Sect. 3. No person shall be a Senator or Representative in Congress, or elector of President or Vice President, or hold any office, civil or military, under the United States, or under any State, who, having previously taken an oath, as a member of Congress, or as an officer of the United States, or as a member of any State legislature, or as an executive or judicial officer of any State, to support the Constitution of the United States, shall have engaged in insurrection or rebellion against the same, or given aid or comfort to the enemies thereof. But Congress may by a vote of two-thirds of each House, remove such disability.

Sect. 4. The validity of the public debt of the United States, authorized by law, including debts incurred for payment of pensions and bounties for services in suppressing insurrection or rebellion, shall not be questioned. But neither the United States nor any State shall assume or pay any debt or obligation incurred in aid of insurrection or rebellion against the United States, or any claim for the loss or emancipation of any slave; but all such debts, obligations and claims shall be held illegal and void.

Sect. 5. The Congress shall have power to enforce, by appropriate legislation, the provisions of this article.

ARTICLE XV

Sect. 1. The right of citizens of the United States to vote shall not be denied or abridged by the United States or by any State on account of race, color, or previous condition of servitude.

Sect. 2. The Congress shall have power to enforce this article by appropriate legislation.

ARTICLE XVI

The Congress shall have power to lay and collect taxes on incomes, from whatever source derived, without apportionment among the several States, and without regard to any census or enumeration.

ARTICLE XVII

The Senate of the United States shall be composed of two Senators from each State, elected by the people thereof, for six years; and each Senator shall have one vote. The electors in each State shall have the qualifications requisite for electors of the most numerous branch of the State legislatures.

When vacancies happen in the representation of any State in the Senate, the executive authority of such State shall issue writs of election to fill such vacancies: Provided, That the legislature of any State may empower the executive thereof to make temporary appointment until the people fill the vacancies by election as the legislature may direct.

This amendment shall not be so construed as to affect the election or term of any Senator chosen before it becomes valid as part of the Constitution.

ARTICLE XVIII

Sect. 1. After one year from the ratification of this article the manufacture, sale, or transportation of intoxicating liquors within, the importation thereof into, or the exportation thereof from the United States and all territory subject to the jurisdiction thereof for beverage purposes is hereby prohibited.

Sect. 2. The Congress and the several States shall have concurrent power to enforce this article by appropriate legislation.

Sect. 3. This article shall be inoperative unless it shall have been ratified as an amendment to the Constitution by the legislatures of the several States, as provided in the Constitution, within seven years from the date of the submission hereof to the States by the Congress.

ARTICLE XIX

The right of citizens of the United States to vote shall not be denied or abridged by the United States or by any State on account of sex.

Congress shall have power to enforce this article by appropriate legislation.

ARTICLE XX

Sect. 1. The terms of the President and Vice President shall end at noon on the 20th day of January, and the terms of Senators and Representatives at noon on the 3rd day of January, of the years in which such terms would have ended if this article had not been ratified; and the terms of their successors shall then begin.

Sect. 2. The Congress shall assemble at least once in every year, and such meeting shall begin at noon on the 3rd day of January, unless they shall by law appoint a different day.

Sect. 3. If, at the time fixed for the beginning of the term of the President, the President elect shall have died, the Vice President elect shall become President. If a President shall not have been chosen before the time fixed for the beginning of his term, or if the President elect shall have failed to qualify, then the Vice President elect shall act as president until a President shall have qualified; and the Congress may by law provide for the case wherein neither a President elect nor a Vice President elect shall have qualified, declaring who shall then act as President, or the manner in which one who is to act shall be selected, and such person shall act accordingly until a President or Vice President shall have qualified.

Sect. 4. The Congress may by law provide for the case of the death of any of the persons from whom the House of Representatives may choose a President whenever the right of choice shall have devolved upon them, and for the case of the death of any of the persons from whom the Senate may choose a Vice President whenever the right of choice shall have devolved upon them.

Sect. 5. Sections 1 and 2 shall take effect on the 15th day of October following the ratification of this article.

Sect. 6. This article shall be inoperative unless it shall have been ratified as an amendment to the Constitution by the legislatures of three- fourths of the several States within seven years from the date of its submission.

ARTICLE XXI

Sect. 1. The eighteenth article of amendment to the Constitution of the United States is hereby repealed.

Sect. 2. The transportation or importation into any State, Territory, or possession of the United States for delivery or use therein of intoxicating liquors, in violation of the laws thereof, is hereby prohibited.

Sect. 3. This article shall be inoperative unless it shall have been ratified as an amendment to the Constitution by conventions in the several States, as provided in the Constitution, within seven years from the date of the submission hereof to the States by the Congress.

ARTICLE XXII

Sect. 1. No person shall be elected to the office of the President more than twice, and no person who has held the office of President, or acted as President, for more than two years of a term to which some other person was elected President shall be elected to the office of the President more than once. But this Article shall not apply to any person holding the office of President when this Article was proposed by the Congress, and shall not prevent any person who may be holding the office of President, or acting as President, during the term within which this Article becomes operative from holding the office of President or acting as President during the remainder of such term.

Sect. 2. This article shall be inoperative unless it shall have been ratified as an amendment to the Constitution by the legislatures of three- fourths of the several States within seven years from the date of its submission to the States by the Congress.

ARTICLE XXIII

Sect. 1. The District constituting the seat of Government of the United States shall appoint in such manner as the Congress may direct:

A number of electors of President and Vice President equal to the whole number of Senators and Representatives in Congress to which the District would be entitled if it were a State, but in no event more than the least populous State; they shall be in addition to those appointed by the States, but they shall be considered, for the purposes of the election of President and Vice President, to be electors appointed by a State; and they shall meet in the District and perform such duties as provided by the twelfth article of amendment.

Sect. 2. The Congress shall have power to enforce this article by appropriate legislation.

ARTICLE XXIV

Sect. 1. The right of citizens of the United States to vote in any primary or other election for President or Vice President, for electors for President or Vice President, or for Senator or Representative in Congress, shall not be denied or abridged by the United States or any State by reason of failure to pay any poll tax or other tax.

Sect. 2. The Congress shall have power to enforce this article by appropriate legislation.

ARTICLE XXV

Sect. 1. In case of the removal of the President from office or of his death or resignation, the Vice President shall become President.

Sect. 2. Whenever there is a vacancy in the office of the Vice President, the President shall nominate a Vice President who shall take office upon confirmation by a majority vote of both Houses of Congress.

Sect. 3. Whenever the President transmits to the President pro tempore of the Senate and the Speaker of the House of Representatives his written declaration that he is unable to discharge the powers and duties of his office, and until he transmits to them a written declaration to the contrary, such powers and duties shall be discharged by the Vice President as

Acting President.

Sect. 4. Whenever the Vice President and a majority of either the principal officers of the executive departments or of such other body as Congress may by law provide, transmit to the President pro tempore of the Senate and the Speaker of the House of Representatives their written declaration that the President is unable to discharge the powers and duties of his office, the Vice President shall immediately assume the powers and duties of the office as Acting President. Thereafter, when the President transmits to the President pro tempore of the Senate and the Speaker of the House of Representatives his written declaration that no inability exists, he shall resume the powers and duties of his office unless the Vice President and a majority of either the principal officers of the executive department or of such other body as Congress may by law provide, transmit within four days to the President pro tempore of the Senate and the Speaker of the House of Representatives their written declaration that the President is unable to discharge the powers and duties of his office. Thereupon Congress shall decide the issue, assembling within forty-eight hours for that purpose if not in session. If the Congress, within twenty-one days after receipt of the latter written declaration, or, if Congress is not in session, within twenty-one days after Congress is required to assemble, determines by two-thirds vote of both Houses that the President is unable to discharge the powers and duties of his office, the Vice President shall continue to discharge the same as Acting President; otherwise, the President shall resume the powers and duties of his office.

ARTICLE XXVI

Sect. 1. The right of citizens of the United States, who are eighteen years of age or older, to vote shall not be denied or abridged by the United States or by any State on account of age.

Sect. 2. The Congress shall have power to enforce this article by appropriate legislation.

ARTICLE XXVII

No law, varying the compensation for the services of the Senators and Representatives, shall take effect, until an election of Representatives shall have intervened.

Universal Declaration of Human Rights

United Nations

PREAMBLE

Whereas recognition of the inherent dignity and of the equal and inalienable rights of all members of the human family is the foundation of freedom, justice and peace in the world,

Whereas disregard and contempt for human rights have resulted in barbarous acts which have outraged the conscience of mankind, and the advent of a world in which human beings shall enjoy freedom of speech and belief and freedom from fear and want has been proclaimed as the highest aspiration of the common people,

Whereas it is essential, if man is not to be compelled to have recourse, as a last resort, to rebellion against tyranny and oppression, that human rights should be protected by the rule of law,

Whereas it is essential to promote the development of friendly relations between nations,

Whereas the peoples of the United Nations have in the Charter reaffirmed their faith in fundamental human rights, in the dignity and worth of the human person and in the equal rights of men and women and have determined to promote social progress and better standards of life in larger freedom,

Whereas Member States have pledged themselves to achieve, in co-operation with the United Nations, the promotion of universal respect for and observance of human rights and fundamental freedoms,

Whereas a common understanding of these rights and freedoms is of the greatest importance for the full realization of this pledge,

Now, Therefore THE GENERAL ASSEMBLY proclaims THIS UNIVERSAL DECLARATION OF HUMAN RIGHTS as a common standard of achievement for all peoples and all nations, to the end that every individual and every organ of society, keeping this Declaration constantly in mind, shall strive by teaching and education to promote respect for these rights and freedoms and by progressive measures, national and international, to secure their universal and effective recognition and observance, both among the peoples of Member States themselves and among the peoples of territories under their jurisdiction.

Article 1.

All human beings are born free and equal in dignity and rights. They are endowed with reason and conscience and should act towards one another in a spirit of brotherhood.

Article 2.

Everyone is entitled to all the rights and freedoms set forth in this Declaration, without distinction of any kind, such as race, colour, sex, language, religion, political or other opinion, national or social origin, property, birth or other status. Furthermore, no distinction shall be made on the basis of the political, jurisdictional or international status of the country or territory to which a person belongs, whether it be independent, trust, non-self-governing or under any other limitation of sovereignty.

Article 3.

Everyone has the right to life, liberty and security of person.

Article 4.

No one shall be held in slavery or servitude; slavery and the slave trade shall be prohibited in all their forms.

Article 5.

No one shall be subjected to torture or to cruel, inhuman or degrading treatment or punishment.

Article 6.

Everyone has the right to recognition everywhere as a person before the law.

Article 7.

All are equal before the law and are entitled without any discrimination to equal protection of the law. All are entitled to equal protection against any discrimination in violation of this Declaration and against any incitement to such discrimination.

Article 8.

Everyone has the right to an effective remedy by the competent national tribunals for acts violating the fundamental rights granted him by the constitution or by law.

Article 9.

No one shall be subjected to arbitrary arrest, detention or exile.

Article 10.

Everyone is entitled in full equality to a fair and public hearing by an independent and impartial tribunal, in the determination of his rights and obligations and of any criminal charge against him.

Article 11.

(1) Everyone charged with a penal offence has the right to be presumed innocent until proved guilty according to law in a public trial at which he has had all the guarantees necessary for his defence.

(2) No one shall be held guilty of any penal offence on account of any act or omission which did not constitute a penal offence, under national or international law, at the time when it was committed. Nor shall a heavier penalty be imposed than the one that was applicable at the time the penal offence was committed.

Article 12.

No one shall be subjected to arbitrary interference with his privacy, family, home or correspondence, nor to attacks upon his honour and reputation. Everyone has the right to the protection of the law against such interference or attacks.

Article 13.

(1) Everyone has the right to freedom of movement and residence within

the borders of each state.

(2) Everyone has the right to leave any country, including his own, and to return to his country.

Article 14.

(1) Everyone has the right to seek and to enjoy in other countries asylum from persecution.

(2) This right may not be invoked in the case of prosecutions genuinely arising from non-political crimes or from acts contrary to the purposes and principles of the United Nations.

Article 15.

(1) Everyone has the right to a nationality.

(2) No one shall be arbitrarily deprived of his nationality nor denied the right to change his nationality.

Article 16.

(1) Men and women of full age, without any limitation due to race, nationality or religion, have the right to marry and to found a family. They are entitled to equal rights as to marriage, during marriage and at its dissolution.

(2) Marriage shall be entered into only with the free and full consent of the intending spouses.

(3) The family is the natural and fundamental group unit of society and is entitled to protection by society and the State.

Article 17.

(1) Everyone has the right to own property alone as well as in association with others.

(2) No one shall be arbitrarily deprived of his property.

Article 18.

Everyone has the right to freedom of thought, conscience and religion; this right includes freedom to change his religion or belief, and freedom, either alone or in community with others and in public or private, to manifest his religion or belief in teaching, practice, worship and observance.

Article 19.

Everyone has the right to freedom of opinion and expression; this right includes freedom to hold opinions without interference and to seek, receive and impart information and ideas through any media and regardless of frontiers.

Article 20.

(1) Everyone has the right to freedom of peaceful assembly and association.

(2) No one may be compelled to belong to an association.

Article 21.

(1) Everyone has the right to take part in the government of his country, directly or through freely chosen representatives.

(2) Everyone has the right of equal access to public service in his country.

(3) The will of the people shall be the basis of the authority of government; this will shall be expressed in periodic and genuine elections which shall be by universal and equal suffrage and shall be held by secret vote or by equivalent free voting procedures.

Article 22.

Everyone, as a member of society, has the right to social security and is entitled to realization, through national effort and international co-operation and in accordance with the organization and resources of each State, of the economic, social and cultural rights indispensable for his dignity and the free development of his personality.

Article 23.

(1) Everyone has the right to work, to free choice of employment, to just and favourable conditions of work and to protection against unemployment.

(2) Everyone, without any discrimination, has the right to equal pay for equal work.

(3) Everyone who works has the right to just and favourable remuneration ensuring for himself and his family an existence worthy of human dignity, and supplemented, if necessary, by other means of social protection.
(4) Everyone has the right to form and to join trade unions for the protection of his interests.

Article 24.

Everyone has the right to rest and leisure, including reasonable limitation of working hours and periodic holidays with pay.

Article 25.

(1) Everyone has the right to a standard of living adequate for the health and well-being of himself and of his family, including food, clothing, housing and medical care and necessary social services, and the right to security in the event of unemployment, sickness, disability, widowhood, old age or other lack of livelihood in circumstances beyond his control.
(2) Motherhood and childhood are entitled to special care and assistance. All children, whether born in or out of wedlock, shall enjoy the same social protection.

Article 26.

(1) Everyone has the right to education. Education shall be free, at least in the elementary and fundamental stages. Elementary education shall be compulsory. Technical and professional education shall be made generally available and higher education shall be equally accessible to all on the basis of merit.

(2) Education shall be directed to the full development of the human personality and to the strengthening of respect for human rights and fundamental freedoms. It shall promote understanding, tolerance and

friendship among all nations, racial or religious groups, and shall further the activities of the United Nations for the maintenance of peace.

(3) Parents have a prior right to choose the kind of education that shall be given to their children.

Article 27.

(1) Everyone has the right freely to participate in the cultural life of the community, to enjoy the arts and to share in scientific advancement and its benefits.

(2) Everyone has the right to the protection of the moral and material interests resulting from any scientific, literary or artistic production of which he is the author.

Article 28.

Everyone is entitled to a social and international order in which the rights and freedoms set forth in this Declaration can be fully realized.

Article 29.

(1) Everyone has duties to the community in which alone the free and full
development of his personality is possible.

(2) In the exercise of his rights and freedoms,
everyone shall be subject only to such limitations as are determined by law solely for the purpose of securing due recognition and respect for the rights and freedoms of others and of meeting the just requirements of morality, public order and the general welfare in a democratic society.

(3) These rights and freedoms may in no case be exercised contrary to the purposes and principles of the United Nations.

Article 30.

Nothing in this Declaration may be interpreted as implying for any State, group or person any right to engage in any activity or to perform any act aimed at the destruction of any of the rights and freedoms set forth herein.

4.4

Critique of the Doctrine of Inalienable, Natural Rights

Jeremy Bentham

PRELIMINARY OBSERVATIONS

The Declaration of Rights—I mean the paper published under that name by the French National Assembly in 1791—assumes for its subject-matter a field of disquisition as unbounded in point of extent as it is important in its nature. But the more ample the extent given to any proposition or string of propositions, the more difficult it is to keep the import of it confined without deviation, within the bounds of truth and reason. If in the smallest corners of the field it ranges over, it fail of coinciding with the line of rigid rectitude, no sooner is the aberration pointed out, than (inasmuch as there is no medium between truth and falsehood) its pretensions to the appellation of truism are gone, and whoever looks upon it must recognize it to be false and erroneous,—and if, as here, political conduct be the theme, so far as the error extends and fails of being detected, pernicious.

In a work of such extreme importance with a view to practice, and which throughout keeps practice so closely and immediately and professedly in view, a single error may be attended with the most fatal consequences. The more extensive the propositions, the more consummate will be the knowledge, the more exquisite the skill, indispensably requisite to confine them in all points within the pale of truth. The most consummate ability in the whole nation could not have been too much for the task—one may venture to say, it would not have been equal to it. But that, in the sanctioning of each proposition, the most consummate ability should happen to be vested in the heads of the sorry

---

Jeremy Bentham. "Anarchical Fallacies" *Works of Jeremy Bentham*. Vol. 2. Ed. John Bowring Edinburgh: William Tait, 1843.

majority in whose hands the plenitude of power happened on that same occasion to be vested, is an event against which the chances are almost as infinity to one.

Here, then, is a radical and all-pervading error—the attempting to give to a work on such a subject the sanction of government; especially of such a government—a government composed of members so numerous, so unequal in talent, as well as discordant in inclinations and affections. Had it been the work of a single hand, and that a private one, and in that character given to the world, every good effect would have been produced by it that could be produced by it when published as the work of government, without any of the bad effects which in case of the smallest error must result from it when given as the work of government.

The revolution which threw the government into the hands of the penners and adopters of this declaration, having been the effect of insurrection, the grand object evidently is to justify the cause. But by justifying it, they invite it: in justifying past insurrections they plant and cultivate a propensity to perpetual insurrection in time future; they sow the seeds of anarchy broadcast: in justifying the demolition of existing authorities, they undermine all future ones, their own consequently in the number. Shallow and reckless vanity! They imitate in their conduct the author of that fabled law, according to which the assassination of the prince upon the throne gave to the assassin a title to succeed him. *"People, behold your rights! If a single article of them be violated, insurrection is not your right only, but the most sacred of your duties."* Such is the constant language, for such is the professed object of this source and model of all laws—this self-consecrated oracle of all nations....

The great enemies of public peace are the selfish and dissocial passions:—necessary as they are—the one to the very existence of each individual, the other to his security. On the part of these affections, a deficiency in point of strength is never to be apprehended: all that is to be apprehended in respect of them, is to be apprehended on the side of their excess. Society is held together only by the sacrifices that men can be induced to make of the gratifications they demand: to obtain these sacrifices is the great difficulty, the great task of government. What has been the object, the perpetual and palpable object, of this declaration of pretended rights? To add as much force as possible to these passions, already but too strong,—to burst the cords that hold them in,—to say to the selfish passions, there—everywhere—is your prey!—to the angry passions, there—everywhere—is your enemy.

Such is the morality of this celebrated manifesto, rendered famous by the same qualities that gave celebrity to the incendiary of the Ephesian temple.

The logic of it is of a piece with its morality:—a perpetual vein of nonsense, flowing from a perpetual abuse of words,—words having a variety of meanings, where words with single meanings were equally at hand—the same words used in a variety of meanings in the same page, — words used in meanings not their own, where proper words were equally at hand, —words and propositions of the most unbounded signification, turned loose without any of those exceptions or modifications which are so necessary on every occasion to reduce their import within the compass, not only of right reason, but even of the design in hand, of whatever nature it may be; —the same inaccuracy, the same inattention in the penning of this cluster of truths on which the fate of nations was to hang, as if it had been an oriental tale, or an allegory for a magazine:—stale epigrams, instead of necessary distinctions,—figurative expressions preferred to simple ones, —sentimental conceits, as trite as they are unmeaning, preferred to apt and precise expressions,—frippery ornament preferred to the majestic simplicity of good sound sense, —and the acts of the senate loaded and disfigured by the tinsel of the playhouse....

Article II

The end in view of every political association is the preservation of the natural and imprescriptible rights of man. These rights are liberty, property, security, and resistance to oppression.

Sentence 1. The end in view of every political association, is the preservation of the natural and imprescriptible rights of man.

More confusion—more nonsense,—and the nonsense, as usual, dangerous nonsense. The words can scarcely be said to have a meaning: but if they have, or rather if they had a meaning, these would be the propositions either asserted or implied: —

1. That there are such things as rights anterior to the establishment of governments: for natural, as applied to rights, if it mean anything, is meant to stand in opposition to *legal*—to such rights as are acknowledged to owe their existence to government, and are consequently posterior in their date to the establishment of government.
2. That these rights *cannot* be abrogated by government: for *cannot* is implied in the form of the word imprescriptible, and the sense it wears when so applied, is the cut-throat sense above

explained.

3. That the governments that exist derive their origin from formal associations or what are now called *conventions*: associations entered into by a partnership contract, with all the members for partners,—entered into at a day prefixed, for a predetermined purpose, the formation of a new government where there was none before (for as to formal meetings held under the control of an existing government, they are evidently out of question here) in which it seems again to be implied in the way of inference, though a necessary and an unavoidable inference, that all governments (that is, self-called governments, knots of persons exercising the powers of government) that have had any other origin than an association of the above description, are illegal, that is, no governments at all; resistance to them and subversion of them, lawful and commendable; and so on.

Such are the notions implied in this first part of the article. How stands the truth of things? That there are no such things as natural rights—no such things as rights anterior to the establishment of government—no such things as natural rights opposed to, in contradistinction to, legal: that the expression is merely figurative; that when used, in the moment you attempt to give it a literal meaning it leads to error, and to that sort of error that leads to mischief—to the extremity of mischief.

We know what it is for men to live without government—and living without government, to live without rights: we know what it is for men to live without government, for we see instances of such a way of life—we see it in many savage nations, or rather races of mankind; for instance, among the savages of New South Wales, whose way of living is so well known to us: no habit of obedience, and thence no government -- no government, and thence no laws—no laws, and thence no such things as rights—no security—no property:—liberty, as against regular control, the control of laws and government—perfect; but as against all irregular control, the mandates of stronger individuals, none. In this state, at a time earlier than the commencement of history—in this same state, judging from analogy, we the inhabitants of the part of the globe we call Europe, were;—no government, consequently no rights: no rights, consequently no property—no legal security—no legal liberty: security not more than belongs to beasts—forecast and sense of insecurity keener—consequently in point of happiness below the level of the brutal race.

In proportion to the want of happiness resulting from the want of rights, a reason exists for wishing that there were such things as rights.

But reasons for wishing there were such things as rights, are not rights;—a reason for wishing that a certain right were established, is not that right—want is not supply—hunger is not bread.

That which has no existence cannot be destroyed—that which cannot be destroyed cannot require anything to preserve it from destruction. *Natural rights* is simple nonsense: natural and imprescriptible rights, rhetorical nonscnse,—nonsense upon stilts. But this rhetorical nonsense ends in the old strain of mischievous nonsense for immediately a list of these pretended natural rights is given, and those are so expressed as to present to view legal rights. And of these rights, whatever they are, there is not, it seems, any one of which any government *can*, upon any occasion whatever, abrogate the smallest particle.

So much for terrorist language. What is the language of reason and plain sense upon the same subject? That in proportion as it is *right or proper*, i.e. advantageous to the society in question, that this or that right—a right to this or that effect—should be established and maintained, in that same proportion it is wrong that it should be abrogated: but that as there is no right, which ought not to be maintained so long as it is upon the whole advantageous to the society that it should be maintained, so there is no right which, when the abolition of it is advantageous to society, should not be abolished. To know whether it would be more for the advantage of society that this or that right should be maintained or abolished, the time at which the question about maintaining or abolishing is proposed, must be given, and the circumstances under which it is proposed to maintain or abolish it; the right itself must be specifically described, not jumbled with an undistinguishable heap of others, under any such vague general terms as property, liberty, and the like.

One thing, in the midst of all this confusions is but too plain. They know not of what they are talking under the name of natural rights, and yet they would have them imprescriptible—proof against all the power of the laws—pregnant with occasions summoning the members of the community to rise up in resistance against the laws. What, then, was their object in declaring the existence of imprescriptible rights, and without specifying a single one by any such mark as it could be known by? This and no other—to excite and keep up a spirit of resistance to all laws—a spirit of insurrection against all governments—against the governments of all other nations instantly,—against the government of their own nation—against the government they themselves were pretending to establish—even that, as soon as their own reign should be at an end. In us is the perfection of virtue and wisdom: in all mankind besides, the extremity of wickedness and folly. Our will shall consequently reign without control, and forever: reign now we are living—reign after we are dead.

All nations—all future ages—shall be, for they are predestined to be, our Slaves.

Future governments will not have honesty enough to be trusted with the determination of what rights shall be maintained, what abrogated— what laws kept in force, what repealed. Future subjects (I should say future citizens, for French government does not admit of subjects) will not have wit enough to be trusted with the choice whether to submit to the determination of the government of their time, or to resist it. Governments, citizens—all to the end of time—all must be kept in chains.

Such are their maxims—such their premises—for it is by such premises only that the doctrine of imprescriptible rights and unrepealable laws can be supported.

What is the real source of these imprescriptible rights—these unrepealable laws? Power turned blind by looking from its own height: self-conceit and tyranny exalted into insanity. No man was to have any other man for a servant, yet all men are forever to be their slaves. Making laws with imposture in their mouths, under pretence of declaring them— giving for laws anything that came uppermost, and these unrepealable ones, on pretence of finding them ready made. Made by what? Not by a God—they allow of none; but by their goddess, Nature.

The origination of governments from a contract is a pure fiction, or in other words, a falsehood. It never has been known to be true in any instance; the allegation of it does mischief, by involving the subject in error and confusion, and is neither necessary nor useful to any good purpose.

All governments that we have any account of have been gradually established by habit, after having been formed by force; unless in the instance of governments formed by individuals who have been emancipated, or have emancipated themselves, front governments already formed, the governments under which they were born—a rare case, and from which nothing follows with regard to the rest. What signifies it how governments are formed? Is it the less proper—the less conducive to the happiness of society—that the happiness of society should be the one object kept in view by the members of the government in all their measures? Is it the less the interest of men to be happy—less to be wished that they may be so—less the moral duty of their governors to make them so, as far as they can, at Mogadore than at Philadelphia.

Whence is it, but from government, that contracts derive their binding force? Contracts came from government, not government from contracts. It is from the habit of enforcing contracts, and seeing them enforced that governments are chiefly indebted for whatever disposition they have to observe them.

Sentence 2. These rights [these imprescriptible as well as natural rights,] are liberty, property, security, and resistance to oppression.

Observe the extent of these pretended rights, each of them belonging to every man, and all of them without bounds. Unbounded liberty; that is, amongst other things, the liberty of doing or not doing on every occasion whatever each man pleases:—Unbounded property; that is, the right of doing with everything around him (with every*thing* at least, if not with every person,) whatsoever he pleases; communicating that right to anybody and withholding it from anybody:—Unbounded security; that is, security for such his liberty, for such his property and for his person, against every defalcation that can be called for on any account in respect of any of them:— Unbounded resistance to oppression; that is, unbounded exercise of the faculty of guarding himself against whatever unpleasant circumstance may present itself to his imagination or his passions under that name. Nature, say some of the interpreters of the pretended law of nature—nature gave to each man a right to everything; which is, in effect, but another way of saying—nature has given no such right to anybody; for in regard to most rights, it is as true that what is every man's right is no man's right, as that what is every man's business is no man's business. Nature gave—gave to every man a right to everything—be it so—true; and hence the necessity of human government and human laws, to give to every man his own right, without which no right whatsoever would amount to anything. Nature gave every man a right to everything before the existence of laws, and in default of laws. This nominal universality and real nonentity of right, set up provisionally by nature in default of laws, the French oracle lays hold of, and perpetuates it under the law and in spite of laws. These anarchical rights which nature had set out with, democratic art attempts to rivet down, and declares indefeasible.

Unbounded liberty—I must still say unbounded liberty;—for though the next article but one returns to the charge, and gives such a definition of liberty as seems intended to set bounds to it, yet in effect the limitation amounts to nothing; and when, as here, no warning is given of any exception in the texture of the general rule, every exception which turns up is, not a confirmation but a contradiction of the rule: —liberty, without any preannounced or intelligent bounds; and as to the other rights, they remain unbounded to the end: rights of man composed of a system of contradictions and impossibilities.

In vain would it be said, that though no bounds are here assigned to any of these rights, yet it is to be understood as taken for granted and tacitly admitted and assumed, that they are to have bounds; viz. such bounds as it is understood will be set them by the laws. Vain, I say, would be this apology; for the supposition would be contradictory to the express declaration of the article itself, and would defeat the very object which the whole declaration has in view. It would be self-contradictory, because these rights are, in the same breath in which their existence is declared, declared to be imprescriptible; and imprescriptible, or as we in England should say, indefeasible, means nothing unless it exclude the interference of the laws.

It would be not only inconsistent with itself, but inconsistent with the declared and sole object of the declaration, if it did not exclude the interference of the laws. It is against the laws themselves, and the laws only, that this declaration is leveled. It is for the hands of the legislator and all legislators, and none but legislators, that the shackles it provides are intended,—it is against the apprehended encroachments of legislators that the rights in question, the liberty and property, and so forth, are intended to be made secure,— it is to such encroachments, and damages, and dangers, that whatever security it professes to give has respect. Precious security for unbounded rights against legislators, if the extent of those rights in every direction were purposely left to depend upon the will and pleasure of those very legislators!

Nonsensical or nugatory, and in both cases mischievous such is the alternative.

So much for all these pretended indefeasible rights in the lump: their inconsistency with each other, as well as the inconsistency of them in the character of indefeasible rights with the existence of government and all peaceable society, will appear still more plainly when we examine them one by one.

1. *Liberty*, then, is imprescriptible—incapable of being taken away— out of the power of any government ever to take away liberty,—that is, every branch of liberty—every individual exercise of liberty; for no line is drawn—no distinction—no exception made. What these instructors as well as governors of mankind appear not to know, is, that all rights are made at the expense of liberty—all laws by which rights are created or confirmed. No right without a correspondent obligation. Liberty, as against the coercion of the law, may, it is true, be given by the simple removal of the obligation by which that coercion was applied—by the simple repeal of the coercing law. But as against the coercion applicable by individual to individual, no liberty can be given to one man but in

proportion as it is taken front another. All coercive laws, therefore (that is, all laws but constitutional laws and laws repealing or modifying coercive laws,) and in particular all laws creative of liberty are, as far as they go, abrogative of liberty. Not here and there a law only—not this or that possible law, but almost all laws, are therefore repugnant to these natural and inprescriptible rights consequently null and void, calling for resistance and insurrection, and so on, as before.

Laws creative of rights of property are also struck at by the same anathema. How is property given? By restraining liberty; that is, by taking it away so far as is necessary for the purpose. How is your house made yours? By debarring every one else from the liberty of entering it without your leave.

2. *Property*. Property stands second on the list,—proprietary rights are in the number of the natural and imprescriptible rights of man—of the rights which a man is not indebted for to the laws, and which cannot be taken from him by the laws. Men—that is, every man (for a general expression given without exception is an universal one) has a right to property, to proprietary rights, *a right which* cannot be taken away from him by the laws. To proprietary rights. Good: but in relation to what subject? for as to proprietary rights—without a subject to which they are referable—without a subject in or in relation to which they can be exercised—they will hardly be of much value, they will hardly be worth taking care of, with so much solemnity. In vain would all the laws in the world have ascertained that I have a right to something. If this be all they have done for me —if there be no specific subject in relation to which my proprietary rights are established, I must either take what I want without right, or starve. As there is no such subject specified with relation to each man, or to any man (indeed how could there be?) the necessary inference (taking the passage literally) is, that every man has all manner of proprietary rights with relation to every subject of property without exception: in a word, that every man has a right to everything. Unfortunately, in most matters of property, what is every man's right is no man's right; so that the effect of this part of the oracle, if observed, would be, not to establish property, but to extinguish it—to render it impossible ever to be revived: and this is one of the rights declared to be imprescriptible.

It will probably be acknowledged, that according to this construction, the clause in question is equally ruinous and absurd—and hence the inference may be, that this was not the construction—this was not the meaning in view. But by the same rule, every possible construction which the words employed can admit of, might be proved not to have been the meaning in view nor is this clause a whit more absurd or ruinous than all that goes before it, and a great deal of what comes after it. And, in short, if this be not the meaning of it, what is? Give it a sense—give it any sense whatever, it is—mischievous—to save it from that imputation, there is but one course to take, which is to acknowledge it to be nonsense.

Thus much could be clear, if anything were clear in it, that according to this clause, whatever proprietary rights, whatever property a man once has, no matter how, being imprescriptible, can never be taken away from him by any law: or of what use or meaning is the clause? So that the moment it is acknowledged in relation to any article, that such article is my property, no matter how or when it became so, that moment it is acknowledged that it can never be taken away from me: therefore, for example, all laws and all judgments, whereby anything is taken away from me without my free consent—all taxes, for example, and all fines—are void, and, as such call for resistance and insurrection, and so forth, as before.

3. *Security*. Security stands the third on the list of these natural and imprescriptible rights which laws did not give, and which laws are not in any degree to be suffered to take away. Under the head of security, liberty might have been included, so likewise property: since security for liberty, or the enjoyment of liberty, may be spoken of as a branch of security:—security for property, or the enjoyment of proprietary rights, as another. Security for person is the branch that seems here to have been understood: security for each man's person, as against all those hurtful or disagreeable impressions (exclusive of those which consist in the mere disturbance of the enjoyment of liberty,) by which a man is affected in his person; loss of life—loss of limbs—loss of the use of limbs—wounds, bruises, and the like. All laws are null and void then, which on any account or in any manner seek to expose the person of any man to any risk—which appoint capital or other corporal punishment—which expose a man to personal hazard in the service of the military power against foreign enemies, or in that of the judicial power against delinquents—all laws which, to preserve the country from pestilence, authorize the immediate execution of a suspected person, in the event of his transgressing certain bounds

4. *Resistance to oppression*. Fourth and last in the list of natural and imprescriptible rights, resistance to oppression—meaning, I suppose, the right to resist oppression. What is oppression? Power misapplied to the prejudice of some individual. What is it that a man has in view when he speaks of oppression? Some exertion of power which he looks upon as misapplied to the prejudice of some individual—to the producing on the

part of such individual some sufferings to which (whether as forbidden by the laws or otherwise) we conceive he ought not to have been subjected. But against everything that can come under the name of oppression, provision has been already made, in the manner we have seen, by the recognition of the three preceding rights; since no oppression can fall upon a man which is not all infringement of his rights in relation to liberty, rights in relation to property, or rights in relation to security, as above described. Where, then, is the difference?—to what purpose this fourth clause after the three first? To this purpose: the mischief they seek to prevent, the rights they seek to establish are the same; the difference lies in the nature of the remedy endeavored to be applied. To present the mischief in question, the endeavor of the three former clauses is, to tie the hand of the legislator and his subordinates, by the fear of nullity, and the remote apprehension of general resistance and insurrection. The aim of this fourth clause is to raise the hand of the individual concerned to prevent the apprended infraction of his rights at the moment when he looks upon it as about to take place.

Whenever you are about to be oppressed, you have a right to resist oppression: whenever you conceive yourself to be oppressed, conceive yourself to have a right to make resistance, and act accordingly. In proportion as a law of any kind—any act of power, supreme or subordinate, legislative, administrative, or judicial, is unpleasant to a man, especially if, in consideration of such its unpleasantness, his opinion is, that such act of power ought not to have been exercised, he of course looks upon it as oppression: as often as anything of this sort happens to a man—as often as anything happens to a man to inflame his passions,—this article, for fear his passions should not be sufficiently inflamed of themselves, sets itself to work to blow the flame, and urges him to resistance. Submit not to any decree or other act of power, of the justice of which you are not yourself perfectly convinced. If a constable call upon you to serve in the militia, shoot the constable and not the enemy—if the commander of a press-gang trouble you, push him into the sea—if a bailiff, throw him out of the window. If a judge sentences you to be imprisoned or put to death, have a dagger ready, and take a stroke first at the judge.

Happiness and Moral Virtue
Aristotle

BOOK ONE

1. The Good as the End of All Action

Every art and every inquiry, and similarly every action and pursuit, is thought to aim at some good; and for this reason the good has rightly been declared to be that at which all things aim. But a certain difference is found among ends; some are activities, others are products apart from the activities that produce them. Where there are ends apart from the actions, it is the nature of the products to be better than the activities.

Now, as there are many actions, arts, and sciences, their ends also are many; the end of the medical art is health, that of shipbuilding a vessel, that of strategy victory, that of economics wealth. But where such arts fall under a single capacity—as bridle-making and the other arts concerned with the equipment of horses fall under the art of riding, and this and every military action under strategy, in the same way other arts fall under yet others—in all of these the ends of the master arts are to be preferred to all the subordinate ends; for it is for the sake of the former that the latter are pursued. It makes no difference whether the activities themselves are the ends of the actions, or something else apart from the activities, as in the case of the sciences just mentioned....

4. Happiness as the Supreme Good

Let us resume our inquiry and state, in view of the fact that all knowledge and every pursuit aims at some good, what it is that we say political science aims at and what is the highest of all goods achievable by action. Verbally there is very general agreement; for both the general run of men

Aristotle. *Nicomachean Ethics*. Trans. W.D. Ross. Oxford: Clarendon Press, 1908. The text has been updated by the editor.

and people of superior refinement say that it is happiness (*eudaimonia*), and identify living well and doing well with being happy; but with regard to what happiness is they differ, and the many do not give the same account as the wise. For the former think it is some plain and obvious thing, like pleasure, wealth, or honour; they differ, however, from one another—and often even the same man identifies it with different things, with health when he is ill, with wealth when he is poor; but, conscious of their ignorance, they admire those who proclaim some great ideal that is above their comprehension. Now some thought that apart from these many goods there is another which is self-subsistent and causes the goodness of all these as well. To examine all the opinions that have been held were perhaps somewhat fruitless; enough to examine those that are most prevalent or that seem to be arguable.

5. Mistaken Views Concerning the Supreme Good

...Now the mass of mankind are evidently quite slavish in their tastes, preferring a life suitable to beasts, but they get some ground for their view from the fact that many of those in high places share the tastes of Sardanapallus. A consideration of the prominent types of life shows that people of superior refinement and of active disposition identify happiness with honor; for this is, roughly speaking, the end of the political life. But it seems too superficial to be what we are looking for, since it is thought to depend on those who bestow honor rather than on him who receives it, but the good we divine to be something proper to a man and not easily taken from him.

Further, men seem to pursue honor in order that they may be assured of their goodness; at least it is by men of practical wisdom that they seek to be honored, and among those who know them, and on the ground of their virtue; clearly, then, according to them, at any rate, virtue is better. And perhaps one might even suppose this to be, rather than honor, the end of the political life. But even this appears somewhat incomplete; for possession of virtue seems actually compatible with being asleep, or with lifelong inactivity, and, further, with the greatest sufferings and misfortunes; but a man who was living so no one would call happy, unless he were maintaining a thesis at all costs. But enough of this; for the subject has been sufficiently treated even in the current discussions. Third comes the contemplative life, which we shall consider later.

The life of money-making is one undertaken under compulsion, and wealth is evidently not the good we are seeking; for it is merely useful and for the sake of something else. And so one might rather take the aforenamed objects to be ends; for they are loved for themselves. But it is evident that not even these are ends; yet many arguments have been thrown away in support of them. Let us leave this subject, then....

7. Happiness and the "Function" of Human Beings

...Presumably, however, to say that happiness is the chief good seems a platitude, and a clearer account of what it is still desired. This might perhaps be given, if we could first ascertain the function of man. For just as for a flute-player, a sculptor, or an artist, and, in general, for all things that have a function or activity, the good and the 'well' is thought to reside in the function, so would it seem to be for man, if he has a function. Have the carpenter, then, and the tanner certain functions or activities, and has man none? Is he born without a function? Or as eye, hand, foot, and in general each of the parts evidently has a function, may one lay it down that man similarly has a function apart from all these? What then can this be? Life seems to be common even to plants, but we are seeking what is peculiar to man. Let us exclude, therefore, the life of nutrition and growth. Next there would be a life of perception, but it also seems to be common even to the horse, the ox, and every animal.

There remains, then, an active life of the element that has a rational principle; of this, one part has such a principle in the sense of being obedient to one, the other in the sense of possessing one and exercising thought. And, as 'life of the rational element' also has two meanings, we must state that life in the sense of activity is what we mean; for this seems to be the more proper sense of the term. Now if the function of man is an activity of soul which follows or implies a rational principle, and if we say 'so-and-so-and 'a good so-and-so' have a function which is the same in kind, e.g. a lyre, and a good lyre-player, and so without qualification in all cases, eminence in respect of goodness being added to the name of the function (for the function of a lyre-player is to play the lyre, and that of a good lyre-player is to do so well): if this is the case, and we state the function of man to be a certain kind of life, and this to be an activity or actions of the soul implying a rational principle, and the function of a good man to be the good and noble performance of these, and if any action is well performed when it is performed in accordance with the appropriate excellence: if this is the case, human good turns out to be activity of soul in accordance with virtue (*arete*), and if there are more than one virtue, in accordance with the best and most complete.

BOOK TWO

1. Moral Virtue and Habit

Virtue, then, being of two kinds, intellectual and moral, intellectual virtue in the main owes both its birth and its growth to teaching (for which reason it requires experience and time), while moral virtue comes about as a result of habit, whence also its name (*ethike*) is one that is formed by a slight variation from the word ethos (habit). From this it is also plain that none of the moral virtues arises in us by nature; for nothing that exists by nature can form a habit contrary to its nature. For instance the stone which by nature moves downwards cannot be habituated to move upwards, not even if one tries to train it by throwing it up ten thousand times; nor can fire be habituated to move downwards, nor can anything else that by nature behaves in one way be trained to behave in another. Neither by nature, then, nor contrary to nature do the virtues arise in us; rather we are adapted by nature to receive them, and are made perfect by habit.

Again, of all the things that come to us by nature we first acquire the potentiality and later exhibit the activity (this is plain in the case of the senses; for it was not by often seeing or often hearing that we got these senses, but, on the contrary, we had them before we used them, and did not come to have them by using them); but the virtues we get by first exercising them, as also happens in the case of the arts as well. For the things we have to learn before we can do them, we learn by doing them, e.g. men become builders by building and lyreplayers by playing the lyre; so too we become just by doing just acts, temperate by doing temperate acts, brave by doing brave acts.

This is confirmed by what happens in states; for legislators make the citizens good by forming habits in them, and this is the wish of every legislator, and those who do not effect it miss their mark, and it is in this that a good constitution differs from a bad one.

Again, it is from the same causes and by the same means that every virtue is both produced and destroyed, and similarly every art; for it is from playing the lyre that both good and bad lyre-players are produced. And the corresponding statement is true of builders and of all the rest; men will be good or bad builders as a result of building well or badly. For if this were not so, there would have been no need of a teacher, but all men would have been born good or bad at their craft. This, then, is the case with the virtues also; by doing the acts that we do in our transactions with other men we become just or unjust, and by doing the acts that we do in the presence of danger, and being habituated to feel fear or confidence, we become brave or cowardly. The same is true of appetites and feelings of anger; some men become temperate and good-tempered, others self-indulgent and irascible, by behaving in one way or the other in the appropriate circumstances. Thus, in one word, states of character arise out of like activities. This is why the activities we exhibit must be of a certain kind; it is because the states of character correspond to the differences between these. It makes no small difference, then, whether we form habits of one kind or of another from our very youth; it makes a very great difference, or rather all the difference....

3. Pleasure and Pain as the Test of Virtue

We must take as a sign of states of character the pleasure or pain that ensues on acts; for the man who abstains from bodily pleasures and delights in this very fact is temperate, while the man who is annoyed at it is self-indulgent, and he who stands his ground against things that are terrible and delights in this or at least is not pained is brave, while the man who is pained is a coward. For moral excellence is concerned with pleasures and pains; it is on account of the pleasure that we do bad things, and on account of the pain that we abstain from noble ones. Hence we ought to have been brought up in a particular way from our very youth, as Plato says, so as both to delight in and to be pained by the things that we ought; for this is the right education.

Again, if the virtues are concerned with actions and passions, and every passion and every action is accompanied by pleasure and pain, for this reason also virtue will be concerned with pleasures and pains. This is indicated also by the fact that punishment is inflicted by these means; for it is a kind of cure, and it is the nature of cures to be effected by contraries.

Again, as we said but lately, every state of soul has a nature relative to and concerned with the kind of things by which it tends to be made worse or better; but it is by reason of pleasures and pains that men become bad, by pursuing and avoiding these—either the pleasures and pains they ought not or when they ought not or as they ought not, or by going wrong in one of the other similar ways that may be distinguished. Hence men even define the virtues as certain states of impassivity and rest; not well, however, because they speak absolutely, and do not say 'as one ought' and 'as one ought not' and 'when one ought or ought not', and the other things that may be added. We assume, then, that this kind of excellence tends to do what is best with regard to pleasures and pains, and vice does the contrary.

The following facts also may show us that virtue and vice are concerned with these same things. There being three objects of choice and three of avoidance, the noble, the advantageous, the pleasant, and their contraries, the base, the injurious, the painful, about all of these the good man tends to go right and the bad man to go wrong, and especially about pleasure; for this is common to the animals, and also it accompanies all objects of choice; for even the noble and the advantageous appear pleasant.

Again, it has grown up with us all from our infancy; this is why it is difficult to rub off this passion, engrained as it is in our life. And we measure even our actions, some of us more and others less, by the rule of pleasure and pain. For this reason, then, our whole inquiry must be about these; for to feel delight and pain rightly or wrongly has no small effect on our actions.

Again, it is harder to fight with pleasure than with anger, to use Heraclitus' phrase, but both art and virtue are always concerned with what is harder; for even the good is better when it is harder. Therefore, for this reason also the whole concern both of virtue and of political science is with pleasures and pains; for the man who uses these well will be good, he who uses them badly will be bad.

That virtue, then, is concerned with pleasures and pains, and that by the acts from which it arises it is both increased and, if they are done differently, destroyed, and that the acts from which it arose are those in which it actualizes itself—let this be taken as said.

4. Becoming Virtuous

The question might be asked, what we mean by saying that we must become just by doing just acts, and temperate by doing temperate acts; for if men do just and temperate acts, they are already just and temperate, exactly as, if they do what is in accordance with the laws of grammar and of music, they are grammarians and musicians.

Or is this not true even of the arts? It is possible to do something that is in accordance with the laws of grammar, either by chance or at the suggestion of another. A man will be a grammarian, then, only when he has both done something grammatical and done it grammatically; and this means doing it in accordance with the grammatical knowledge in himself.

Again, the case of the arts and that of the virtues are not similar; for the products of the arts have their goodness in themselves, so that it is enough that they should have a certain character, but if the acts that are in accordance with the virtues have themselves a certain character it does not follow that they are done justly or temperately. The agent also must be in a certain condition when he does them; in the first place he must have knowledge, secondly he must choose the acts, and choose them for their own sakes, and thirdly his action must proceed from a firm and unchangeable character. These are not reckoned as conditions of the possession of the arts, except the bare knowledge; but as a condition of the possession of the virtues knowledge has little or no weight, while the other conditions count not for a little but for everything, i.e. the very conditions which result from often doing just and temperate acts.

Actions, then, are called just and temperate when they are such as the just or the temperate man would do; but it is not the man who does these that is just and temperate, but the man who also does them as just and temperate men do them. It is well said, then, that it is by doing just acts that the just man is produced, and by doing temperate acts the temperate man; without doing these no one would have even a prospect of becoming good.

But most people do not do these, but take refuge in theory and think they are being philosophers and will become good in this way, behaving somewhat like patients who listen attentively to their doctors, but do none of the things they are ordered to do. As the latter will not be made well in body by such a course of treatment, the former will not be made well in soul by such a course of philosophy.

6a. Defining Virtue

We must, however, not only describe virtue as a state of character, but also say what sort of state it is. We may remark, then, that every virtue or excellence both brings into good condition the thing of which it is the excellence and makes the work of that thing be done well; e.g. the excellence of the eye makes both the eye and its work good; for it is by the excellence of the eye that we see well. Similarly the excellence of the horse makes a horse both good in itself and good at running and at carrying its rider and at awaiting the attack of the enemy. Therefore, if this is true in every case, the virtue of man also will be the state of character which makes a man good and which makes him do his own work well.

How this is to happen we have stated already, but it will be made plain also by the following consideration of the specific nature of virtue. In everything that is continuous and divisible it is possible to take more, less, or an equal amount, and that either in terms of the thing itself or relatively to us; and the equal is an intermediate between excess and defect. By the intermediate in the object I mean that which is equidistant from each of the extremes, which is one and the same for all men; by the intermediate relatively to us that which is neither too much nor too little—and this is not one, nor the same for all. For instance, if ten is many and two is few, six is the intermediate, taken in terms of the object; for it exceeds and is exceeded by an equal amount; this is intermediate according to arithmetical proportion. But the intermediate relatively to us is not to be taken so; if ten pounds are too much for a particular person to eat and two too little, it does not follow that the trainer will order six pounds; for this also is perhaps too much for the person who is to take it, or too little—too little for Milo, too much for the beginner in athletic exercises. The same is true of running and wrestling. Thus a master of any art avoids excess and defect, but seeks the intermediate and chooses this—the intermediate not in the object but relatively to us.

If it is thus, then, that every art does its work well—by looking to the intermediate and judging its works by this standard (so that we often say of good works of art that it is not possible either to take away or to add anything, implying that excess and defect destroy the goodness of works of art, while the mean preserves it; and good artists, as we say, look to this in their work), and if, further, virtue is more exact and better than any art, as nature also is, then virtue must have the quality of aiming at the intermediate. I mean moral virtue; for it is this that is concerned with passions and actions, and in these there is excess, defect, and the intermediate. For instance, both fear and confidence and appetite and anger and pity and in general pleasure and pain may be felt both too much and too little, and in both cases not well; but to feel them at the right times, with reference to the right objects, towards the right people, with the right motive, and in the right way, is what is both intermediate and best, and this is characteristic of virtue. Similarly with regard to actions also there is excess, defect, and the intermediate. Now virtue is concerned with passions and actions, in which excess is a form of failure, and so is defect, while the intermediate is praised and is a form of success; and being praised and being successful are both characteristics of virtue. Therefore virtue is a kind of mean, since, as we have seen, it aims at what is intermediate.

Again, it is possible to fail in many ways..., while to succeed is possible only in one way (for which reason also one is easy and the other difficult- to miss the mark easy, to hit it difficult); for these reasons also, then, excess and defect are characteristic of vice, and the mean of virtue;

For men are good in but one way, but bad in many.

6b. The Golden Mean

Virtue, then, is a state of character concerned with choice, lying in a mean, i.e. the mean relative to us, this being determined by a rational principle, and by that principle by which the man of practical wisdom would determine it. Now it is a mean between two vices, that which depends on excess and that which depends on defect; and again it is a mean because the vices respectively fall short of or exceed what is right in both passions and actions, while virtue both finds and chooses that which is intermediate. Hence in respect of its substance and the definition which states its essence virtue is a mean, with regard to what is best and right an extreme.

But not every action nor every passion admits of a mean; for some have names that already imply badness, e.g. spite, shamelessness, envy, and in the case of actions adultery, theft, murder; for all of these and suchlike things imply by their names that they are themselves bad, and not the excesses or deficiencies of them. It is not possible, then, ever to be right with regard to them; one must always be wrong. Nor does goodness or badness with regard to such things depend on committing adultery with the right woman, at the right time, and in the right way, but simply to do any of them is to go wrong. It would be equally absurd, then, to expect that in unjust, cowardly, and voluptuous action there should be a mean, an excess, and a deficiency; for at that rate there would be a mean of excess and of deficiency, an excess of excess, and a deficiency of deficiency. But as there is no excess and deficiency of temperance and courage because what is intermediate is in a sense an extreme, so too of the actions we have mentioned there is no mean nor any excess and deficiency, but however they are done they are wrong; for in general there is neither a mean of excess and deficiency, nor excess and deficiency of a mean.

7. Illustrating the Mean

We must, however, not only make this general statement, but also apply it to the individual facts. For among statements about conduct those which are general apply more widely, but those which are particular are more genuine, since conduct has to do with individual cases, and our statements must harmonize with the facts in these cases. We may take these cases from our table. With regard to feelings of fear and confidence courage is the mean..., while the man who exceeds in confidence is foolhardy, and he who exceeds in fear and falls short in confidence is a coward.

With regard to pleasures and pains—not all of them, and not so much with regard to the pains—the mean is temperance, the excess self-indulgence. Persons deficient with regard to the pleasures are not often found; hence such persons also have received no name. But let us call them 'insensible'.

With regard to giving and taking of money the mean is generosity, the excess and the defect extravagance and stinginess. In these actions people exceed and fall short in contrary ways; the prodigal exceeds in spending and falls short in taking, while the mean man exceeds in taking and falls short in spending. (At present we are giving a mere outline or summary, and are satisfied with this; later these states will be more exactly determined.)....

With regard to honour and dishonour the mean is proper pride, the excess is known as a sort of 'empty vanity', and the deficiency is undue humility....

With regard to anger also there is an excess, a deficiency, and a mean. Although they can scarcely be said to have names, yet since we call the intermediate person good-tempered let us call the mean good temper; of the persons at the extremes let the one who exceeds be called irascible, and his vice irascibility, and the man who falls short [can be called] an apathetic sort of person....

With regard to pleasantness in the giving of amusement the intermediate person is witty and the disposition wittiness, the excess is buffoonery and the person characterized by it a buffoon, while the man who falls short is a sort of boor and his state is boorishness....

9. Three Rules for Guidance

That moral virtue is a mean, then, and in what sense it is so, and that it is a mean between two vices, the one involving excess, the other deficiency, and that it is such because its character is to aim at what is intermediate in passions and in actions, has been sufficiently stated. Hence also it is no easy task to be good. For in everything it is no easy task to find the middle, e.g. to find the middle of a circle is not for every one but for him who knows; so, too, anyone can get angry—that is easy—or give or spend money; but to do this to the right person, to the right extent, at the right time, with the right motive, and in the right way, that is not for every one, nor is it easy; it is for this reason that goodness is both rare and laudable and noble.

(1) Hence he who aims at the intermediate must first depart from what is the more contrary to it, as Calypso advises: "Hold the ship out beyond that surf and spray." For of the extremes one is more erroneous, one less so; therefore, since to hit the mean is hard in the extreme, we must as a second best, as people say, take the least of the evils; and this will be done best in the way we describe. But we must consider the things towards which we ourselves also are easily carried away; for some of us tend to one thing, some to another; and this will be recognizable from the pleasure and the pain we feel. We must drag ourselves away to the contrary extreme; for we shall get into the intermediate state by drawing well away from error, as people do in straightening sticks that are bent.

(2) Now in everything the pleasant or pleasure is most to be guarded against; for we do not judge it impartially. We ought, then, to feel towards pleasure as the elders of the people felt towards Helen, and in all circumstances repeat their saying; for if we dismiss pleasure thus we are less likely to go astray. It is by doing this, then, (to sum the matter up) that we shall best be able to hit the mean.

(3) But this is no doubt difficult, and especially in individual cases; for it is not easy to determine both how and with whom and on what provocation and how long one should be angry; for we too sometimes praise those who fall short and call them good-tempered, but sometimes we praise those who get angry and call them manly. The man, however, who deviates little from goodness is not blamed, whether he do so in the direction of the more or of the less, but only the man who deviates more widely; for he does not fail to be noticed. But up to what point and to what extent a man must deviate before he becomes blameworthy it is not easy to determine by reasoning, any more than anything else that is perceived by the senses; such things depend on particular facts, and the decision rests with perception. So much, then, is plain, that the intermediate state is in all things to be praised, but that we must incline sometimes towards the excess, sometimes towards the deficiency; for so shall we most easily hit the mean and what is right....

5.2

The Virtues
Aristotle

Courage

That it is a mean with regard to feelings of fear and confidence has
already been made evident; and plainly the things we fear are terrible
things, and these are, to speak without qualification, evils; for which
reason people even define fear as expectation of evil.

Now we fear all evils, e.g. disgrace, poverty, disease, friendlessness,
death, but the brave man is not thought to be concerned with all; for
to fear some things is even right and noble, and it is base not to fear
them—e.g. disgrace; he who fears this is good and modest, and he who
does not is shameless. He is, however, by some people called brave, by a
transference of the word to a new meaning; for he has in him something
which is like the brave man, since the brave man also is a fearless person.
Poverty and disease we perhaps ought not to fear, nor in general the
things that do not proceed from vice and are not due to a man himself.
But not even the man who is fearless of these is brave. Yet we apply the
word to him also in virtue of a similarity; for some who in the dangers
of war are cowards are liberal and are confident in face of the loss of
money. Nor is a man a coward if he fears insult to his wife and children
or envy or anything of the kind; nor brave if he is confident when he is
about to be flogged.

With what sort of terrible things, then, is the brave man concerned?
Surely with the greatest; for no one is more likely than he to stand his
ground against what is awe-inspiring. Now death is the most terrible
of all things; for it is the end, and nothing is thought to be any longer
either good or bad for the dead. But the brave man would not seem to be
concerned even with death in all circumstances, e.g. at sea or in disease.
In what circumstances, then? Surely in the noblest. Now such deaths are
those in battle; for these take place in the greatest and noblest danger.

Aristotle. *Nicomachean Ethics.* 3.6-7; 4.1, 3, 5. Trans. W.D. Ross. Oxford: Clarendon Press,
1908.

And these are correspondingly honoured in city-states and at the courts of monarchs.

Properly, then, he will be called brave who is fearless in face of a noble death, and of all emergencies that involve death; and the emergencies of war are in the highest degree of this kind. Yet at sea also, and in disease, the brave man is fearless, but not in the same way as the seaman; for he has given up hope of safety, and is disliking the thought of death in this shape, while they are hopeful because of their experience. At the same time, we show courage in situations where there is the opportunity of showing prowess or where death is noble; but in these forms of death neither of these conditions is fulfilled.

7. What is terrible is not the same for all men; but we say there are things terrible even beyond human strength. These, then, are terrible to every one—at least to every sensible man; but the terrible things that are not beyond human strength differ in magnitude and degree, and so too do the things that inspire confidence. Now the brave man is as dauntless as man may be. Therefore, while he will fear even the things that are not beyond human strength, he will face them as he ought and as the rule directs, for honour's sake; for this is the end of virtue. But it is possible to fear these more, or less, and again to fear things that are not terrible as if they were. Of the faults that are committed one consists in fearing what one should not, another in fearing as we should not, another in fearing when we should not, and so on; and so too with respect to the things that inspire confidence.

The man, then, who faces and who fears the right things and from the right motive, in the right way and from the right time, and who feels confidence under the corresponding conditions, is brave; for the brave man feels and acts according to the merits of the case and in whatever way the rule directs. Now the end of every activity is conformity to the corresponding state of character. This is true, therefore, of the brave man as well as of others. But courage is noble. Therefore the end also is noble; for each thing is defined by its end. Therefore it is for a noble end that the brave man endures and acts as courage directs.

Of those who go to excess he who exceeds in fearlessness has no name (we have said previously that many states of character have no names), but he would be a sort of madman or insensible person if he feared nothing, neither earthquakes nor the waves, as they say the Celts do not; while the man who exceeds in confidence about what really is terrible is rash. The rash man, however, is also thought to be boastful and only a pretender to courage; at all events, as the brave man is with regard to what is terrible, so the rash man wishes to appear; and so he imitates him in situations where he can. Hence also most of them are a mixture of rashness and cowardice; for, while in these situations they display confidence, they do not hold their ground against what is really terrible.

The man who exceeds in fear is a coward; for he fears both what he ought not and as he ought not, and all the similar characterizations attach to him. He is lacking also in confidence; but he is more conspicuous for his excess of fear in painful situations. The coward, then, is a despairing sort of person; for he fears everything. The brave man, on the other hand, has the opposite disposition; for confidence is the mark of a hopeful disposition. The coward, the rash man, and the brave man, then, are concerned with the same objects but are differently disposed towards them; for the first two exceed and fall short, while the third holds the middle, which is the right, position; and rash men are precipitate, and wish for dangers beforehand but draw back when they are in them, while brave men are keen in the moment of action, but quiet beforehand.

As we have said, then, courage is a mean with respect to things that inspire confidence or fear, in the circumstances that have been stated; and it chooses or endures things because it is noble to do so, or because it is base not to do so. But to die to escape from poverty or love or anything painful is not the mark of a brave man, but rather of a coward; for it is softness to fly from what is troublesome, and such a man endures death not because it is noble but to fly from evil.

Generosity

Let us speak next of generosity. It seems to be the mean with regard to wealth; for the generous man is praised not in respect of military matters, nor of those in respect of which the temperate man is praised, nor of judicial decisions, but with regard to the giving and taking of wealth, and especially in respect of giving. Now by 'wealth' we mean all the things whose value is measured by money. Further, extravagance and stinginess are excesses and defects with regard to wealth; and stinginess we always impute to those who care more than they ought for wealth, but we sometimes apply the word 'extravagance' in a complex sense; for we call those men extravagant who are incontinent and spend money on self-indulgence. Hence also they are thought the poorest characters; for they combine more vices than one. Therefore the application of the word to them is not its proper use; for a 'extravagant' means a man who has a single evil quality, that of wasting his substance; since an extravagant person is one who is being ruined by his own fault, and the wasting of substance is thought to be a sort of ruining of oneself, life being held to depend on possession of substance.

This, then, is the sense in which we take the word 'extravagant'. Now the things that have a use may be used either well or badly; and riches is a useful thing; and everything is used best by the man who has the virtue concerned with it; riches, therefore, will be used best by the man who has the virtue concerned with wealth; and this is the generous man. Now spending and giving seem to be the using of wealth; taking and keeping rather the possession of it. Hence it is more the mark of the genrous man to give to the right people than to take from the right sources and not to take from the wrong. For it is more characteristic of virtue to do good than to have good done to one, and more characteristic to do what is noble than not to do what is base; and it is not hard to see that giving implies doing good and doing what is noble, and taking implies having good done to one or not acting basely. And gratitude is felt towards him who gives, not towards him who does not take, and praise also is bestowed more on him. It is easier, also, not to take than to give; for men are apter to give away their own too little than to take what is another's. Givers, too, are called generous; but those who do not take are not praised for generosity but rather for justice; while those who take are hardly praised at all. And the generous are almost the most loved of all virtuous characters, since they are useful; and this depends on their giving.

Now virtuous actions are noble and done for the sake of the noble. Therefore the generous man, like other virtuous men, will give for the sake of the noble, and rightly; for he will give to the right people, the right amounts, and at the right time, with all the other qualifications that accompany right giving; and that too with pleasure or without pain; for that which is virtuous is pleasant or free from pain—least of all will it be painful. But he who gives to the wrong people or not for the sake of the noble but for some other cause, will be called not liberal but by some other name. Nor is he generous who gives with pain; for he would prefer the wealth to the noble act, and this is not characteristic of a genrous man. But no more will the generous man take from wrong sources; for such taking is not characteristic of the man who sets no store by wealth. Nor will he be a ready asker; for it is not characteristic of a man who confers benefits to accept them lightly. But he will take from the right sources, e.g. from his own possessions, not as something noble but as a necessity, that he may have something to give. Nor will he neglect his own property, since he wishes by means of this to help others. And he will refrain from giving to anybody and everybody, that he may have something to give to the right people, at the right time, and where it is noble to do so.

It is highly characteristic of a generous man also to go to excess in giving, so that he leaves too little for himself; for it is the nature of a genrous man not to look to himself. The term 'generosity' is used relatively to a man's substance; for generosity resides not in the multitude of the gifts but in the state of character of the giver, and this is relative to the giver's substance. There is therefore nothing to prevent the man who gives less from being the more generous man, if he has less to give those are thought to be more liberal who have not made their wealth but inherited it; for in the first place they have no experience of want, and secondly all men are fonder of their own productions, as are parents and poets. It is not easy for the generous man to be rich, since he is not apt either at taking or at keeping, but at giving away, and does not value wealth for its own sake but as a means to giving. Hence comes the charge that is brought against fortune, that those who deserve riches most get it least. But it is not unreasonable that it should turn out so; for he cannot have wealth, any more than anything else, if he does not take pains to have it. Yet he will not give to the wrong people nor at the wrong time, and so on; for he would no longer be acting in accordance with liberality, and if he spent on these objects he would have nothing to spend on the right objects. For, as has been said, he is generous who spends according to his substance and on the right objects; and he who exceeds is prodigal. Hence we do not call despots prodigal; for it is thought not easy for them to give and spend beyond the amount of their possessions.

Generosity, then, being a mean with regard to giving and taking of wealth, the generous man will both give and spend the right amounts and on the right objects, alike in small things and in great, and that with pleasure; he will also take the right amounts and from the right sources. For, the virtue being a mean with regard to both, he will do both as he ought; since this sort of taking accompanies proper giving, and that which is not of this sort is contrary to it, and accordingly the giving and taking that accompany each other are present together in the same man, while the contrary kinds evidently are not. But if he happens to spend in a manner contrary to what is right and noble, he will be pained, but moderately and as he ought; for it is the mark of virtue both to be pleased and to be pained at the right objects and in the right way. Further, the generous man is easy to deal with in money matters; for he can be got the better of, since he sets no store by money, and is more annoyed if he has not spent something that he ought than pained if he has spent something that he ought not, and does not agree with the saying of Simonides.

The extravagant errs in these respects also; for he is neither pleased nor pained at the right things or in the right way; this will be more evident as we go on. We have said that extravagance and stinginess are excesses and deficiencies, and in two things, in giving and in taking; for we include spending under giving. Now extravagance exceeds in giving and not taking, while stinginess falls short in giving, and exceeds in taking, except in small things.

The characteristics of extravagance are not often combined; for it is not easy to give to all if you take from none; private persons soon exhaust their substance with giving, and it is to these that the term extravagant is applied—though a man of this sort would seem to be in no small degree better than a mean man. For he is easily cured both by age and by poverty, and thus he may move towards the middle state. For he has the characteristics of the generous man, since he both gives and refrains from taking, though he does neither of these in the right manner or well. Therefore if he were brought to do so by habituation or in some other way, he would be generous; for he will then give to the right people, and will not take from the wrong sources. This is why he is thought to have not a bad character; it is not the mark of a wicked or ignoble man to go to excess in giving and not taking, but only of a foolish one. The man who is extravagant in this way is thought much better than the stingy man both for the aforesaid reasons and because he benefits many while the other benefits no one, not even himself.

But most extravagant people, as has been said, also take from the wrong sources, and are in this respect mean. They become apt to take because they wish to spend and cannot do this easily; for their possessions soon run short. Thus they are forced to provide means from some other source. At the same time, because they care nothing for honour, they take recklessly and from any source; for they have an appetite for giving, and they do not mind how or from what source. Hence also their giving is not generous; for it is not noble, nor does it aim at nobility, nor is it done in the right way; sometimes they make rich those who should be poor, and will give nothing to people of respectable character, and much to flatterers or those who provide them with some other pleasure. Hence also most of them are self-indulgent; for they spend lightly and waste money on their indulgences, and incline towards pleasures because they do not live with a view to what is noble.

The extravagant man, then, turns into what we have described if he is left untutored, but if he is treated with care he will arrive at the intermediate and right state. But stinginess is both incurable (for old age and every disability is thought to make men miserly) and more innate in men than extravagance; for most men are fonder of getting money than of giving. It also extends widely, and is multiform, since there seem to be many kinds of stinginess.

For it consists in two things, deficiency in giving and excess in taking, and is not found complete in all men but is sometimes divided; some men go to excess in taking, others fall short in giving. Those who are called by such names as 'miserly', 'close', 'stingy', all fall short in giving, but do not covet the possessions of others nor wish to get them. In some this is due to a sort of honesty and avoidance of what is disgraceful (for some seem, or at least profess, to hoard their money for this reason, that they may not some day be forced to do something disgraceful; to this class belong the cheeseparer and every one of the sort; he is so called from his excess of unwillingness to give anything); while others again keep their hands off the property of others from fear, on the ground that it is not easy, if one takes the property of others oneself, to avoid having one's own taken by them; they are therefore content neither to take nor to give.

Others again exceed in respect of taking by taking anything and from any source, e.g. those who ply sordid trades, pimps and all such people, and those who lend small sums and at high rates. For all of these take more than they ought and from wrong sources. What is common to them is evidently sordid love of gain; they all put up with a bad name for the sake of gain, and little gain at that. For those who make great gains but from wrong sources, and not the right gains, e.g. despots when they sack cities and spoil temples, we do not call stingy but rather wicked, impious, and unjust. But the gamester and the footpad and the highwayman belong to the class of the mean, since they have a sordid love of gain. For it is for gain that both of them ply their craft and endure the disgrace of it, and the one faces the greatest dangers for the sake of the booty, while the other makes gain from his friends, to whom he ought to be giving. Both, then, since they are willing to make gain from wrong sources, are sordid lovers of gain; therefore all such forms of taking are mean.

And it is natural that stinginess is described as the contrary of generosity; for not only is it a greater evil than extravagance, but men err more often in this direction than in the way of extravagance as we have described it.

So much, then, for generosity and the opposed vices....

Pride

Pride seems even from its name to be concerned with great things; what sort of great things, is the first question we must try to answer. It makes no difference whether we consider the state of character or the man characterized by it. Now the man is thought to be proud who thinks himself worthy of great things, being worthy of them; for he who does so beyond his deserts is a fool, but no virtuous man is foolish or silly. The proud man, then, is the man we have described. For he who is worthy of little and thinks himself worthy of little is temperate, but not proud; for pride implies greatness, as beauty implies a good-sized body, and little people may be neat and well-proportioned but cannot be beautiful. On the other hand, he who thinks himself worthy of great things, being unworthy of them, is vain; though not everyone who thinks himself worthy of more than he really is worthy of in vain. The man who thinks himself worthy of worthy of less than he is really worthy of is unduly humble, whether his deserts be great or moderate, or his deserts be small but his claims yet smaller. And the man whose deserts are great would seem most unduly humble; for what would he have done if they had been less? The proud man, then, is an extreme in respect of the greatness of his claims, but a mean in respect of the rightness of them; for he claims what is accordance with his merits, while the others go to excess or fall short.

If, then, he deserves and claims great things, and above all the great things, he will be concerned with one thing in particular. Desert is relative to external goods; and the greatest of these, we should say, is that which we render to the gods, and which people of position most aim at, and which is the prize appointed for the noblest deeds; and this is honour; that is surely the greatest of external goods. Honours and dishonours, therefore, are the objects with respect to which the proud man is as he should be. And even apart from argument it is with honour that proud men appear to be concerned; for it is honour that they chiefly claim, but in accordance with their deserts. The unduly humble man falls short both in comparison with his own merits and in comparison with the proud man's claims. The vain man goes to excess in comparison with his own merits, but does not exceed the proud man's claims.

Now the proud man, since he deserves most, must be good in the highest degree; for the better man always deserves more, and the best man most. Therefore the truly proud man must be good. And greatness in every virtue would seem to be characteristic of a proud man. And it would be most unbecoming for a proud man to fly from danger, swinging his arms by his sides, or to wrong another; for to what end should he do disgraceful acts, he to whom nothing is great? If we consider him point by point we shall see the utter absurdity of a proud man who is not good. Nor, again, would he be worthy of honour if he were bad; for honour is the prize of virtue, and it is to the good that it is rendered. Pride, then, seems to be a sort of crown of the virtues; for it makes them greater, and it is not found without them. Therefore it is hard to be truly proud; for it is impossible without nobility and goodness of character. It is chiefly with honours and dishonours, then, that the proud man is concerned; and at honours that are great and conferred by good men he will be moderately Pleased, thinking that he is coming by his own or even less than his own; for there can be no honour that is worthy of perfect virtue, yet he will at any rate accept it since they have nothing greater to bestow on him; but honour from casual people and on trifling grounds he will utterly despise, since it is not this that he deserves, and dishonour too, since in his case it cannot be just. In the first place, then, as has been said, the proud man is concerned with honours; yet he will also bear himself with moderation towards wealth and power and all good or evil fortune, whatever may befall him, and will be neither over-joyed by good fortune nor over-pained by evil. For not even towards honour does he bear himself as if it were a very great thing. Power and wealth are desirable for the sake of honour (at least those who have them wish to get honour by means of them); and for him to whom even honour is a little thing the others must be so too. Hence proud men are thought to be disdainful.

The goods of fortune also are thought to contribute towards pride. For men who are well-born are thought worthy of honour, and so are those who enjoy power or wealth; for they are in a superior position, and everythingthat has a superiority in something good is held in greater honour. Hence even such things make men prouder; for they are honoured by some for having them; but in truth the good man alone is to be honoured; he, however, who has both advantages is thought the more worthy of honour. But those who without virtue have such goods are neither justified in making great claims nor entitled to the name of 'proud'; for these things imply perfect virtue. Disdainful and insolent, however, even those who have such goods become. For without virtue it is not easy to bear gracefully the goods of fortune; and, being unable to bear them, and thinking themselves superior to others, they despise others and themselves do what they please. They imitate the proud man without being like him, and this they do where they can; so they do not act virtuously, but they do despise others. For the proud man despises justly (since he thinks truly), but the many do so at random.

He does not run into trifling dangers, nor is he fond of danger, because he honours few things; but he will face great dangers, and when he is in danger he is unsparing of his life, knowing that there are conditions on which life is not worth having. And he is the sort of man to confer benefits, but he is ashamed of receiving them; for the one is the mark of a superior, the other of an inferior. And he is apt to confer greater benefits in return; for thus the original benefactor besides being paid will incur a debt to him, and will be the gainer by the transaction. They seem also to remember any service they have done, but not those they have received (for he who receives a service is inferior to him who has done it, but the proud man wishes to be superior), and to hear of the former with pleasure, of the latter with displeasure; this, it seems, is why Thetis did not mention to Zeus the services she had done him, and why the Spartans did not recount their services to the Athenians, but those they had received. It is a mark of the proud man also to ask for nothing or scarcely anything, but to give help readily, and to be dignified towards people who enjoy high position and good fortune, but unassuming towards those of the middle class; for it is a difficult and lofty thing to be superior to the former, but easy to be so to the latter, and a lofty bearing over the former is no mark of ill-breeding, but among humble people it is as vulgar as a display of strength against the weak. Again, it is characteristic of the proud man not to aim at the things commonly held in honour, or the things in which others excel; to be sluggish and to hold back except where great honour or a great work is at stake, and to be a man of few deeds, but of great and notable ones. He must also be open in his hate and in his love (for to conceal one's feelings, i.e. to care less for truth than for what people will think, is a coward's part), and must speak and act openly; for he is free of speech because he is contemptuous, and he is given to telling the truth, except when he speaks in irony to the vulgar. He must be unable to make his life revolve round another, unless it be a friend; for this is slavish, and for this reason all flatterers are servile and people lacking in self-respect are flatterers. Nor is he given to admiration; for nothing to him is great. Nor is he mindful of wrongs; for it is not the part of a proud man to have a long memory, especially for wrongs, but rather to overlook them. Nor is he a gossip; for he will speak neither about himself nor about another, since he cares not to be praised nor for others to be blamed; nor again is he given to praise; and for the same reason he is not an evil-speaker, even about his enemies, except from haughtiness. With regard to necessary or small matters he is least of all me given to lamentation or the asking of favours; for it is the part of one who takes such matters seriously to behave so with respect to them. He is one who will possess beautiful and profitless things rather than profitable and useful ones; for this is more proper to a character that suffices to itself.

Further, a slow step is thought proper to the proud man, a deep voice, and a level utterance; for the man who takes few things seriously is not likely to be hurried, nor the man who thinks nothing great to be excited, while a shrill voice and a rapid gait are the results of hurry and excitement.

Such, then, is the proud man; the man who falls short of him is unduly humble, and the man who goes beyond him is vain. Now even these are not thought to be bad (for they are not malicious), but only mistaken. For the unduly humble man, being worthy of good things, robs himself of what he deserves, and to have something bad about him from the fact that he does not think himself worthy of good things, and seems also not to know himself; else he would have desired the things he was worthy of, since these were good. Yet such people are not thought to be fools, but rather unduly retiring. Such a reputation, however, seems actually to make them worse; for each class of people aims at what corresponds to its worth, and these people stand back even from noble actions and undertakings, deeming themselves unworthy, and from external goods no less. Vain people, on the other hand, are fools and ignorant of themselves, and that manifestly; for, not being worthy of them, they attempt honourable undertakings, and then are found out; and tetadorn themselves with clothing and outward show and such things, and wish their strokes of good fortune to be made public, and speak about them as if they would be honoured for them. But undue humility is more opposed to pride than vanity is; for it is both commoner and worse.

Good Temper

Good temper is a mean with respect to anger; the middle state being unnamed, and the extremes almost without a name as well, we place good temper in the middle position, though it inclines towards the deficiency, which is without a name. The excess might called a sort of 'irascibility'. For the passion is anger, while its causes are many and diverse.

The man who is angry at the right things and with the right people, and, further, as he ought, when he ought, and as long as he ought, is praised. This will be the good-tempered man, then, since good temper is praised. For the good-tempered man tends to be unperturbed and not to be led by passion, but to be angry in the manner, at the things, and for the length of time, that the rule dictates; but he is thought to err rather in the direction of deficiency; for the good-tempered man is not revengeful, but rather tends to make allowances.

The deficiency, whether it is a sort of 'irascibility' or whatever it is, is blamed. For those who are not angry at the things they should be angry at are thought to be fools, and so are those who are not angry in the right way, at the right time, or with the right persons; for such a man is thought not to feel things nor to be pained by them, and, since he does not get angry, he is thought unlikely to defend himself; and to endure being insulted and put up with insult to one's friends is slavish.

The excess can be manifested in all the points that have been named (for one can be angry with the wrong persons, at the wrong things, more than is right, too quickly, or too long); yet all are not found in the same person. Indeed they could not; for evil destroys even itself, and if it is complete becomes unbearable. Now hot-tempered people get angry quickly and with the wrong persons and at the wrong things and more than is right, but their anger ceases quickly—which is the best point about them. This happens to them because they do not restrain their anger but retaliate openly owing to their quickness of temper, and then their anger ceases. By reason of excess choleric people are quick-tempered and ready to be angry with everything and on every occasion; whence their name. Sulky people are hard to appease, and retain their anger long; for they repress their passion. But it ceases when they retaliate; for revenge relieves them of their anger, producing in them pleasure instead of pain. If this does not happen they retain their burden; for owing to its not being obvious no one even reasons with them, and to digest one's anger in oneself takes time. Such people are most troublesome to themselves and to their dearest friends. We call had-tempered those who are angry at the wrong things, more than is right, and longer, and cannot be appeased until they inflict vengeance or punishment.

To good temper we oppose the excess rather than the defect; for not only is it commoner since revenge is the more human), but bad-tempered people are worse to live with.

What we have said in our earlier treatment of the subject is plain also from what we are now saying—namely, that it is not easy to define how, with whom, at what, and how long one should be angry, and at what point right action ceases and wrong begins. For the man who strays a little from the path, either towards the more or towards the less, is not blamed; since sometimes we praise those who exhibit the deficiency, and call them good-tempered, and sometimes we call angry people manly, as being capable of ruling. How far, therefore, and how a man must stray before he becomes blameworthy, it is not easy to state in words; for the decision depends on the particular facts and on perception. But so much at least is plain, that the middle state is praiseworthy—that in virtue of which we are angry with the right people, at the right things, in the right way, and so on, while the excesses and defects are blameworthy— slightly so if they are present in a low degree, more if in a higher degree, and very much if in a high degree. Evidently, then, we must cling to the middle state. Enough of the states relative to anger....

5.3

A Program for Moral Improvement

Benjamin Franklin

It was about this time I conceived the bold and arduous project of arriving at moral perfection. I wished to live without committing any fault at any time; I would conquer all that either natural inclination, custom, or company might lead me into. As I knew, or thought I knew, what was right and wrong, I did not see why I might not always do the one and avoid the other. But I soon found I had undertaken a task of more difficulty than I had imagined. While my care was employed in guarding against one fault, I was often surprised by another; habit took the advantage of inattention; inclination was sometimes too strong for reason. I concluded, at length, that the mere speculative conviction that it was our interest to be completely virtuous was not sufficient to prevent our slipping, and that the contrary habits must be broken, and good ones acquired and established, before we can have any dependence on a steady, uniform rectitude of conduct. For this purpose I therefore contrived the following method. In the various enumerations of the moral virtues I met in my reading, I found the catalogue more or less numerous, as different writers included more or fewer ideas under the same name. Temperance, for example, was by some confined to eating and drinking, while by others it was extended to mean the moderating every other pleasure, appetite, inclination, or passion, bodily or mental, even to our avarice and ambition. I proposed to myself, for the sake of clearness, to use rather more names, with fewer ideas annexed to each, than a few names with more ideas; and I included under thirteen names of virtues all that at that time occurred to me as necessary or desirable, and annexed to each a short precept, which fully expressed the extent I gave to its meaning.

These names of virtues, with their precepts were:

1. Temperance

Benjamin Franklin. *Autobiography* (1791).

Eat not to dullness; drink not to elevation.

2. Silence
    Speak not but what may benefit others or yourself; avoid
    trifling conversation.

3. Order
    Let all your things have their places; let each part of your
    business have its time.

4. Resolution
    Resolve to perform what you ought; perform without fail what
    you resolve.

5. Frugality
    Make no expense but to do good to others or yourself, i.e.,
    waste nothing.

6. Industry
    Lose no time; be always employed in something useful; cut off
    all unnecessary actions.

7. Sincerity.
    Use no hurtful deceit; think innocently and justly, and, if you
    speak, speak accordingly.

8. Justice
    Wrong none by doing injuries or omitting the benefits that are
    your duty.

9. Moderation
    Avoid extremes; forbear resenting injuries so much as you
    think they deserve.

10. Cleanliness
    Tolerate no uncleanliness in body, clothes, or habitation.

11. Tranquillity
    Be not disturbed at trifles, or at accidents common or
    unavoidable.

12. Chastity
    Rarely use venery but for health or offspring, never to dullness,
    weakness, or the injury of your own or another's peace or

reputation.

13. Humility
   Imitate Jesus and Socrates.

My intention being to acquire the *habitude* of all these virtues, I judged it would be well not to distract my attention by attempting the whole at once, but to fix it on one of them at a time, and, when I should be master of that, then to proceed to another, and so on, till I should have gone thro' the thirteen; and, as the previous acquisition of some might facilitate the acquisition of certain others, I arranged them with that view, as they stand above. Temperance first, as it tends to procure that coolness and clearness of head which is so necessary where constant vigilance was to be kept up, and guard maintained against the unremitting attraction of ancient habits and the force of perpetual temptations. This being acquired and established, Silence would be more easy; and my desire being to gain knowledge at the same time that I improved in virtue, and considering that in conversation it was obtained rather by the use of the ears than of the tongue, and therefore wishing to break a habit I was getting into prattling, punning, and joking, which only made me acceptable to trifling company, I gave *Silence* the second place. This and the next, *Order*, I expected would allow me more time for attending to my project and my studies. Resolution, once because habitual, would keep me firm in my endeavors to obtain all the subsequent virtues; *Frugality* and Industry, freeing me from my remaining debt, and producing affluence and independence, would make more easy the practice of Sincerity and Justice, etc., Conceiving, then, that, agreeably to the advice of Pythagoras in his Garden Verses, daily examination would be necessary, I contrived the following method for conducting that examination. I made a little book, in which I allotted a page for each of the virtues. I ruled each page with red ink, so as to have seven columns, one for each day of the week, marking each column with a letter for the day. I crossed these columns with thirteen red lines, marking the beginning of each line with the first letter of one of the virtues, on which line, and in its proper column, I might mark, by a little black spot, every fault I found upon examination to have been committed respecting that virtue upon that day.
   I determined to give a week's strict attention to each of the virtues successively. Thus, in the first week, my great guard was to avoid every the least offense against *Temperance*, leaving the other virtues to their ordinary chance, only marking every evening the faults of the day. Thus, if in the first week I could keep my first line, marked T, clear of spots, I supposed the habit of that virtue so much strengthened, and its opposite weakened, that I might venture extending my attention to

include the next, and for the following week keep both lines clear of spots. Proceeding thus to the last, I could go thro' a course complete in thirteen weeks, and four courses in a years. And like him who, having a garden to weed, does not attempt to eradicate all the bad herbs at once, which would exceed his reach and his strength, but works on one of the beds at a time, and, having accomplished the first, proceeds to a second, so I should have, I hoped, the encouraging pleasure of seeing on my pages the progress I made in virtue, by clearing successively my lines of their spots, till in the end, by a number of courses, I should be happy in viewing a clean book, after a thirteen weeks' daily examination. This my little book had for its motto these lines from *Addison's "Cato"*:

> *Here will I hold. If there's a power above us (And that there is, all nature cries aloud Thro' all her works), He must delight in virtue; And that which He delights in must be happy.*

Another from Cicero:

> *O vitae Philosophia dux! O virtutum indagatrix expultrixque vitiorum! Unus dies, bene et ex praeceptis tuis actus, peccanti immortalitati est anteponendus.*

Another from the Proverbs of Solomon, speaking of wisdom or virtue:

> *Length of days is in her right hand; and in her left hand riches and honor. Her ways are ways of pleasantness, and all her paths are peace (iii. 16, 17).*

And conceiving God to be the fountain of wisdom, I thought it right and necessary to solicit His assistance for obtaining it; to this end I formed the following little prayer, which was prefixed to my tables of examination, for daily use:

> *O powerful Goodness! bountiful Father! merciful Guide! increase in me that wisdom which discovers my truest interest. Strengthen my resolutions to perform what that wisdom dictates. Accept my kind offices to Thy other children as the only return in my power for Thy continual favors to me.*

I used also sometimes a little prayer which I took from *Thomson's* "Poems," viz.:

> *Father of light and life, thou Good Supreme! O teach me what is good; teach me Thyself!*

Save me from folly, vanity, and vice,
From every low pursuit; and fill my soul
With knowledge, conscious peace, and virtue pure;
Sacred, substantial, never-fading bliss!

The precept of Order requiring that *every part of my business should have its allotted time*, one page in my little book contained the following scheme of employment for the twenty-four hours of a natural day:

I entered upon the execution of this plan for self-examination, and continued it, with occasional intermissions, for some time. I was surprised to find myself so much fuller of faults than I had imagined; but I had the satisfaction of seeing them diminish. To avoid the trouble of renewing now and then my little book, which, by scraping out the marks on the paper of old faults to make room for new ones in a new course, became full of holes, I transferred my tables and precepts to the ivory leaves of a memorandumbook, on which the lines were drawn with red ink, that made a durable strain, and on those lines I marked my faults with a black leading pencil, which marks I could easily wipe out with a wet sponge. After a while I went thro' one course only in a year, and afterward only one in several years, till at length I omitted them entirely, being employed in voyages and business abroad, with a multiplicity of affairs that interfered; but I always carried my little book with me.

My scheme of Order gave me the most trouble; and I found that, tho' it might be practicable where a man's business was such as to leave him the disposition of his time, that of a journeyman printer, for instance, it was not possible to be exactly observed by a master, who must mix with the world, and often receive people of business at their own hours. Order, too, with regard to places for things, papers, etc., I found extremely difficult to acquire. I had not been early accustomed to it, and, having an exceeding good memory, I was not so sensible of the inconvenience attending want of method. This article, therefore, cost me so much painful attention, and my faults in it vexed me so much, and I made so little progress in amendment, and had such frequent relapses, that I was almost ready to give up the attempt, and content myself with a faulty character in that respect, like the man who, in buying an ax of a smith, my neighbor, desired to have the whole of its surface as bright as the edge. The smith consented to grind it bright for him if he would turn the wheel; he turned, while the smith pressed the broad face of the ax hard and heavily on the stone, which made the turning of it very fatiguing. The man came every now and then from the wheel to see how the work went on, and at length would take his ax as it was, without farther grinding. " No," said the smith; " turn on, turn on; we shall have it bright by and by; as yet, it is only speckled." "Yes," says the man, *"but I think I like a apeckled ax best."* And I believe this may have been the case

with many, who, having, for want of some such means as I employed,
found the difficulty of obtaining good and breaking bad habits in other
points of vice and virtue, have given up the struggle, and concluded that
" *a speckled ax was best*" for something, that pretended to be reason,
was every now and then suggesting to me that such extreme nicety as
I exacted of myself might be a kind of foppery in morals, which, if it
were known, would make me ridiculous; that a perfect character might
be attended with the inconvenience of being envied and hated; and that a
benevolent man should allow a few faults in himself, to keep his friends
in countenance.

In truth, I myself incorrigible with respect to Order; and now I am
grown old, and my memory bad, I feel very sensibly the want of it.
But, on the whole, tho' I never arrived at the perfection I had been so
amblitious of obtaining, but fell far short of it, yet I was, by the endeavor,
a better and a happier man than I otherwise should have been if I had
not attempted it; as those who aim at perfect writing by imitating the
engraved copies, tho' they never reach the wished-for excellence of
those copies, their hand is mended by the endeavor, and tolerable, while
it continues fair and legible.

It may be well my posterity should be informed that to this little
artifice, with the blessing of God, their ancestor owned the constant
felicity of his life down to his seventyninth year, in which this is written.
What reverses may attend the remainder is in the hand of Providence;
but, if they arrive, the reflection on past happiness enjoyed ought to help
his bearing them with more resignation. To Temperance he ascribe his
long-continued health and what is still left to him of a good constitution;
to Industry and Frugality, the early easiness of his circumstances and
acquisition of his fortune, with all that knowledge that enabled him to be
a useful citizen, and obtained for him some degree of reputation among
the learned; to Sincerity and Justice, the confidence of his country, and
the honorable employs it conferred upon him; and to the joint influence
of the whole mass of the virtues, even in the imperfect state he was able
to acquire them, all that evenness of temper, and that cheerfulness in
conversation, which makes his company still sought for, and agreeable
even to his younger acquaintance. I hope, therefore, that some of my
descendants may follow the example and reap the benefit.

It will be remarked that, tho' my scheme was not wholly without
religion, there was in it no mark of the distinguishing tenets of any
particular sect. I had purposely avoided them; for, being fully persuaded
of the utility and excellency of my method, and that it might be
serviceable to people in all religions, and intending some time or other
to publish it, I would not have anything in it that should prejudice any
one,of any sect, against it. I purposed writing a little comment on each
virtue, in which I would have shown the advantages of possessing it,

and the mischiefs attending its opposite vice; and I should have called my book "The Art of Virtue," 1 because it would have shown the means and manner of obtaining virtue, which would have distinguished it from the mere exhortation to be good, that does not instruct and indicate the means, but is like the apostle's man of verbal charity, who only, without showing to the naked and hungry how or where they might get clothes or victuals, exhorted themto be fed and clothed (James ii. 15,16).

But it so happened that my intention of writing and publishing this comment was never fulfilled. I did, indeed, from time to time, put down short hints of the sentiments, reasonings, etc., to be made use of in it, some of which I have still by me: But the necessary close Attention to private Business in the earlier part of Life, and public Business since, have occasioned my postponing it. For it being connected in my Mind with a *great and extensive Project* that require the whole man to execute, and which an unforeseen Secession of Employs prevented my attending to, it has hitherto remain'd unfinish'd.

In this piece it was my design to explain and enforce this doctrine, that vicious actions are not hurtful because they are forbidden, but forbidden because they are hurtful, the nature of man alone considered; that it was, therefore, every one's interest to be virtuous who wished to be happy even in this world; and I should, from this circumstance (there being always in the world a number of rich merchants, nobility, states, and princes, who have need of honest instruments for the management of their affairs, and such being so rare), have endeavored to convince young persons that no qualities were so likely to make a poor man's fortune as those of probity and integrity.

My list of virtues continued at first but twelve; but a Quaker friend having kindly informed me that I was generally thought proud, that my pride showed itself frequently in conversation, that I was not content with being in the right when discussing any point, but was overbearing and rather insolent, of which he convinced me by mentioning several instances, I determined endeavoring to cure myself, if I could, of this vice or folly among the rest, and I added *Humility* to my list, giving an extensive meaning to the word.

I cannot boast of much success in acquiring the *reality* of this virtue, but I had a good deal with regard to the *appearance* of it. I made it a rule to forbear all direct contradiction to the sentiments of others, and all positive assertion of my own. I even forbid myself, agreeably to the old laws of our Junto, the use of every word or expression in the language that imported a fixed opinion, such as *certainly, undoubtedly,* etc., and I adopted, instead of them, I *conceive,* I *apprehend,* or I *imagine* a thing to be so or so, or it so *appears* to me at *present.* When another asserted something that I thought an error, I denied myself the pleasure of contradicting him abruptly and of showing immediately some absurdity in his proposition; and in answering, I began by observing that in certain cases or circumstances his opinion would be right, but in the present case there *appeared* or *seemed* to me some difference, etc. I soon found the advantage of this charge in my manner; the conversations I engaged in went on more pleasantly.

The modest way in which I proposed my opinions procured them a readier reception and less contradiction; I had less mortification when I was found to be in the wrong, and I more easily prevailed with other to give up their mistakes and join with me when I happened to be in the right.

And this mode, which I at first put on with some violence to natural inclination, became at length so easy, and so habitual to me, that perhaps for these fifty years past no one has ever heard a dogmatical expression escape me. And to this habit (after my character of integrity) I think it principally owing that I had early so much weight with my fellow-citizens when I proposed new institutions, or alterations in the old, and so much influence in public councils when I became a member; for I was but a bad speaker, never eloquent, subject to much hesitation in my choice of words, hardly correct in language, and yet I generally carried my points.

In reality, there is, perhaps, no one of our natural passions so hard to subdue as *pride*. Disguise it, struggle with it, beat it down, stifle it, mortify it as much as one pleases, it is still alive, and will every now and then peep out and show itself; you will see it, perhaps, often in this history; for, even if I could conceive that I had completely overcome it, I should probably be proud of my humility.

5.4

Malicious Joy, Envy, and Revenge

Friedrich Nietzsche

27. Explanation of Malicious Joy

Malicious joy arises when a man consciously finds himself in evil plight and feels anxiety or remorse or pain. The misfortune that overtakes B. makes him equal to A., and A. is reconciled and no longer envious. If A. is prosperous, he still hoards up in his memory B.'s misfortune as a capital, so as to throw it in the scale as a counter-weight when he himself suffers adversity. In this case too he feels "malicious joy" (*Schadenfreude*). The sentiment of equality thus applies its standard to the domain of luck and chance. Malicious joy is the commonest expression of victory and restoration of equality, even in a higher state of civilization. This emotion has only been in existence since the time when man learnt to look upon another as his equal—in other words, since the foundation of society.

28. The Arbitrary Element in the Award of Punishment

To most criminals punishment comes just as illegitimate children come to women. They have done the same thing a hundred times without any bad consequences. Suddenly comes discovery, and with discovery punishment. Yet habit should make the deed for which the criminal is punished appear more excusable, for he has developed a propensity that is hard to resist. Instead of this, the criminal is punished more severely if the suspicion of habitual crime rests on him, and habit is made a valid reason against all extenuation. On the other hand, a model life, wherein crime shows up in more terrible contrast, should make the guilt appear more heavy! But here the custom is to soften the punishment. Everything

Friedrich Nietzsche. *Human, All-Too-Human*. Trans. Paul V. Cohn. London: T.N. Foulis, 1911.

is measured not from the standpoint of the criminal but from that of society and its losses and dangers. The previous utility of an individual is weighed against his one nefarious action, his previous criminality is added to that recently discovered, and punishment is thus meted out as highly as possible. But if we thus punish or reward a man's past (for in the former case the diminution of punishment is a reward) we ought to go farther back and punish and reward the cause of his past—I mean parents, teachers, society. In many instances we shall then find the judges somehow or other sharing in the guilt. It is arbitrary to stop at the criminal himself when we punish his past: if we will not grant the absolute excusability of every crime, we should stop at each individual case and probe no farther into the past—in other words, isolate guilt and not connect it with previous actions. Otherwise we sin against logic. The teachers of free will should draw the inevitable conclusion from their doctrine of "free will" and boldly decree: "No action has a past."

29. Envy and Her Nobler Sister

Where equality is really recognized and permanently established, we see the rise of that propensity that is generally considered immoral, and would scarcely be conceivable in a state of nature—envy. The envious man is susceptible to every sign of individual superiority to the common herd, and wishes to depress every one once more to the level—or raise himself to the superior plane. Hence arise two different modes of action, which Hesiod designated good and bad Eris. In the same way, in a condition of equality there arises indignation if A. is prosperous above and B. unfortunate beneath their deserts and equality. These latter, however, are emotions of nobler natures. They feel the want of justice and equity in things that are independent of the arbitrary choice of men—or, in other words, they desire the equality recognized by man to be recognized as well by Nature and chance. They are angry that men of equal merits should not have equal fortune.

30. The Envy of the Gods

"The envy of the Gods" arises when a despised person sets himself on an equality with his superior (like Ajax), or is made equal with him by the favor of fortune (like Niobe, the too favored mother). In the social class system this envy demands that no one shall have merits above his station, that his prosperity shall be on a level with his position, and especially that his self-consciousness shall not outgrow the limits of his rank. Often the victorious general, or the pupil who achieves a masterpiece, has experienced "the envy of the gods."

31. Vanity as an Anti-Social Aftergrowth

As men, for the sake of security, have made themselves equal in order to found communities, but as also this conception is imposed by a sort of constraint and is entirely opposed to the instincts of the individual, so, the more universal security is guaranteed, the more do new offshoots of the old instinct for predominance appear. Such offshoots appear in the setting-up of class distinctions, in the demand for professional dignities and privileges, and, generally speaking, in vanity (manners, dress, speech, and so forth). So soon as danger to the community is apparent, the majority, who were unable to assert their preponderance in a time of universal peace, once more bring about the condition of equality, and for the time being the absurd privileges and vanities disappear. If the community, however, collapses utterly and anarchy reigns supreme, there arises the state of nature: an absolutely ruthless inequality as recounted by Thucydides in the case of Corcyra. Neither a natural justice nor a natural injustice exists.

32. Equity

Equity is a development of justice, and arises among such as do not come into conflict with the communal equality. This more subtle recognition of the principle of equilibrium is applied to cases where nothing is prescribed by law. Equity looks forwards and backwards, its maxim being, "Do unto others as you would that they should do unto you." *Aequum* means: "This principle is conformable to our equality; it tones down even our small differences to an appearance of equality, and expects us to be indulgent in cases where we are not compelled to pardon."

33. Elements of Revenge

The word "revenge" is spoken so quickly that it almost seems as if it could not contain more than one conceptual and emotional root. Hence we are still at pains to find this root. Our economists, in the same way, have never wearied of scenting a similar unity in the word "value," and of hunting after the primitive root idea of value. As if all words were not pockets, into which this or that or several things have been stuffed at once! So "revenge" is now one thing, now another, and sometimes more composite. Let us first distinguish that defensive counter-blow, which we strike, almost unconsciously, even at inanimate objects (such as machinery in motion) that have hurt us. The notion is to set a check to the object that has hurt us, by bringing the machine to a stop. Sometimes the force of this counter-blow, in order to attain its object, will have to be strong enough to shatter the machine. If the machine be too strong to be disorganized by one man, the latter will all the same strike the most violent blow he can—as a sort of last attempt. We behave similarly towards persons who hurt us, at the immediate sensation of the hurt. If we like to call this an act of revenge, well and good: but we must remember that here self-preservation alone has set its cog-wheels of reason in motion, and that after all we do not think of the doer of the injury but only of ourselves. We act without any idea of doing injury in return, only with a view to getting away safe and sound. It needs time to pass in thought from oneself to one's adversary and ask oneself at what point he is most vulnerable. This is done in the second variety of revenge, the preliminary idea of which is to consider the vulnerability and susceptibility of the other. The intention then is to give pain. On the other hand, the idea of securing himself against further injury is in this case so entirely outside the avenger's horizon, that he almost regularly brings about his own further injury and often foresees it in cold blood. If in the first sort of revenge it was the fear of a second blow that made the counter-blow as strong as possible, in this case there is an almost complete indifference to what one's adversary will do: thestrength of the counter-blow is only determined by what he has already done to us. Then what has he done? What profit is it to us if he is now suffering, after we have suffered through him? This is a case of readjustment, whereas the first act of revenge only serves the purpose of self-preservation. It may be that through our adversary we have lost property, rank, friends, children—these losses are not recovered by revenge, the readjustment only concerns a subsidiary loss which is added to all the other losses. The revenge of readjustment does not preserve one from further injury, it does not make good the injury already suffered—except in one case. If our honor has suffered through our adversary, revenge can restore it. But in any case honor has suffered an injury if intentional harm has been done us, because our adversary proved thereby that he was not afraid of us. By revenge we prove that we are not afraid of him either, and herein lies the settlement, the readjustment. (The intention of showing their complete lack of fear goes so far in some people that the dangers of revenge— loss of health or life or other losses--are in their eyes an indispensable condition of every vengeful act. Hence they practice the duel, although the law also offers them aid in obtaining satisfaction for what they have suffered. They are not satisfied with a safe means of recovering their honor, because this would not prove their fearlessness.)—In the first-named variety of revenge it is just fear that strikes the counter-blow; in the second case it is the absence of fear, which, as has been said, wishes to manifest itself in the counter-blow. Thus nothing appears more different than the motives of the two courses of action which are designated by the one word "revenge." Yet it often happens that the avenger is not precisely certain as to what really prompted his deed: perhaps he struck the counterblow from fear and the instinct of self-preservation, but in the background, when he has time to reflect upon the standpoint of wounded honor, he imagines that he has avenged himself for the sake of his honor—this motive is in any case more reputable than the other. An essential point is whether he sees his honor injured in the eyes of others (the world) or only in the eyes of his offenders: in the latter case he will prefer secret, in the former open revenge. Accordingly, as he enters strongly or feebly into the soul of the doer and the spectator, his revenge will be more bitter or more tame. If he is entirely lacking in this sort of imagination, he will not think at all of revenge, as the feeling of "honor" is not present in him, and accordingly cannot be wounded. In the same way, he will not think of revenge if he despises the offender and the spectator; because as objects of his contempt they cannot give him honor, and accordingly cannot rob him of honor. Finally, he will forego revenge in the not uncommon case of his loving the offender. It is true that he then suffers loss of honor in the other's eyes, and will perhaps become less worthy of having his love returned. But even to renounce all requital of love is a sacrifice that love is ready to make when its only object is to avoid hurting the beloved object: this would mean hurting oneself more than one is hurt by the sacrifice. Accordingly, everyone will avenge himself, unless he be bereft of honor or inspired by contempt or by love for the offender. Even if he turns to the law-courts, he desires revenge as a private individual; but also, as a thoughtful, prudent man of society, he desires the revenge of society upon one who does not respect it. Thus by legal punishment private honor as well as that of society is restored—that is to say, punishment is revenge. Punishment undoubtedly contains the first-mentioned element of revenge, in as far as by its means society helps to preserve itself, and strikes a counter-blow in self-defense. Punishment desires to prevent further injury, to scare other offenders. In this way the two elements of revenge, different as they are, are united in punishment, and this may perhaps tend most of all to maintain the above-mentioned confusion of ideas, thanks to which the individual avenger generally does not know what he really wants.

The Fisherman and His Wife
Jacob and Wilhelm Grimm

There was once a fisherman who lived with his wife in a pigsty, close by the seaside. The fisherman used to go out all day long a-fishing; and one day, as he sat on the shore with his rod, looking at the sparkling waves and watching his line, all on a sudden his float was dragged away deep into the water: and in drawing it up he pulled out a great fish. But the fish said, 'Pray let me live! I am not a real fish; I am an enchanted prince: put me in the water again, and let me go!' 'Oh, ho!' said the man, 'you need not make so many words about the matter; I will have nothing to do with a fish that can talk: so swim away, sir, as soon as you please!' Then he put him back into the water, and the fish darted straight down to the bottom, and left a long streak of blood behind him on the wave.

When the fisherman went home to his wife in the pigsty, he told her how he had caught a great fish, and how it had told him it was an enchanted prince, and how, on hearing it speak, he had let it go again. 'Did not you ask it for anything?' said the wife, 'we live very wretchedly here, in this nasty dirty pigsty; do go back and tell the fish we want a snug little cottage.'

The fisherman did not much like the business: however, he went to the seashore; and when he came back there the water looked all yellow and green. And he stood at the water's edge, and said:

'O man of the sea!
Hearken to me!
My wife Ilsabill
Will have her own will,
And hath sent me to beg a boon of thee!'

Then the fish came swimming to him, and said, 'Well, what is her

Jacob and Wilhelm Grimm. *Grimms' Fairy Tales*. Trans. Edgar Taylor and Marian Edwardes. London: R. Meek and Co., 1876.

will? What does your wife want?' 'Ah!' said the fisherman, 'she says that when I had caught you, I ought to have asked you for something before I let you go; she does not like living any longer in the pigsty, and wants a snug little cottage.' 'Go home, then,' said the fish; 'she is in the cottage already!' So the man went home, and saw his wife standing at the door of a nice trim little cottage. 'Come in, come in!' said she; 'is not this much better than the filthy pigsty we had?' And there was a parlour, and a bedchamber, and a kitchen; and behind the cottage there was a little garden, planted with all sorts of flowers and fruits; and there was a courtyard behind, full of ducks and chickens. 'Ah!' said the fisherman, 'how happily we shall live now!' 'We will try to do so, at least,' said his wife.

Everything went right for a week or two, and then Dame Ilsabill said, 'Husband, there is not near room enough for us in this cottage; the courtyard and the garden are a great deal too small; I should like to have a large stone castle to live in: go to the fish again and tell him to give us a castle.' 'Wife,' said the fisherman, 'I don't like to go to him again, for perhaps he will be angry; we ought to be easy with this pretty cottage to live in.' 'Nonsense!' said the wife; 'he will do it very willingly, I know; go along and try!'

The fisherman went, but his heart was very heavy: and when he came to the sea, it looked blue and gloomy, though it was very calm; and he went close to the edge of the waves, and said:

'O man of the sea!
Hearken to me!
My wife Ilsabill
Will have her own will,
And hath sent me to beg a boon of thee!'

'Well, what does she want now?' said the fish. 'Ah!' said the man, dolefully, 'my wife wants to live in a stone castle.' 'Go home, then,' said the fish; 'she is standing at the gate of it already.' So away went the fisherman, and found his wife standing before the gate of a great castle. 'See,' said she, 'is not this grand?' With that they went into the castle together, and found a great many servants there, and the rooms all richly furnished, and full of golden chairs and tables; and behind the castle was a garden, and around it was a park half a mile long, full of sheep, and goats, and hares, and deer; and in the courtyard were stables and cow-houses. 'Well,' said the man, 'now we will live cheerful and happy in this beautiful castle for the rest of our lives.' 'Perhaps we may,' said the wife; 'but let us sleep upon it, before we make up our minds to that.' So they went to bed.

The next morning when Dame Ilsabill awoke it was broad daylight, and she jogged the fisherman with her elbow, and said, 'Get up, husband, and bestir yourself, for we must be king of all the land.' 'Wife, wife,' said the man, 'why should we wish to be the king? I will not be king.' 'Then I will,' said she. 'But, wife,' said the fisherman, 'how can you be king—the fish cannot make you a king?' 'Husband,' said she, 'say no more about it, but go and try! I will be king.' So the man went away quite sorrowful to think that his wife should want to be king. This time the sea looked a dark grey colour, and was overspread with curling waves and the ridges of foam as he cried out:

'O man of the sea!
Hearken to me!
My wife Ilsabill
Will have her own will,
And hath sent me to beg a boon of thee!'

'Well, what would she have now?' said the fish. 'Alas!' said the poor man, 'my wife wants to be king.' 'Go home,' said the fish; 'she is king already.'

Then the fisherman went home; and as he came close to the palace he saw a troop of soldiers, and heard the sound of drums and trumpets. And when he went in he saw his wife sitting on a throne of gold and diamonds, with a golden crown upon her head; and on each side of her stood six fair maidens, each a head taller than the other. 'Well, wife,' said the fisherman, 'are you king?' 'Yes,' said she, 'I am king.' And when he had looked at her for a long time, he said, 'Ah, wife! what a fine thing it is to be king! Now we shall never have anything more to wish for as long as we live.' 'I don't know how that may be,' said she; 'never is a long time. I am king, it is true; but I begin to be tired of that, and I think I should like to be emperor.' 'Alas, wife! why should you wish to be emperor?' said the fisherman. 'Husband,' said she, 'go to the fish! I say I will be emperor.' 'Ah, wife!' replied the fisherman, 'the fish cannot make an emperor, I am sure, and I should not like to ask him for such a thing.' 'I am king,' said Ilsabill, 'and you are my slave; so go at once!'

So the fisherman was forced to go; and he muttered as he went along, 'This will come to no good, it is too much to ask; the fish will be tired at last, and then we shall be sorry for what we have done.' He soon came to the seashore; and the water was quite black and muddy, and a mighty whirlwind blew over the waves and rolled them about, but he went as near as he could to the water's brink, and said:

'O man of the sea!
Hearken to me!
My wife Ilsabill
Will have her own will,
And hath sent me to beg a boon of thee!'

'What would she have now?' said the fish. 'Ah!' said the fisherman, 'she wants to be emperor.' 'Go home,' said the fish; 'she is emperor already.'

So he went home again; and as he came near he saw his wife Ilsabill sitting on a very lofty throne made of solid gold, with a great crown on her head full two yards high; and on each side of her stood her guards and attendants in a row, each one smaller than the other, from the tallest giant down to a little dwarf no bigger than my finger. And before her stood princes, and dukes, and earls: and the fisherman went up to her and said, 'Wife, are you emperor?' 'Yes,' said she, 'I am emperor.' 'Ah!' said the man, as he gazed upon her, 'what a fine thing it is to be emperor!' 'Husband,' said she, 'why should we stop at being emperor? I will be pope next.' 'O wife, wife!' said he, 'how can you be pope? there is but one pope at a time in Christendom.' 'Husband,' said she, 'I will be pope this very day.' 'But,' replied the husband, 'the fish cannot make you pope.' 'What nonsense!' said she; 'if he can make an emperor, he can make a pope: go and try him.'

So the fisherman went. But when he came to the shore the wind was raging and the sea was tossed up and down in boiling waves, and the ships were in trouble, and rolled fearfully upon the tops of the billows. In the middle of the heavens there was a little piece of blue sky, but towards the south all was red, as if a dreadful storm was rising. At this sight the fisherman was dreadfully frightened, and he trembled so that his knees knocked together: but still he went down near to the shore, and said:

'O man of the sea!
Hearken to me!
My wife Ilsabill
Will have her own will,
And hath sent me to beg a boon of thee!'

'What does she want now?' said the fish. 'Ah!' said the fisherman, 'my wife wants to be pope.' 'Go home,' said the fish; 'she is pope already.'

Then the fisherman went home, and found Ilsabill sitting on a throne that was two miles high. And she had three great crowns on her head, and around her stood all the pomp and power of the Church. And on each side of her were two rows of burning lights, of all sizes, the greatest as large as the highest and biggest tower in the world, and the least no larger than a small rushlight. 'Wife,' said the fisherman, as he looked at all this greatness, 'are you pope?' 'Yes,' said she, 'I am pope.' 'Well, wife,' replied he, 'it is a grand thing to be pope; and now you must be easy, for you can be nothing greater.' 'I will think about that,' said the wife. Then they went to bed: but Dame Ilsabill could not sleep all night for thinking what she should be next. At last, as she was dropping asleep, morning broke, and the sun rose. 'Ha!' thought she, as she woke up and looked at it through the window, 'after all I cannot prevent the sun rising.' At this thought she was very angry, and wakened her husband, and said, 'Husband, go to the fish and tell him I must be lord of the sun and moon.' The fisherman was half asleep, but the thought frightened him so much that he started and fell out of bed. 'Alas, wife!' said he, 'cannot you be easy with being pope?' 'No,' said she, 'I am very uneasy as long as the sun and moon rise without my leave. Go to the fish at once!'

Then the man went shivering with fear; and as he was going down to the shore a dreadful storm arose, so that the trees and the very rocks shook. And all the heavens became black with stormy clouds, and the lightnings played, and the thunders rolled; and you might have seen in the sea great black waves, swelling up like mountains with crowns of white foam upon their heads. And the fisherman crept towards the sea, and cried out, as well as he could:

> 'O man of the sea!
> Hearken to me!
> My wife Ilsabill
> Will have her own will,
> And hath sent me to beg a boon of thee!'

'What does she want now?' said the fish. 'Ah!' said he, 'she wants to be lord of the sun and moon.' 'Go home,' said the fish, 'to your pigsty again.'

And there they live to this very day.

Made in United States
North Haven, CT
14 July 2024